Mechanisms & Devices

A Little More Help From a Friend

First Edition

By Douglas Packard

Published by Douglas T. Packard

Mechanisms & Devices A Little More Help From a Friend

© 2013 by Douglas Packard

Editor: Douglas T Packard

Book design: Douglas T. Packard

Composition: Douglas T. Packard

Cover design: Douglas Packard & Kyle Hickey

Please direct any comments, questions, or suggestions regarding this book to Douglas Packard, at the address below.

dphandbook38@gmail.com

Printed in the United States of America

First Edition.

TABLE OF CONTENTS

LIST OF FIGURES

Chapter 1   Introduction

Purpose of this Document

Hi! My name is Doug Packard. Originally, just prior to my retirement in the fall of 2000, I wrote a Design Handbook as a guide for young engineers who were "fresh out" of school and starting to design mechanisms at the Jet Propulsion Lab. The title was: "Aerospace Mechanism-Tips and Speed Secrets (A Little Help From a Friend). I understand that it is now called "Packard 101".

I have decided that similar but updated information may be of interest to a wider audience. Not just us nerds who put "stuff" into space and on to (or into) other planets. Welcome aboard, Education is a Right!

James Michener in his fictional book, "Space", wrote of an event that occurred in July of the year 1054. A super nova occurred in the constellation Taurus. Michener tells us: "That this great star which must have been the most extraordinary sight in the history of the heavens was noted in many places in the world, as we have their written records to prove it". Michener then continues, " we know the event took place, for with a telescope today we can see the remnants of the super nova hiding in Taurus, but we searched every library in the western world without finding a single shred of evidence that the learned people of Europe even bothered to notice what was happening about them". **"An age is called Dark not because the light fails to shine, but because people refuse to see it".**

I will strive to shine more than a little light! Prepare yourself! You are about to be shined-on!

Who's Douglas Packard

My dad, Ed Packard, hired into Lockheed in the fall of 1937. I was born in February 1938. My bedtime stories were right out of the material presented in a movie called : "The Right Stuff".

Dad relocated our family to Dayton, Ohio in 1946. He worked in the Lockheed Corporate Office there until 1952.One hot, humid afternoon in October 1947, Dad took me and a friend out to the flight line at Wright-Patterson airfield (in Dayton, Ohio). We were told that we were going to see a real jet airplane up-close. Sure enough, a P80 jet landed and taxied to a stop near us. A pilot emerged wearing a sweat soaked flight suit and walked over to us.

Dad spoke briefly to the pilot. A lifetime later, after his death, I discovered that dad hadn't been truthful (there were secrets even then). Actually, we had not gone to see the machine but to meet the man. Hours before over the high desert in California, the pilot, a man named "Chuck Yeager", "challenged that demon that lives out in the thin air". He had just become the first man to fly faster than the speed of sound.

I graduated from Cal Poly (San Luis Obispo) in June 1960 with a degree in Aero Engineering. I went to work at Lockheed Missiles and within a few years was the lead mechanical engineer responsible for all equipment installations and optional kits for the Standard Agena Program. I moved to Lockheed's special projects in 1966, and worked on numerous Lockheed Projects including the responsibility for Lockheed mechanisms configuration work on the Space Telescope.

Ronald Reagan, in August 1984, wrote a letter to a small group of people, both inside and outside the government: "A generation of this Nation's youth has grown up unaware that, in large measure, their security was insured by the dedicated work of your employees. National security interests prohibit me from rewarding you with the public recognition which you so richly deserve".

That "small group" mentored me and I hope that this manuscript will be a lasting tribute to all of them.

I joined the Jet Propulsion Lab in the summer of 1978 and worked on the Galileo Project. I helped make JPL successful on later projects including SIR-B, SIR-C, SRTM, Cassini, Mars Pathfinder, TES and Galax. I returned to Lockheed in 1985 as an independent contractor (Type A consultant) and worked on classified projects in Space Systems and Ocean Systems at Lockheed until the Fall of 1990. I returned to JPL just as the Soviet Union collapsed and I spent the next ten years designing and developing more space hardware for JPL including: The Mars Pathfinder HGA Gimbal, SIR-C Tri Drive, The idea for the SRTM 200 foot long, athermalized boom, and the Galax 18 inch diameter deployable cover (not quite as big as the ST main aperture door). I also found time to work on an automated version of a 2-D gel box (protein separation) for Cal Tech's Beckman Institute. I formally retired from JPL on Oct 1, 2000. But, I just kept ticking, doing more independent contracting including patented work with Alcon Labs (A three degree of freedom gimbal for the Display and Touch Pad used on Alcon's eye surgery equipment). If you suffer a loss of vision due to Cataracts and your vision is saved by surgery, I probably had a small part to do with the save.

After 54+ years in the aerospace design business, I have become a highly experienced generalist instead of focused expert with a limited field of view.

Collective Knowledge from Generations of Nerdy Engineers

(A) There is no Substitute for a Thinking Human Being.

Are you at risk of becoming a Mushroom?

Do they feed you poop?

Are you kept in the dark.

Is there a chance you might get canned?

(B) Keep Designs Simple.

(C) Develop Alternate Concepts for New Designs.

(D) Select the Best Concept or combination of Concepts:

Then run like hell because money can't buy you time (illusions of love yes, time no).

(E) Provide Time and Money for Development:

"They weren't Born Knowing"

(F) Dare to be Different:

"All Rules of Science and Engineering Were Made to Be Broken". But, please remember what Uncle Earl Said":

"Nature's laws are complete and coordinated, whether we know them all or not. They are also self-enforcing and the penalty for violation is always exacted to the precise degree that the offense has earned. About the only thing in common between the laws of nature and those of man is that ignorance of the law is no defense."   Earl Buckingham

"Design of Gear Drives for Extreme Conditions"   AGMA 109.10, June 1957

It's good to think outside the box! But, remember to avoid un-natural activities!

(G) Avoid Too Much Help:

A thousand hour job won't get done in one hour with a Thousand Engineers working on it. Hell, you can't learn all their names that fast!

(H) Be sure that the Resources and the Pain are shared equally:

Do Not Allow part of the System to be simplified at everyone else's expense (however, this only applies if it doesn't involve the Boss's close friends / relatives).

(I) Always Use Protection:

Consider the failure modes of the mechanism and protect against them) (see Ch 17).

(J) Avoid the trap:

Avoid 10 years at one job if total knowledge learned is actually one year of experience, ten times over. You can lose a job, or benefits. But, no one can take back what you have learned.

(K) Avoid the Ego Trip:

You are not indispensable and you are not special! Remember how many companies are doing just fine without you. Likewise, no single company is indispensable to your future for the same reason. Don't lock yourself into a bad situation!

(L) MICE Aren't Nice:

I just discussed EGO (Item K). EGO has three equally dangerous family members: MONEY, IDEOLOGY, and COMPROMISE. Watch out for all members of the MICE family. One or more of the family members will always appear when you are the target for persuasion or manipulation. Sound engineering judgment is easily defeated when the MICE come in to play.

More Common Sense Rules

(M) Avoid Friction:

It's never there when you want it and it is always there when you don't want it. But, also remember rule (F) (see Chapters 6 and 18)

(N) Optimize Lubrication:

Grease is good sometimes, Oil is good sometimes, and Dry Film Lube is good sometimes. Read this document and learn what to use and when to use it.(see Ch 3).

(O) Don't Gild the Lily:

Carefully consider whether you really want to use the finest spin bearing oil in an actuator (see Ch 3).

Some of you younger folks may not understand the term "Gild the Lily". The lily is a thing of beauty and a wonder to behold. Shall we now also plate it with gold?

Rules for Procurement of Critical Mechanism Component Parts

(P) Demand Design Details:

You can't tell a book by its cover and that Pretty Solid Model of the outside of an actuator doesn't help much either (see Ch 2 and 18).

(Q) Be Alert for what is not said or shown:

During a design review, you will be shown the best not the worst. The supplier may not even recognize a problem.(see Ch 2 for more discussion).

(R) Avoid Complex Contractual Relationships:

(The Buck stops at the first level of sub-contract and the sub-tier suppliers starve).(see Ch 2)

(S) The Seller is not necessarily your friend:

The term "Sharing Lunch" can be misunderstood. (Come and sit beside me said the Spider to the Fly !)

(T) Vendor Hopping:

Multi sourcing is great! Hopping from a qualified source to a non-qualified source to save "chump change" is not.

This item relates to item (H). (see Ch 18). Saving "chump change" gives the Procurement Group bragging rights. While Engineering spends far more (than was saved) to qualify the "new source".

Chapter 2   How Did He Do That?

The Work Environment

I was very lucky during my working years in the Aerospace Industry. I have had the opportunity to work many years in each of the environments which I am about to discuss. I will try to give "newcomers" an understanding of how the "Space Business" works. I was also lucky enough to work for and with some of the best people in the fledgling Space Technology business. But, in that area I can only provide you with my opinion as the players are always changing as time marches on and most of my mentors are long gone. The information which I present targets individual working engineers but "managers" would be wise to understand the things which I will discuss because your jobs will be very much easier if you provide your engineers with the ability to do their work as I suggest here.

I realize that more than a few smart young graduate engineers come out of school with the "fast track" placed before them. My dad's cousin, David (Packard) was one of those young "fast tracked" engineers when he graduated from Stanford. He did OK!

I have worked with many others who became infected with self importance and developed seriously enlarged "Egos". You probably already know that the "Ego" is one of the most sensitive organs in the human body. It is very difficult to be a thinking human being when your "Ego" becomes enlarged.

Recall my words from Chapter One: Avoid the Ego Trip: You are not indispensable and you are not special! Remember how many companies are doing just fine without you.

The three work environments which I will discuss include:

(1) High Volume Production

(2) Small Self Contained Developmental Programs

(3) The Laboratory Environment

High Volume Production

This type of program is easily identified by the management structure. The Manufacturing Manager is more powerful than the Engineering Manager. The term "Works Manager" was common within the Aircraft Industry. This arrangement is necessary because hardware production and delivery is the top priority.

Manufacturing controls all aspects of production using a manufacturing group referred to as "Manufacturing Control". The "Controls" group establishes a Master Schedule for a new program and everyone on the program must comply. This is not done in isolation. It is a team effort. Engineering begins to create a definition of the end product and simultaneously, the Manufacturing Planning group develops a step by step plan for the fabrication and assembly of each piece of the "Deliverable Product" This plan becomes the basis for the "First Article Master Schedule".

Once these formalities are completed, the fun begins. A committee is formed with the purpose of obtaining commitments from each group involved in the production process. The FAMSCO (First Article Master Scheduling Committee) has sit down meetings where representatives of Engineering, Manufacturing, Tool Design, and Subcontracts / Purchasing where each group member signs up to meet delivery dates for their parts of the project. Programs which have very short development time frames usually have the individual design engineers attend the FAMSCO and commit to release drawings by specific dates and in a specific order:

Drawings for long lead purchases first. Then detail drawings, then subassembly drawings, and finally Top Assembly drawings. The releases are scheduled with standard manufacturing "set-backs" (maybe 30 days) for each type of release. Manufacturing Planning watches this whole operation and specifies the order of drawing release. The schedules do not just happen. They are the end products of tedious negotiations.

Any changes to the original plan must be negotiated with a "Change Board" which assesses the impact to the original schedule.

This is not a fun world to work in! It is highly structured and a very high pressure environment. But, the experience is necessary in order to learn discipline. You need to learn the rules. It's like learning to separate the fly poop from the pepper. Don't stay too long or you will get one years experience (x) times over.

High Volume Production Programs may be completely open or they may limit access.
The degree to which a program limits access should not reduce the level of discipline. High volume production must be disciplined.

Small Self Contained Developmental Programs

Spacecraft programs usually involve metallic and non-metallic structure where standard tolerances are +/- .03 inches for sheet metal and +/- .005 inches for machined parts. The structures are usually stuffed with electronics, batteries, cables and functional devices. These functional devices may be very complex, moving, mechanical assemblies. The standard tolerances may approach +/- .0001 inch. You drop one of those drawings into a typical spacecraft manufacturing planning group and standby for the fireworks. Your tight tolerances are applicable to machine tools or jet / rocket engines, not to spacecrafts! This type of product is better suited to a small self contained development program where the design engineer, assembly technician and the machinist work together. You still need a manufacturing control function but it may only require one, single, very knowledgeable person from manufacturing. This type of organization is a true partnership of the involved workers. After working on a production program, coming into this type of program is like leaving Wonderland and returning to Kansas. Any "Moving Mechanical Assembly" is better suited to the small program environment.

The Laboratory Environment

If you have extensive experience in the other two work environments before you work at "The Laboratory", you will love the "Lab". Why? Because Anarchy Reigns! If you are a cognizant engineer, you will call the shots for your piece of the action. But, if you do not know how to use this freedom, you will be heading off a cliff.

You still need a planning and control function. You will have to know how to "master schedule" the whole job yourself. But, do not fall in love with the "Schedules and Budgets" task. Your pride and joy "Schedule and Budget" will go obsolete within hours of its publication. Shortly, I will explain which elements of a job are schedule critical. The "Budgets" part of the job will take care of itself if you do the job efficiently.

If you are "fresh out" of school and want to work in a lab environment do not push for leadership until you gain experience. Any fool can get a job done given enough time and money. The trick is to make the correct decisions quickly. Contingency planning is also very important. There will always be a few uncertainties for any complex development job and contingency plans are fundamentally important. Don't wait for a problem to appear. Anticipate problems and have solutions ready for implementation. Succeed in completing a job quickly and costs will be minimized.

A true Laboratory Environment has numerous programs simultaneously competing for resources. This results in numerous resources being available including an assortment of captive shops with varying precision capabilities and the ability for you to direct pieces of your job to outside sources. You can make your own drawings, have a captive drafting room do it or send the drafting job to an outside source. Those decisions are yours. Remember, the more that you do yourself the better your control of the job will be. This relates directly to your level of experience.

Developing Individual Mechanisms

An actuator is an individual mechanism. It may contain many purchased components: a motor, a potentiometer, or a special ball screw plus numerous purchased parts like ball bearings or metal bellows. Aperture covers and associated release / deploy mechanisms also represent individual mechanisms.

After I gained experience, I became able to develop individual mechanisms within about one year if the work environment allowed me the opportunity to move quickly. I will show you how I do it in the remainder to this chapter.

Systems containing Numerous Mechanisms

Systems which contain numerous individual mechanisms are developed in the same manner. But require more time for serial developments or more workers for parallel efforts. But remember, you can't complete a 1,000 hour job in one hour using 1,000 workers. More people on the job always means more total cost.

How Did He Do That ?

The Concept Phase

The development of a mechanism or mechanism system always starts with a concept layout phase. I believe that this is best done with a 2D Cad layout because 3D models of complex mechanisms require too much time. It's fine to have a 3D picture! But save time. Just make it from the 2D layout. Think of this time as your last chance to "get it right". I always recommend that three different concepts for doing the job be developed. Equal effort should be put into each. One of the hardest but most valuable lessons I have learned over the years is the ability to put a recently completed design concept totally out of mind and begin a second or third try. There is a tendency to get married to the design in progress. But, with discipline and serious effort, a second or third idea may prove even more inviting. Only when you stand back and look at all ideas will you know which is actually the best or even which combination of ideas is best.

Once you commit to a specific concept and start development the "concrete" begins to set and you will have less and less flexibility to revise the concept. This is the time to get it right and to address secondary issues like protective devices such as clutches and stops (always use protection).

The concept layouts must contain enough information so that critical procurements can be identified. You must confirm that you have a viable source for each critical item. This information is vital to the final concept decision. Your concept layout should be complete enough that you can count the number of drawings which will be required. I do this and then multiply by two. This "drawing list" is the starting point for developing job costs. I was taught to assume each detail drawing requires a preparation time of eight hours, each subassembly requires 20 hours and each major assembly requires forty hours. These times are averages. Some drawings will require more and some less. If you just graduated from one of the top engineering schools and are wondering: " What's a Detailed Drawing ?" I hope that you recognize that you got a super education but they could not teach you everything. My purpose with this book is to tell you about the things I learned after graduation.

Preliminary Design and Analysis

A final decision on the concept allows Preliminary Design to begin. Now it's time for that real 3D "Solid Model". But, you must also simultaneously prepare the documentation for critical purchased or subcontracted items. Purchased items include catalog items or slightly modified versions of catalog items and special materials. They also include custom made items like gears. A Source Control Drawing (SCD) is the usual method of documenting these items. But, custom gears or springs may also be documented with detailed drawings. The procurement document is a simple Purchase Order (PO).

Subcontracted items include all critical functional items like motors, encoders, pots and custom items like ball screws. These items require an SCD. But, they also require a Detail Specification (performance and test requirements) and a Statement of Work (SOW) which defines contractual and delivery requirements. The applicable procurement document is a formal Sub-Contract. Always try to complete the documentation before you ask for cost estimates. Every time you expand the documentation, the supplier will add cost to your purchase. Any piece of the documentation is about 70% "boiler plate". Seventy percent of all mechanisms contract documents say the same thing. Learn how to write this 70% piece once and it will apply forever. It is a shame to pay extra because you failed to present the "boiler plate" up-front.

You should have determined which sources you want to use during the Concept Phase of the program and the determination should have included justification of single source/ sole source items. If competitive bids are required, you must start that process early. You must get all critical purchases and contracts placed. The "agreed to" delivery dates are milestone items for your schedule. You really don't have a real budget or schedule until all critical purchases / subcontracts are locked into place.

Obtain Quality Certifications with all purchases so that all of the items you buy will be useable for end item units. Do this and you won't have to make a second buy for end item units.

It is wise to break the modeling effort into rational subassemblies if possible so that individual job packages can begin fabrication early. These early items should include any components which are needed for engineering evaluations (dev testing).

While the model is being generated, you need to perform preliminary analysis to assure that you are not buying scrap. Determining the loading conditions to use for your analysis can be a problem.. JPL uses something they call the mass-acceleration curve (check it out on-line). It is a very useful tool for preliminary design. If you can estimate the mass of your mechanism, the curve tells you how many G's to apply for preliminary analysis.

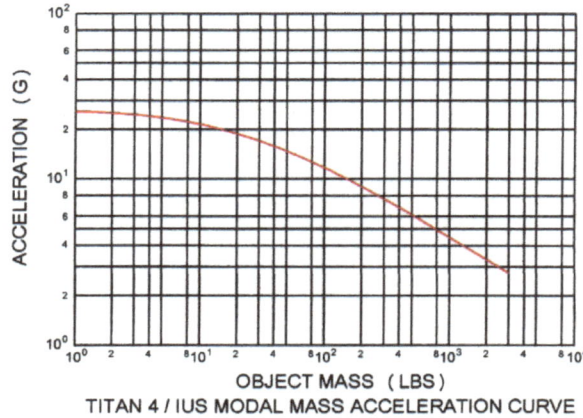

TITAN 4 / IUS MODAL MASS ACCELERATION CURVE

Figure 1 The MAC

Detail Design

Completion of the Solid Model initiates detail drawing preparation. All drawings should be prepared in a releasable condition without the need for a total redraw before the production release. The completed drawing should allow part fabrication to begin even before all drawings are finished. This process of starting fabrication before all the design is completed is called "concurrent engineering". You have to be agile to successfully achieve concurrency. But, if you succeed, you can significantly shorten the overall program schedule. The little things become very important. Early on, you needed to decide who obtains the necessary raw materials. It is best that the shop do it well before you have drawings completed. Or, you can obtain the materials and kit them. This will save the shop days of time. If you decide to supply raw material, you will need to coordinate the effort with the shop. They will need to tell you how much extra material is required for each piece of raw stock in order to create each final finished part.

Fabrication

I prefer to use a single shop for all fabrication effort. I request that the shop assign one experienced lead machinist to coordinate all fabrication, the work will flow smoothly and your parts will all fit when you are finished. The inspections should be done "in-process" while parts are still "in the machine". Early fit checks are possible because all mating parts are in a single place. Your lead machinist will probably want access to your purchased gears and ball bearings for these fit checks. You will need an up-front agreement with your own Quality Assurance organization for source inspection to happen. Don't wait until the parts are completed to ask for source inspection. If you do, you will probably find yourself in what "us" gentlemen call "a pissing contest" while QA "thinks about it" and your job grinds to a halt.

There is another even more important reason to fabricate precision parts together. The precision tolerances of the parts are so tight that shop temperature becomes a critical factor. If two 10 inch diameter steel or titanium rings are machined in different shops having environmental temperatures which are different by only 10°F, the final parts will have a diameter difference of .0006 inches when they come together at the same temperature. Ball bearings and gears would fit poorly or not at all. If you design with materials which have matching coefficients of thermal expansion, you don't need to specify a specific fabrication temperature. But, you do need to have all parts machined at the same temperature.

Use Cost Saving Techniques

(1) Parallel Production of Dev and End Item Components (When only a few end items are to be built).

(2) Use "Red Line" control of all Shop Drawings. Drawing changes may be hand written on the shop fabrication drawing for incorporation into the drawing before final inspection.

(3) Use "In-process" inspections

(4) Strive for "End Item" quality for all components. This allows expensive development parts to be recycled through inspection and then be available for end item usage.

(5) Obtain Inspection Certifications with all Purchases

(6) Use Identical Inspection Techniques for development unit and end items

(7) Assure that all changes (including red lines) are incorporated and drawings are released for final inspections.

Note: This is a disciplined approach which need not be followed. But, you will finish the whole job more quickly and at a lower cost if you follow these rules!

A short time after Dev Unit completion, you will be ready to assemble the Qualification Test Unit and Flight Unit. Actually, you can finish the End Item and deliver it to the Spacecraft before the Qualification Test Unit is assembled.

Design Tooling and Test Fixtures

you will need to consider how to support the mechanism during assembly and test. You will also need to design / fab or purchase test equipment. The best time to consider these items is during the last 25% of the detail design phase. If you do this at that time, any needed items like attachment points can be designed in the first time around. Rework of completed parts will not be necessary.

A carefully thought out plan for handling your mechanism is fundamentally important to avoiding damaging accidents. Good tooling will protect the costly end item hardware. I discuss this in Chapter 18 called "Sailor Proofing".

Assembly Drawings

The solid model will generate an assembly picture and a list of materials. But, much other very important information will only get onto the drawing if the cognizant engineer is experienced enough to know that it is needed. The solid model is not that smart!

(1) Provide an assembly drawing that clearly depicts the assembled system, including critical steps, and warns of high risks.

(2) Augment the assembly drawing with step-by-step procedures in the form of drawing notes.

(3) Be sure that your top assembly drawing clearly identifies all warnings that must apply to higher assembly levels.

(4) Use drawing notes to specify "in-process" tests and inspections.

(5) Annotate the field of the drawing with interface information such as electrical connector identity and identifying information for the unit (part number, serial, number and assembly name).

I have found that the best way to accomplish this "not so fun" task is to take a pre-release copy of the assembly drawing and hand write the missing information on to the copy. Then return the copy to the drawing maker so that it can be entered into the cad data base. If you are the drawing maker, you don't need this step and a little more time is saved.

First Article Assembly (The Dev Unit)

Assign an "End Item" certified assembly technician

He will:

(1) Prepare a Parts Kit which contains one units worth of parts including all inspection records, certifications, and component test records

(2) Confirm that records are complete including certifications and test records.

(3) Assure that all parts are cleaned, packaged, and identified per the drawing.

(4) Assure that all tools and fixtures are clean and calibrated as required.

(5) Assemble the Dev unit with the cog engineer witnessing.

(6) Prepare and maintain a log book for the Dev unit (containing all records)

Assign an "End Item" certified inspector

He will:

(1) Review the log book

(2) Work with the assembly tech and Cog engineer to identify in-process inspection point for later use with end item units.

The Assembly Procedure

Define what type of documentation will be used to assemble "End Items"

Will it be a Manufacturing Document or an Engineering Document? Obtain the blank forms and prepare the procedure in "real time" as the development unit is assembled.

Note: What I have described here is a dress rehearsal for the End Item assembly. Get this one right and your End Items will be:

(1) A cake walk

(2) A piece of cake

(3) A breeze

(4) All of the above

Test Procedures

Two types of formal testing are usually required. The first end item unit is acceptance tested and then retested to higher qualification test levels. All other End Items receive only Acceptance Testing. Procedures for both types of testing are virtually identical except the Qualification Test levels are more stringent. Always use the Dev Unit Testing as a dress rehearsal for the Formal Acceptance and Qualification testing.

Chapter 3   Lubrication in a (Space) Environment

Introduction:

Great effort was expended in the last half of the 1960's to develop much longer component life times. We learned quickly that proper lubrication was mandatory for uniform/long life performance. And, we also learned which lubes provided months of continuous operation with minimal degradation of the lubricant. My own involvement started in mid 1966. A major part of my work for the next six years involved the development of lubrication technology for space actuators.

Development began in the mid-1960s on a family of electromechanical devices including potentiometers, tachometers, encoders, actuators, and motors. The initial life requirement for these custom items was only a few days on-orbit and only a few thousand revs of operation. But, after six years of performance upgrades, orbital life of months was achieved and no component failures occurred on-orbit. We knew with great certainty that many years of "on-orbit" service was possible.

The period from 1966 to 1972 was a time of design improvement with a goal of much longer orbital lifetime and a correspondingly reduced launch rate. Ironically, other folks were suggesting that we should develop a Space Shuttle to provide higher launch rates! Surprise, surprise. By 1972, we began development of a "next generation" of far more advanced spacecrafts. Launches of these new systems began after 1975 and vehicle launch rates fell from a peak of 74 tries in 1966 to 16 perfect launches in 1979 and years of active orbital lifetime were achieved. Proper lubrication was fundamental to these successful programs.

I have grouped the chapters which discuss ball bearings, gears and lubrication together in this manuscript. Actuator design is dependent on these technologies. We found, in the late 1960's, that achievable life was a step function. Incorrectly designed and /or improperly lubricated units would fail after only a few thousand revolutions. But once we got it right, millions and millions of revolutions of trouble free life was possible. Hell, it only took us six or seven years to figure it out! So soon old and so late smart!!

I discuss the difference between actuators and spin systems in the ball bearings chapter. Lubrication for spin systems is totally different than actuator lubrication. Unfortunately, advocates of these two technologies have pushed their solutions as the right way for all lubricated devices. Most young engineers become very confused because they hear touted solutions which really apply specifically to actuators or specifically to spin systems. Both solutions are correct but that is not made clear.

I define two very different lubrication applications in the introduction to Chapter 4, (1)spin systems and (2) actuators. So far, we have been assuming liquid lubrication, oils or greases. But, a third category also exists. Dry films (DFL's) and non-metallic rolling elements also have a place of their own. Liquid lubes can't be used in very hot or very cold environments. They will evaporate away or freeze solid. Those extreme temperature applications are candidates for dry lube technology. The problem with DFL's is load sensitivity. The operating contact stresses must be kept at or below 150,000 psi (max hertzian stress) and sliding contacts must be avoided. The usual allowable maximum stress in a liquid lubricated system is about four times that value. The significance of this difference is that allowable load must reduce by a factor of eight in order to reduce the contact stress by two. We need to operate bearings or gears at or below (1/16) of rated load if DFL's are used. That's a really big hit! Presently, I am working on a solution to this problem. I have always despised DFL's with a passion and now I find myself trying to make them work for upcoming interplanetary missions. "What's a nice guy like me doing in a place like this?"

Oils are Good Sometimes

Oils are the preferred lubricant for continuously spinning systems. The idea is to create an oil film which will keep the metallic surfaces from contacting. If separation is achieved, a system will be capable of spinning continuously for years. The typical ball bearings in a Reaction Wheel Assembly (RWA) or a Control Moment Gyro (CMG) will spin for billions of revolutions. This amount of life is never achievable in actuators because they experience "start-stop" conditions. The oil film can't be maintained at or near zero speed. Great effort has gone into the analysis of oil film in spinning systems. Computer programs are now available for determining an adequate oil film is present to assure that metallic surfaces do not contact. Operating temperature, lubricant viscosity, contact stress (system preload), system stiffness and bearing design details like race conformity / race surface finish all have an effect on the ability to create and maintain an oil film. The accuracy of the analysis is fundamentally important. I do not recommend that the novice try to do it! I have been designing space actuators for over 50 years. But, I would seek help from experts in this field.

The oils used in spinning systems have high pour points (they are highly viscose oils) which make them too "stiff" to perform well at cold temperature. Typically, -15° F is a cutoff point. Below that temperature bearing drag will begin to increase causing a need for more and more motor power. This is not a problem because spin systems operate in thermal benign environments, well protected from temperature extremes. Pennzane 2000 and the poly-alpha-olefin oils (PAO's) are presently being offered as the best spin system lubricants. I suggest you read Chapter 8 of the recent book "Space Vehicle Mechanisms" by Peter L. Conley with regard to the newer greases and oils.

Greases are Good Sometimes

The actuators used on the Mars missions have to operate at very low temperatures. The "sun rise" temperature at the "Banana Belt" (the equator) on Mars is -150 °F. Mars actuators place a premium on very low pour point oils and greases. It is a completely different technology than continuously spinning systems.

Each time that an actuator starts or stops the surfaces of the rolling / rotating elements (ball bearings and gears) come into direct contact. This is called "boundary lubrication". It is impossible to maintain an oil film. A magnified view of the contacting surfaces looks somewhat like the surface of a planet in our solar system. There are peaks and valleys on both contacting surfaces. Relative motion of the surfaces causes the asperities to collide, crush and shear off. This produces extreme high temperature at the contacting points and creates microscopic wear debris which accumulates over time. If the method of lubrication uses an oil film only, The debris will accumulate quickly in the oil and eventually cause it to thicken. The thickened oil will lose the ability to lubricate and a wear-out failure will occur.

A paper presented at the (11th AMS, NASA CP-2038) confirms the need for oil:

"Oil lubricated ball bearings are key elements in satellite rotary systems. Reaction wheels, scanning devices, and communication satellite design mechanical assemblies are examples where long life and uniform low torque performance are dependent on rolling element bearings."

This need for an oil supply at rolling elements is also stressed in an earlier paper (10th AMS, Apr 1976, NASA TM-33-777). However, both of these papers address the problem of maintaining oil at the rolling element contacts. One of the papers suggests the use of a very complex relube system (Jiffy Lube in space), see Figure 2.

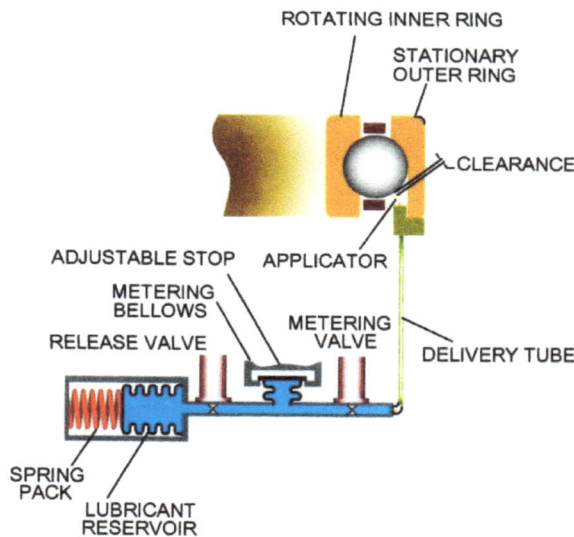

Figure 2 Re-Lube Device for Adding Oil

The applications which they discuss are very special (spin-bearing applications), and the use of oil is justified. However, for every spin-bearing application there are probably 100 boundary lubrication applications (start-stop actuators) where the problems of the oil depletion can be totally avoided by simply using grease. All greases are a mixture of a lubricating oil with a finely ground thickening powder (hopefully, a chemically inert powder). The "thickener" will introduce higher operating torque that, in a spin bearing, will require higher motor power to maintain the stable spin (drag make-up).

But, "start-stop" applications almost always have very much reduced duty cycles. I have never, in 50 years of aerospace work, found it necessary to use "oil only" in these boundary lube applications. A well run-in, light grease plate has friction levels which approach "oil only." This "grease plate" is acceptable for short life applications but, when severe loads and long life are encountered, an added quantity of grease is needed. The next three figures show the condition of the grease on a harmonic drive after 1.1 million input revs. The grease (Brayco 601) is channeled to the edges of the mesh where it acts as a reservoir to feed oil back into the mesh.

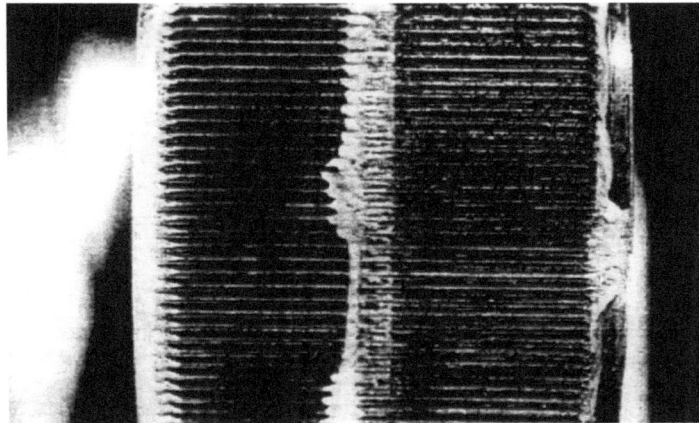

Figure 3 Flexspline (10^6 Input Revs)

Figure 4 Circular Splines (10^6 Input Revs)

Figure 5 W/G Bearing Separator (10^6 Input Revs)

It is of historical interest that these photos were taken at the completion of life testing of the first pancake harmonic drive and the grease used was the first use of the Brayco (low out-gassing/low temp) Grease.

Good Things About Grease:

(1) The Thickener in a Grease Tends to Hold Oil In-Place

(2) The Quantity of Grease Used can be Greater than Oil Only

(3) Grease Plating can Provide Reliable Ops at Low Temps

(4) Simple Visual Inspection can Verify Proper Application

Bad Things About Grease:

(1) Higher Running Friction

(2) Analysis Techniques for Lubricating Film Thickness do not exist.

(3) Allowable Operating Speed with Grease is Lower than Oil Only.

Dry Film Lubes are Good Sometimes

Early in the space program designers turned to the use of dry-film lubrication systems to avoid lubricant evaporation problems, in some cases these DFL's performed satisfactorily. Reports documented the successes (but usually not the failures) when dry-film lubricants were used. These reports left the general impression that DFL's are a panacea for space applications. This is not true. There is a fine thread of evidence to the contrary contained in this same body of data.

In the abstract of the paper "Bearing Lubrication for Long-Term Aerospace Applications," presented at the International Ball Bearing Symposium in June 1973, Ball Brothers Research Corporation states:

"For any long-life bearing application contact stress is a prime consideration in addition to conventional bearing fatigue life factors. Lubricant failure is also stress related. Our general practice is to limit operating bearing contact stresses for dry lubrication systems to 60,000 psi (Hertzian average) and 100,000 psi (Hertzian average) for fluid lubrication systems."

The American Gear Manufacturers Association (AGMA) Standard 370.01 contains the following statements:

Paragraph 11.1.5.1:   "Solid lubricants are not equivalent substitutes for conventional oils and greases..."

Paragraph 11.1.5.4:   "In any design using solid lubricants, the designer must satisfy himself that the type used is adequate for his application."

All too often, these warnings have been overlooked or misunderstood. Dry films have been employed in many applications where they should not have been used. Coupled with inadequate development life testing, this has caused many component and system qualification or operational failures. These failures have most often occurred where dry films have been used to lubricate actuators (i.e., systems where hundreds of thousands or millions of cycles of operation are required). Failures occurred because dry-film lubricants introduce a failure mode not present in liquid lubricated systems. Dry-film lubricated systems fail as a result of increasing frictional torque, which eventually exceeds the available drive torque. Failures occur because users fail to understand the 150,000 psi max hertzian (100,000 psi mean hertzian) contact stress limit. This limit is real and has been verified by many tests since the early 1970's.

Good Things About DFL

(1) Very Wide Operating Temp Range is Possible

Bad Things About DFL

(1) Very Low Operating Contact Stress is Mandatory

(2) Many DFL's Produce Debris which is far worse than Oil

(3) DFL's can be Sensitive to Test Environment. Ice formation will mask true test results.

(4) Human Error is a Fundamental Concern in DFL Processing

Well, If That's True Why Bother Using DFL's

Now we get to the heart of the problem. You don't need DFL's to control a perceived out-gassing problem with liquid lubricants which are used within the proven operating temperature range for space oils and greases. The next figure shows the temperature range of space systems. It becomes apparent that there are lots of places we can't go with our proven liquid lubricant technology.

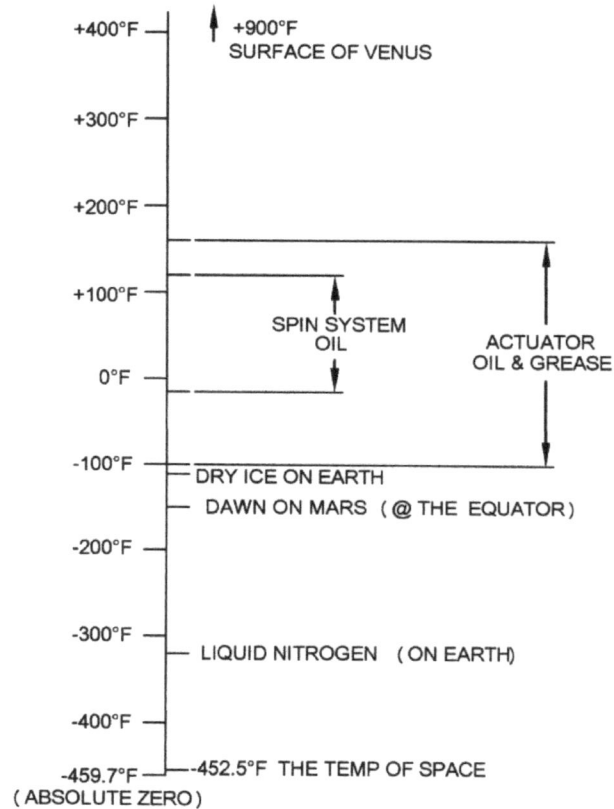

Figure 6 Operating Temperature Range

If we want to operate in many places within our solar system, we need to find a practical way to develop Dry actuators. This technology does not exist. It must be invented. There is no practical Dry wheel drive actuator for a Mars rover today. The contact stress limitations for dry lube applications make it very difficult to configure a small compact actuator.

Effect of Temperature on Out-gassing

The following information was prepared in 1973 by Doug Packard and George Dallimore (George also wrote Chapter 9 of Peter Conley's book) .

The amount of out-gassing is markedly affected by the usage temperature of the polymeric material. In most applications the average usage temperature of polymeric materials in spacecraft is more like 25°C rather than 125°C, and this has a marked effect on both the amount and the molecular weight of the material volatilized. The Stanford Research Institute (SRI) report (which will be discussed next) gives some out-gassing rate data on pure silicone polymers with molecular weights ranging from 458 to 1346 (6 to 18 silicon atoms). These data show that the higher-molecular-weight material has an out-gassing rate that is 2×10^6 times greater at 125°C and 1.3×10^5 times greater at 100°C than its rate at 25°C. The SRI researchers interpreted this data as showing that high molecular weight material released at temperatures near 125°C would condense on surfaces near 25°C and effectively never re-volatilize off these surfaces, remaining as a contaminant. These data can be interpreted another way; namely, that the out-gassing rate determined at 125°C on a high-molecular-weight material is many orders of magnitude too high compared to its out-gassing rate at 25°C, and therefore should not be used as rejection criteria when the intended application is near 25°C.

The SRI report data on the lower molecular weight (458) silicone material showed that its out-gassing rate was 450 times greater at 125°C and 150 times greater at 100°C than its rate at 25°C. These data effectively say that low molecular weight material volatilized at elevated temperatures will revolatilize after condensing on cooler surfaces, provided that the condensed material does not polymerize or become strongly absorbed by the cooler surface.

NASA/SRI Out-gassing Test

Test Method

Stanford Research Institute (SRI), under contract to NASA (Jet Propulsion Laboratory), developed a test method in the early 1970's for determining the out-gassing characteristics of polymeric materials intended for use in spacecraft. The SRI out-gassing test method consists of subjecting small samples (100 mg) of polymers to a temperature of 125°C (257°F) and a vacuum of 10^{-5} Torr or less for 24 hr. The amount of polymeric material lost by this exposure is measured and expresses as percent total weight loss (TWL). The amount of volatilized material that condenses on a 25°C (77°F) cold plate within the vacuum chamber is measured and expressed as percent volatile condensable material (VCM).

The criteria used by SRI in setting up the vacuum out-gassing test method was based on two factors:

(1) That 125°C would be the maximum temperature anticipated in locations where polymeric materials might be used.

(2) That the vacuum/temperature exposure must be maintained for a sufficient time period to remove all the volatile material from the test samples. (The SRI researchers showed that a 24-hour time period was required at 125°C and 10^{-5} Torr (One Torr = one mm mercury) to remove essentially all the volatile material from these small samples of the various polymeric materials used in spacecraft).

The SRI out-gassing test method is basically an accelerated test procedure for determining (in the laboratory within a short time period) the total amount of volatile and condensable material contained in the test specimen. The SRI test method was adopted by most NASA agencies for NASA programs and is now known as the NASA Out-gassing Test.

One Percent Total Weight Loss (TWL)

Based on the above described test method, SRI chose a one-percent limit on the amount of TWL permissible for polymeric materials used in spacecraft. The rationale for the one-percent limit was based on a generalized assumption that release of such small amounts of solvents, absorbed moisture, catalysts, cross-linking agents, etc., would have no effect on the physical properties of most polymeric materials, whereas higher amounts would indicate undesirable volume shrinkage, loss of flexibility, or other effects on physical properties. The one-percent maximum limit chosen is highly debatable for most polymeric materials, since what is lost is more important than how much. For example, the loss of solvent from paint or a coating would generally have no effect, whereas the loss of plasticizer from a rubber or elastomeric material would have a marked effect on physical properties.

One-Tenth Percent Volatile Condensable Material (VCM)

Based on the above described test method, SRI chose a 0.1-percent limit on the amount of VCM permissible for polymeric materials used in spacecraft. The rationale for the 0.1-percent VCM limit was based on the need to prevent condensable organic materials from affecting contamination sensitive surfaces such as optical sensors, thermal control coatings, and electrical contacts. There can be no argument as to the need to keep such sensitive surfaces clean. The 0.1-percent maximum VCM limit appears adequate for a screening test that separates the very low out-gassing materials from those that might cause contamination problems. However, the 0.1-percent maximum VCM limit should be used only to alert the designer that he/she has a potential out-gassing problem that must be analyzed based on the intended applications; i.e., location, amount of out-gassing material present, possible shielding, source and collector, temperature, mission life, other design alternatives, etc.

Applicability of NASA/SRI Out-gassing Criteria

The SRI researchers did an admirable job in developing a screening test for determining the relative out-gassing characteristics of polymeric materials. However, it is important for the user to realize that the NASA Out-gassing Test is an accelerated screening test that may not be applicable to their design, and he should not arbitrarily reject materials that do not meet either the 1 percent TWL or 0.1 percent VCM limits. One of the most important parameters that must be considered is usage temperature.

A New Problem

I described earlier how great effort was expended in the last half of the 1960s to develop much longer component life times. We learned quickly that liquid lubrication (preferably grease) was mandatory for uniform/long life performance of actuators. And, we also learned which lubes provided months of continuous operation with minimal degradation of the lube.

Suddenly, in the early 1970s, the new out-gassing requirements voided all of our efforts. Our lubricants did not meet the arbitrary new standards. But, they did work! The pre-1970 programs were not about to change their qualified systems. But , a whole bunch of new programs were being pushed hard by the new out-gassing test requirements. Things looked bleak! The new programs were all planning to use DFL's without understanding that there was no actuator technology to support that decision. It was a disaster in the making and some of us knew it! The mandatory selection of materials by these arbitrary test methods increased the likelihood that out-gassing characteristics would replace performance characteristics as primary criteria for material selection. I sat with a Lockheed manager of the Space Systems Division, Materials and Processes group on a flight to Boston and I explained the problem to him.

Solving the New Problem

At that point in time, we had managed to trade a hypothetical out-gassing problem for a real actuator design problem. Lockheed M&P worked with Bray Oil Company. A new lubricating oil and grease were introduced by the Bray Oil Co. The products, 815Z (oil) and 3L-38 (grease), are the same products which we use today (40 years later). The grease is now called Brayco 600 -- but it's the same stuff!

With these products we could meet the out-gassing standards and operate at temperatures below -60°F.

That left one final question: Would these lubricants be at least as good at lubricating as our earlier materials?

I was preparing to life-test the drive system shown earlier when these new lubes became available. I selected the Brayco 3L-38 for my life test and by Nov 1974, a total life of 1.1 million wave-generator revolutions was demonstrated with no degradation of the unit. I became a believer (See Figs 3,4 and 5). And, I have continued to use the Brayco grease/oil to this day. My applications always shoot for a max "mean" operating contact stress of 200,000 psi (the lower the better) and minimal preload variation due to thermal gradients. Given these conditions, I have had great success with both alloy steel ball bearings (AISI 52100) and Cres ball bearings (440C) lubricated with Bray 815Z or Brayco 600 (previously 3L-38).

The Early Years of Space Lubrication

There was a relatively small number of lubricant types that found wide usage during the period from 1956 to 1970. The major types included:

(1)   Silicones -- including: F-50 oil

                                    G-300 grease

                                    Royco-13D grease

(2)   Fluorocarbons -- including: Krytox 143AC oil

                                        Krytox 240AC grease

(3)   Fluorosilicones -- including   : FS1265 oil

                                          FS3451 grease

There was also some minor usage of several other lubricant types including:

(4)   Diesters   Electromoly No. 11 grease

(5)   Straight chain hydrocarbon   Apiezon grease

(6)   Mineral oil   Andok C oil

None of the lubricants listed above would meet the NASA out-gassing criteria. Also, the silicones had very poor lubricating qualities.

The silicones did have a very low operating temperature near -100°F. The diesters also operated at temperatures as low as -60°F. All of the other lubes could operate at temperatures as low as -40°F.

We were able, with these lubricants, to develop actuators that provided 10 million to 30 million input shaft revolutions, allowing spacecraft test verified life times of a year or more, although the typical lifetime was 3 to 6 months.

These life-time numbers represent test verified life. All items were still functioning well at the end of life testing.

Lubricant Testing

During the early years, there was no time to conduct extensive lubricant evaluations (remember the launch rate in 1966 was 74 tries). We developed a three-pronged approach to lube testing.

TGA Tests

The thermo-gravimetric analysis (TGA) is a test to evaluate the relative evaporation rate of substances. The next figure shows the resulting evaporation curves for several lube types. The material is heated in an oven, and the oven temperature is increased at a fixed rate. The remaining material mass is measured and plotted against temperature. The upper knee in the curve is most significant as it indicates the temperature at which gross loss of mass begins.

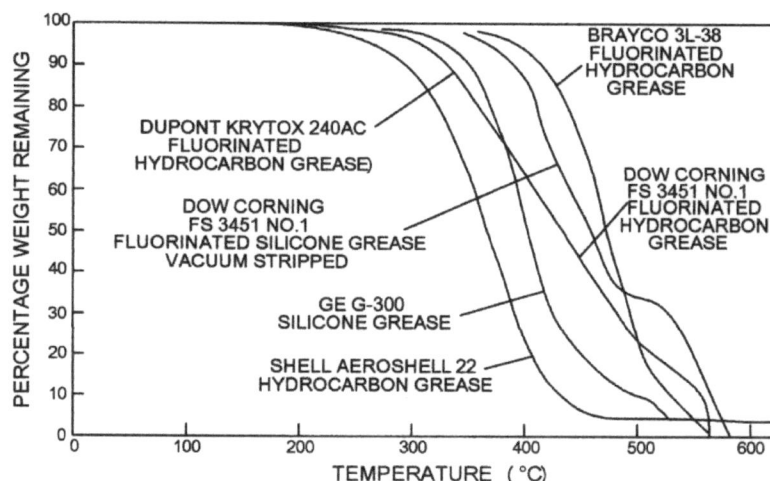

Figure 7 TGA Test Results

Drag Torque Verses Temperature

Drag torque was evaluated by using a single-bearing type with a known preload to evaluate the drag characteristics of several lubricant types .

These two tests provided the basis for trying a lubricant in a real actuator. The actuator would be run-in and operated at both specified temperature extremes. This would provide a no load speed for hot and cold conditions. The stall torque of the unit would then be measured at hot, cold, and ambient. This data could then be used to evaluate motor performance (see Chapter 14). Next, a very severe life test would be performed at ambient pressure. Cold testing was always done in a cold box with GN2 purge. We discovered early that successful ambient pressure testing results provide a virtual guarantee that later vacuum qualification would succeed.

Several years ago [maybe 50] some solid-film advocates tried to sell DFL's which they suggested must always be tested in vacuum. This is nonsense. If their product is that touchy, I don't want it or need it! However, there is a valid reason to do cold testing of DFL's in a vacuum. Any formation of ice (from humidity) on the races would seriously alter the test results.

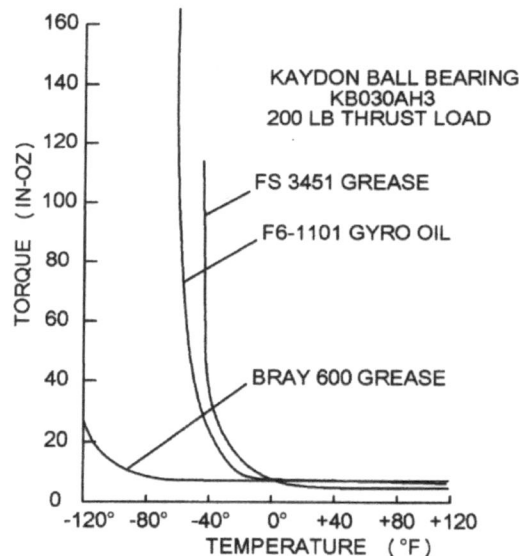

Figure 8 Drag Torque Evaluation

Chapter 4   Ball Bearings

Introduction:

I recently (May 2012) attended a class involving ball bearing design and analysis. The information presented included the related technology of lubrication. I knew many of the attendees personally and also knew "of" many others who attended. This group who I knew and knew "of " represented many of the most experienced ball bearing analysis experts and experienced ball bearing users in America . There was also a group of younger engineers who were there to begin learning about ball bearings.

I found it very interesting that as the two day meeting unfolded, two very different points of view became apparent. This must have been very confusing for those younger engineers who were just beginning to learn about ball bearings.

The experienced old timers represented two very different ball bearing applications. There was a group which was involved with the design and analysis of continuously spinning systems (reaction wheels & gyros) and another group which had put rovers onto the surface of Mars and successfully operated them for years. I will refer to this second group as "The Actuator People". Both groups of experts were very experienced , but in different technologies. This realization was a first for me. It was a revelation. My background was actuators.

I had, for many years, experienced situations where less experienced engineers were proposing "actuator" designs which I knew were not correct. Some of what I viewed as faulty actuator design included non-optimization of straddle, excessively light loading and oil lubrication instead of grease. It turned out that what the newbies were proposing was a completely correct solution......for spin systems. They had read reports and followed the recommendation of the reports without understanding that spin systems and actuators had different optimum solutions. I spend much time in this chapter and in Chapter 3, explaining the differences.

Ball Bearing Terminology

Race conformity is a measure of the conformity of the race to the ball in a plain passing through the bearing axis and transverse to the raceway (see Figure 9). It is expressed as a percentage or a decimal. This feature is important because it is one of the inputs required for calculations of radial play, axial play, and contact stress. The more the contacting surfaces conform the lower the contact stress will be.

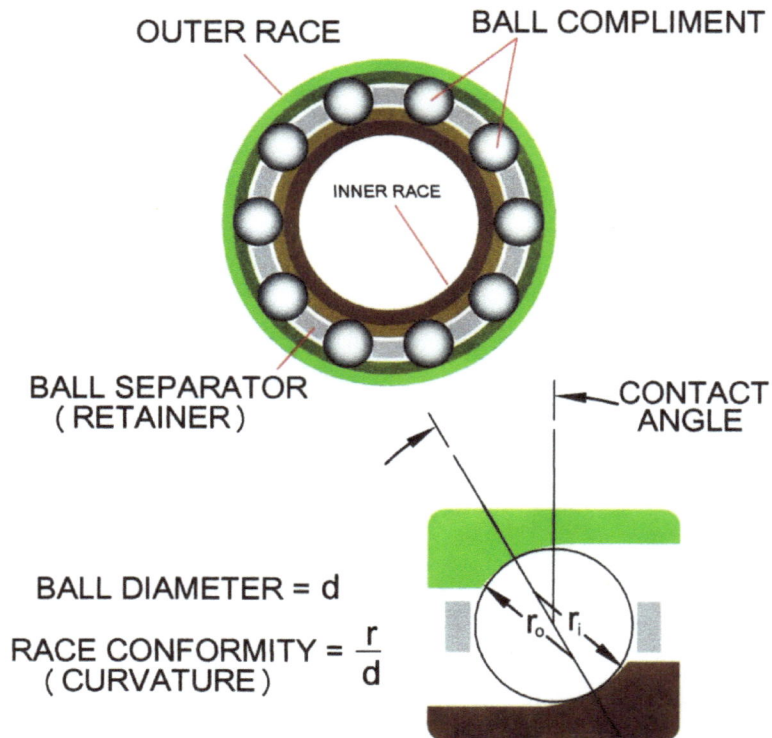

OUTER RACE   BALL COMPLIMENT

INNER RACE

BALL SEPARATOR   CONTACT
(RETAINER)   ANGLE

BALL DIAMETER = d

$$\text{RACE CONFORMITY} = \frac{r}{d}$$
(CURVATURE)

r_o r_i

Figure 9 Ball to Race Conformity

However, use great care when specifying close race conformity (less than 52.5%). A tight fit between race and ball will produce a lower contact stress, but a problem known as "blocking" will probably be introduced. Blocking is an intermittent jamming condition which can cause ball bearing friction to increase by a factor of six.

 The blocking phenomenon is described in detail in a paper from The Proceedings of the 22nd Aerospace Mechanisms Symposium. Once you discover that you have a blocking problem , only two solutions exist: (1) live with it! or (2) get a new bearing (a new bearing with a large conformity number and better dimensional control. Potential blocking problems are a major potential problem for spin systems but may not even be noticed in actuators because bearing losses are such a small part of the overall actuator drag. It can happen repeatedly in an actuator without notice. You could have a pair of very heavily preloaded output bearings which have tightly conforming ball-race contacts in an actuator which develops hundreds of inch-pounds of output torque. Variation of output torque due to blocking would be barely noticeable.

Ball Bearing Analytical Tools and Source Information

The available ball bearing programs make detailed ball bearing analysis practical. The Aerospace Corporation program "BRGS " is well suited to the analysis task and relatively easy to use. You can buy the BRGS program from Alan Leveille.   Examples of the power of "BRGS" are as follows:

EXAMPLE 1   Race Expansion/Contraction

The BRGS program will calculate the race deflections associated with constrained (mounted) races and non-constrained (un-mounted) races. The engineer can then develop a mounting scheme which allows easy bearing installation. The bearing can be slip-fit into place. The outer race will expand into the housing as the preload is applied and the inner race will contract onto the shaft as the preload is applied. The program output simultaneously confirms un-mounted and mounted clearances and confirms preloads.

EXAMPLE 2   Effects of Thermal Gradients

The BRGS program allows input of different inner and outer race temperatures. The changes of preload and deflection are provided simultaneously for each specified thermal gradient condition. The corresponding rolling friction and ball contract stress are also included.

EXAMPLE 3   Effects of External Loading

The BRGS program allows the application of axial, radial, and moment loads simultaneously. The resultant ball load/stress/deflection data is shown for each ball in the bearing. The program also provides the operating contact angle, the size of the contact ellipse, and identifies truncation if it occurs.

EXAMPLE 4   Static (Breakaway) Friction and Dynamic Friction

Dynamic friction (load and lube torques) are calculated for each loading condition. The effects of ball-bearing dynamics are not included in most versions of BRGS. There was a commercially available program called "BABERDYN" which was sold by the Avcon Corporation. Avcon also sold a user-friendly ball-bearing analysis package (Basdrel / Batherm) which is roughly equivalent to BRGS. Other possible software packages include:

Software

This is a list of programs I am familiar with either through literature or experience. Contact the source for up-to-date details. This type of information tends to become obsolete and I recommend that you check for the most current data.

COBRA (Computer Optimized Ball and Roller Bearing Analysis)

Program by J. Poplawski, 910 14th Ave., Bethlehem, PA 18018. Runs on a PC. Can handle up to six bearings of various types on a shaft. Gives deflections, stresses, etc. No high-speed or thermal effects. (This program is being upgraded continually).

SHABERTH

Originally written for NASA by SKF and available from COSMIC, University of GA, 382 Broad St., Athens, GA 30602. Will handle up to six bearings on a shaft. Has all the features one could ever want but is not very user-friendly. COSMIC's version runs on a UNIVAC 1100. Has been ported to the VAX.

SHABERTH-PC

 PC version of above available from SKF, Jamestown, NY.

BBMTI

Single bearing analysis with high speed effects included. Materials properties can be specified. This is basically a computer version of Jones' 1960 paper. Easy to use. MTI, 968 Albany-Shaker Rd., Latham, NY 12110.

A B JONES

The original large bearing analysis software package, now being sold by Jones' son. Will handle up to six bearings on a shaft. Updates and support may be a problem as I understand ABJ is in poor health. Not available for PCs. Jones Engineering Co. 4250 Coldwater Canyon Ave., Unit 207, Studio City, CA 91604.

DREB

Retainer dynamics program available in several versions from P.K. Gupta, 117 Southbury Rd., Clifton Park, NY 12065.

Other Useful Advise

I have found that BRGS is quite adequate for the type of ball-bearing problems which I encounter routinely. The analysis of dynamic effects such as ball skidding, cage oscillation, torque noise, and gyroscopic spin are very special problems best handled by a true bearing expert.

I began using ball bearing computer programs in the spring of 1992. However, I had already spent 30 years working with aerospace ball bearing applications. The classical literature on ball bearing design and analysis has existed for many years. Three of the best sources of information include:

(1) New Departure Analysis of Stress and Deflections

A.B. Jones, 1946

(2) Ball and Roller Bearing Engineering

Arvid Palmgren, 1945

(3) Rolling Bearing Analysis

T.A. Harris, 1966

Every mechanism engineer must be familiar with these books. They define the terminology necessary to operate the bearing computer programs effectively. In fact, all bearing computer programs are based upon these early works.

There is also one additional "source" which addresses the subject of bearing design. This book is important because of its extensive coverage of plain bushing design.

(4)Bearing Design and Application

D.F. Wilcock & E.R. Booser, McGraw-Hill, 1957

Tips and Tricks

In the old'n times, before the computer programs were available, mechanism engineers learned many design tricks through experience. These tricks are equally important today. Their effectiveness can be verified by using the available computer programs.

Understanding Precision

The aerospace industry has used standard drawing tolerances since metallic aircraft structures were first introduced. Sheet metal parts are toleranced to a standard ±0.03 in. Machines part standard tolerances are ±0.01 in. However, precision mechanisms live in a world where the standard tolerance is at or near ±0.0001 inches.

When you become a precision mechanism design engineer, you pass out of the airframe manufacturer's world and into the aircraft engine manufacturer's world. It's a much different place, where the players understand the need for "close" tolerancing.

It is fundamentally important to have a physical feel for the "tenth" or (0.0001). When the novice is asked to describe in common physical terms a tenth, there is usually a long silence and a blank stare.

But, it turns out that the description of a tenth is really very easy!

The paper sheet on which these words are printed is about 0.003 inches thick. You can produce one tenth by using a very sharp razor blade to slice the sheet of paper into 30 equal-sized pieces. (Not 30 small cross sections, but, 30 equally thick sheets each 8-1/2 x 11 inches) (Remember, I said a sharp razor blade). You then have produced 30 objects which are each "one tenth" thick.

Specifying Precision and Play

Precision is controlled by a ball bearing's specified class of precision. The specified ABEC (Annular Bearing Engineers Committee) number defines the tolerances that apply to each element in a bearing.

Many novice bearing users think that the internal play in a ball bearing is controlled by the specified class of precision. This is not true! Precision and play are separate specifications! Both are required. Precision is a tolerance. Play is an allowance, and that allowance sets the operating contact angle.

"Allowance and tolerance differ in that allowance is an intentional and fixed minimum difference between two independent but related dimensions, whereas tolerance is the permissible variation of a dimension. They are related in that tolerance value adds to the allowance effect. This means that there must be consistency between the two."

Precision Gearing Theory and Practice
George Michalec
Wiley 1966

Basic Geometric Relations

The operating characteristics of a ball bearing depends to a great extent upon the internal fit-up. Internal fit-up is generally measured by the diametrical clearance of the bearing.

Figure 10 shows a cross section through a radial, single row bearing. Diametrical clearance is denoted by Pd.

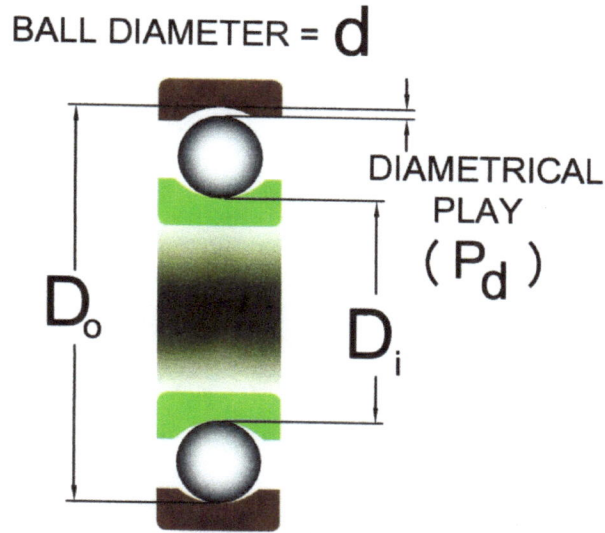

BALL DIAMETER = d

D_o D_i

DIAMETRICAL PLAY

(P_d)

Figure 10 Diametrical Play

From "New Departure Analysis of Stress and Defl." A.B. Jones, 1946

$$P_d = D_o - D_i - 2d$$

Although diametrical clearance is generally used in connection with single row, radial bearings, The above equation is applicable to angular contact bearings as well since there is a definite relation between diametrical clearance, race curvatures and free contact angle.

$$\text{Cos } \alpha = (2Bd - P_d) / 2Bd \qquad \text{Where: } (\alpha) \text{ is the free contact angle}$$

$$\text{And,} \quad B = (f_o + f_i -1) \qquad \text{Where: (f) is the race curvature}$$
$$\text{(inner \& outer races)}$$

Interference Fitting

The vast majority of aerospace ball bearing applications do not require press fits. Normally, the load / life requirements of aerospace actuator applications are so de-rated (see: Chapter 18) that problems do not occur when "push fits" are used.

In some applications, loose fits are unacceptable. The spin-axis bearings on a control moment gyro (CMG) or the spin bearings on a de-spun platform are examples of a very long life and very highly loaded rolling elements which must have interference fits between the bearing /shaft / housing.

A de-spun bearing operating at 60 rpm will accumulate 30 million revs per year of operation. A spin axis bearing in a CMG (3000 rpm) will accumulate 1.5 billion revs/year.

The function of a CMG is to produce inertial torque for attitude control. This torque results from a rotation of the CMG spin vector and is transferred through the spin-axis bearing pair. This combination of a very long life and high loading creates a major problem with regards to bearing/shaft/housing fit-up.

The next figure shows a ball bearing which has a loose inner race, rotating shaft and a large load applied always in the same radial direction. Each revolution of the shaft will cause the shaft and inner race to slip relative to each other. This slip or sliding will accumulate and cause wear between the shaft and inner race. The wear causes fretting and increased clearance which ultimately leads to failure. The slip effect is similar to flex spline /dynamic circular spline motion in a harmonic drive. This problem is primarily a "spin system" problem not an actuator problem. But, even actuator engineers need to be aware of the potential for problems.

A similar problem occurs at the outer race when the radial load vector rotates with the inner race (a spin unbalance would produce this effect).

The reason that interference fitting is not generally used for aerospace actuators is ease of assembly and disassembly. Also, incorrect press fit parts can result in bearing damage for the many instrument size ball bearings use.

The qualified life of a JPL size 14/77:1 dual drive is approximately 26,000 output revolutions (20 million motor revs). And, at least one development unit has been run for 70 million motor revs. Post-test inspection did show a polished race/housing interface but performance was still "in spec."

CASE NO. 1
RADIAL LOAD VECTOR IS FIXED
SHAFT IS LOOSE

RESULT: INNER RACE / SHAFT INTERFACE IS INCREMENTALLY
PRESSED TOGETHER CAUSING SLIPPAGE (FRETTING) OF THE
DIFFERENTIAL CIRCUMFERENCES DURING EACH REV

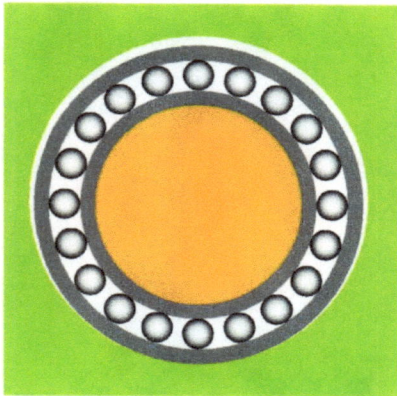

CASE NO. 2
RADIAL LOAD VECTOR ROTATES
HOUSING IS LOOSE

RESULT: OUTER RACE / SHAFT INTERFACE IS INCREMENTALLY
PRESSED TOGETHER CAUSING SLIPPAGE (FRETTING) OF THE
DIFFERENTIAL CIRCUMFERENCES DURING EACH REV

Figure 11 Effects of Shaft / Housing Looseness

The dual drive uses a 0.0002 to 0.0006 inch. diametrical clearance for ball bearing fit-up, and this same tolerance has been used on many other actuators. This fit-up is recommended for all similar applications. It is also important to understand that preloading small thin section bearings will cause the outer race to swell and the inner race to contract. This tightens-up the race-to-shaft-to-housing fits. this works well in actuators where preload variation is not critical. But, the same effect in a spin system where permissible preload variation maybe only a very few pounds would be a disaster.

If press fits (or tight push fits) are required, special provisions must be made in the design to allow tool access for "pulling or pushing" the bearing and race/housing/shaft apart. It is very easy to push small angular contact bearings apart with a rather embarrassing loss of rolling elements (see paragraph titled Truncation). And, if this happens, again, inside the General's favorite spacecraft, Fella, you will loose'em, for sure!

Thermal Gradients (Across a Ball Bearing)

Thermal Expansion of Materials

$$\Delta L = \alpha\, L\, \Delta T$$

Where;

ΔL = Change in length or diameter

α = CTE (coef of thermal expansion)

L = Length (or diameter)

ΔT = Temperature Change

For ball bearings:

$$\frac{\Delta P_d}{\Delta T} = \alpha D$$

P_d = Diameterial Clearance

D = Bearing Diameter

$\dfrac{\Delta P_d}{\Delta T}$ = Change of Diameterical Clearance per Degree (F)

for Steel, Titanium

$$\alpha = CTE = 6 \times (10^{-6})\ \frac{\text{inches}}{(\text{inch})(\text{deg F})}$$

37

The outer race will close in on the inner race by:

$$\Delta D = \frac{1}{2}\left(\frac{\Delta P_d}{\Delta T}\right)$$

BEARING DIAMETER (Inches)	RACE TO RACE APPROACH (Inches / °F)
0.55	0.0000015
3.0	0.000009
9.0	0.000027
90.0	0.00027

Figure 12 Race Approach

A similar decrease of "race approach" would occur if the inner race was heated. These dimensional changes are thermally induced strains (deflections), and the strains must be absorbed by deflections of contacting elements or by reductions of allowed initial clearance. It is generally unacceptable to allow large internal clearance in mounted bearings. The induced strains almost always squeeze hardened metallic elements together. The internal preload changes generated by thermal gradients are very large (see Figure 13).

Each individual ball in the 90 in bearing would experience a load increase of at least 25 lb for each degree F of temperature difference. The increasing ball load would cause higher running friction, and a motor attached to the inner race structure would dissipate even more power, causing more thermal gradient. This condition is very common. It is called a "thermal runaway."

Ball Load / Deflection Characteristics

Figure 13 Ball Load vs Race Approach

(for: 1/8 Dia Ball; "Kaydon" Type A Bearing with 55% Conformity)

A deflection of only .0011 inches will cause a ball load of 140 lbs which will permanently damage the races.

Information Source:

"New Departure Analysis of Stresses and Deflections, "Vol (1) (Eq 135 & Eq 143

But how easy is it to generate substantial thermal gradients? Answer -- it's incredibly easy. A DC brush motor has a wound armature that is thermally isolated by ball bearings. High torque ops can easily dump 14 W (0.5 A @ 28 VDC).

Figure 14 shows that thermal resistance is generally 2-3°F/W for 2.0- to 3.0-in. ball bearings with oil or grease plate. As an upper limit, our 3.0-in. bearing could develop a 40°F gradient (14 W x 3°F/W). The total change would be a race-to-race approach of 0.00036 in. (40°F x 0.000009 in./ °F).

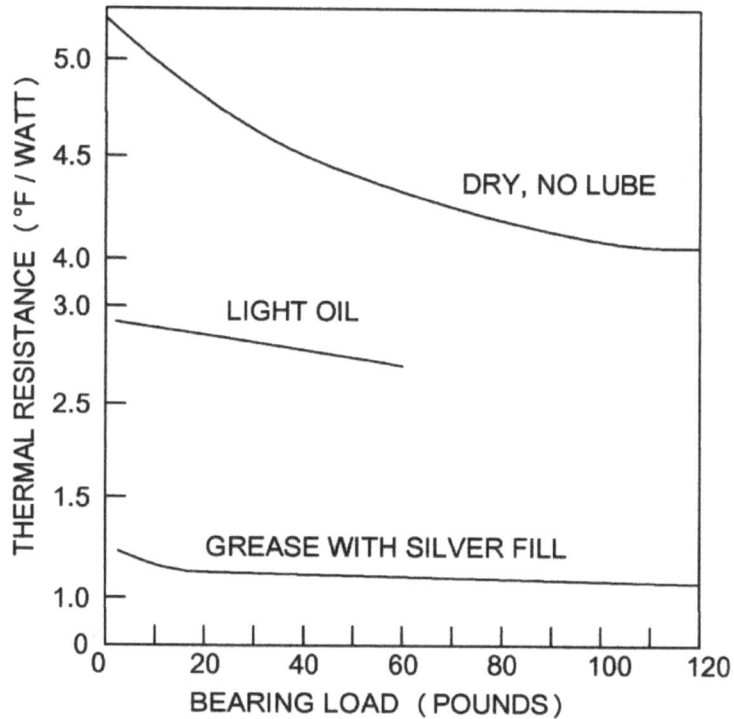

Figure 14 Ball Bearing Thermal Resistance

Can the Higher Capacity Roller Bearing Solve This Problem

The previous analysis and discussion clearly indicates that large diameter preloaded ball bearings will experience serious load variations when conditions of only minor thermal gradients exist across the bearings. This analysis has dealt entirely with ball bearings, and the question may arise regarding roller bearings in similar applications. It is clear that a roller / race contact can support a significantly higher load. However, load capability is not the primary problem! The problem involves a thermally-induced race deflection. A finite strain condition is produced, and that strain must be absorbed by changes of ball / roller / race contact. Obviously, the more compliant ball contacts will produce smaller load changes for a given strain. Or conversely, a roller contact will produce very much higher loads and therefore more rolling friction.

The problem cannot be solved by increasing load-carrying capability. The race strain (deflection) must be controlled, or the mount must be made insensitive to temperature effects.

Differential heaters and controllers can be used in order to maintain these bearings within an acceptable range of temperature gradient. This results in significant electrical power requirements and the introduction of additional functional elements.

The ball-bearing analysis tools that exist allow for a complete evaluation of the effects of thermal gradients. Use the tools!

I continue to hear that "cold lubricant" is causing high actuator friction. But, the Bray oil products which we use cause very little torque increase at or above -40°F. If you experience big friction increases above -40°F, your problem is likely a thermal gradient problem. (See section on optimum straddle).

How do You Diagnose a Thermal Run-Away

The condition is associated with poor heat transfer across the ball bearings in a vacuum. Elimination of the vacuum always causes the condition to disappear. If you note a rapidly increasing motor current during vacuum testing, the first action should be to dump the vacuum by backfilling the chamber with dry GN_2. If running current drops back to original levels, you've most probably experienced a "thermal runaway."

Optimum Straddle

All previous discussions of thermal gradient conditions have involved a reduction of the relative radial clearance within a ball bearing (i.e., one race shrinks or expands relative to another). This is an easy way to introduce the problem (a two dimensional problem).

However, most ball-bearing applications involve at least some axial deflection as well. The balls must contact the races at an angle if thrust loading is to be reacted. A zero-degree contact would produce infinitely high radial ball loads when a small thrust load is applied. In the "real world," preloading and thermal deflections become a three dimensional problem.

The third dimension in the problem is called "straddle." It is the axial center distance between a pair of ball bearings. The figure below shows a bearing pair with optimum straddle. Each ball contacts the races at an angle (α), and the plane of contact is a conical surface with a half angle of (α). When the tips of the conical surfaces (one cone for each bearing) converge exactly at the center of the straddle, the mount becomes virtually insensitive to thermal gradients. It does not matter if the gradient is hot outside/cold inside or cold outside/hot inside.

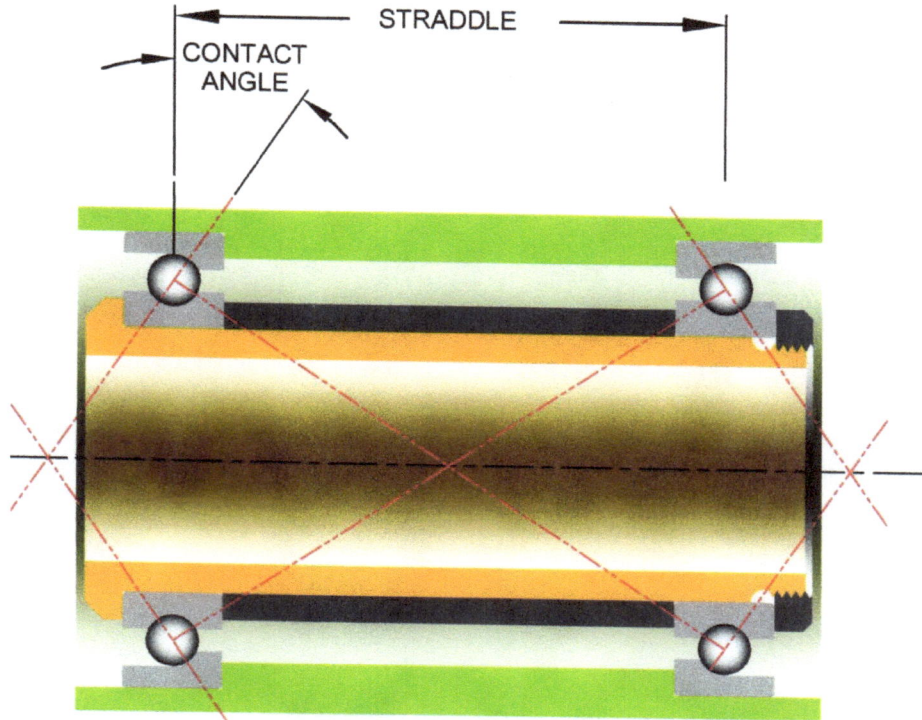

Figure 15 Optimum Straddle

his rather surprising effect occurs because dimensional changes in the axial and radial directions closely balance (not exactly but close) each other and the balls simply ride along the plane of contact without experiencing load changes.

The mounting shown above has diverging contact angles and it is known as a "DB" mount. The straddle of a "DB" mount can be optimized.

If the contact angles converge, an optimum straddle is not possible and thermal gradient problems will exist to some degree. A pair of converging contact angles is known as a "DF" mount.

An understanding of these effects allows a quick visual inspection of an actuator cross-section drawing to establish how sensitive the device may be to running friction changes. When you see a non-optimum straddle and heat dissipation at the device rotor (inner race), be cautious. Likewise, any condition which would cause a colder outer race/housing should also give rise to concerns. Use analysis tools to confirm the problem. Note, most small actuator manufacturers do not have these analysis programs.

Preloading

Many times, I have been told that it is necessary to preload a ball bearing to a load value equal to the maximum externally applied load. This is totally untrue! The concern regarding preload usually comes from a fear of pounding shock/impact. The JPL Guide for Mechanical Engineers (JPL Doc D-16403, pp 50-55) points out that some joint slop is acceptable and provides the techniques for estimating acceptable limits. I will address this subject in more detail in Chapter 8 (Spring Systems). Sadly, the subject of mechanical vibration as taught in engineering school tends to be like wading through waist deep differential equations (or as someone once said : "it's like trying to eat spinach without swallowing").

In some applications, accuracy is a driving requirement. But, even in those applications where joint slop is unacceptable, it is still unnecessary to preload to levels equal to externally applied loads so long as a "hard" preload is used. The next two figures show two common preloading methods. The first figure shows that joint slop (preload relieved) occurs at a load level several times the "hard preload". Chapter 10 (Threaded Devices) describes the preloading of ball screws. Again, the manufactures recommend that preloads not exceed 1/3 of externally applied loads.

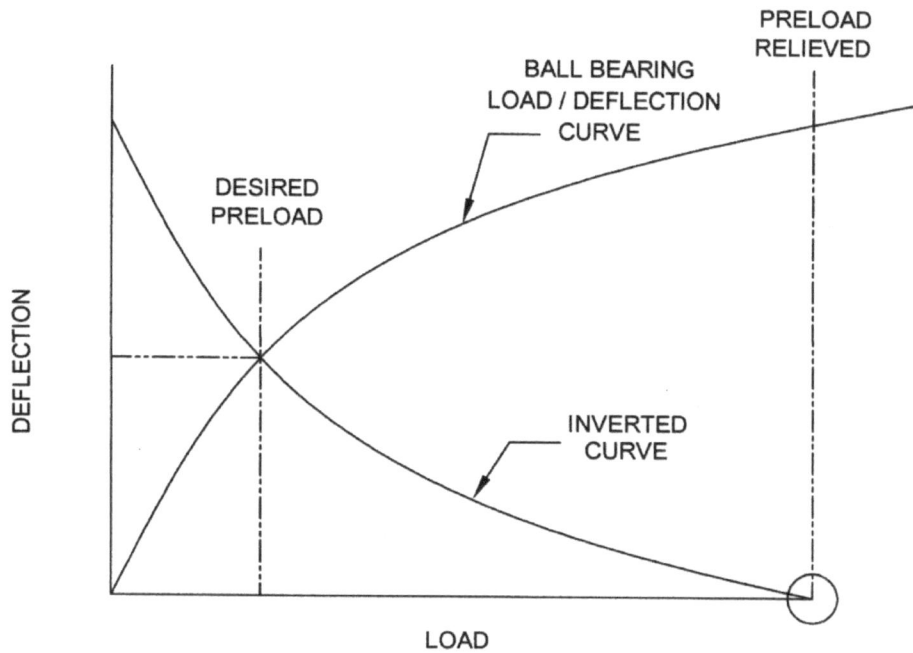

DETERMINING PRELOAD LOSS POINT

INVERT LOAD / DEFLECTION
CURVE AND FIND INTERSECTION
OF INVERTED CURVE WITH LOAD AXIS

Figure 16 Loss of Preload

The preload can be several times less than the worst-case external load. The next figures defines the load/deflection characteristics of any solid preload configuration. The preload levels are far smaller than would be required for a spring preload system with equal external loading. The same information can be obtained by using the available computer programs. This is the way old timers did it.

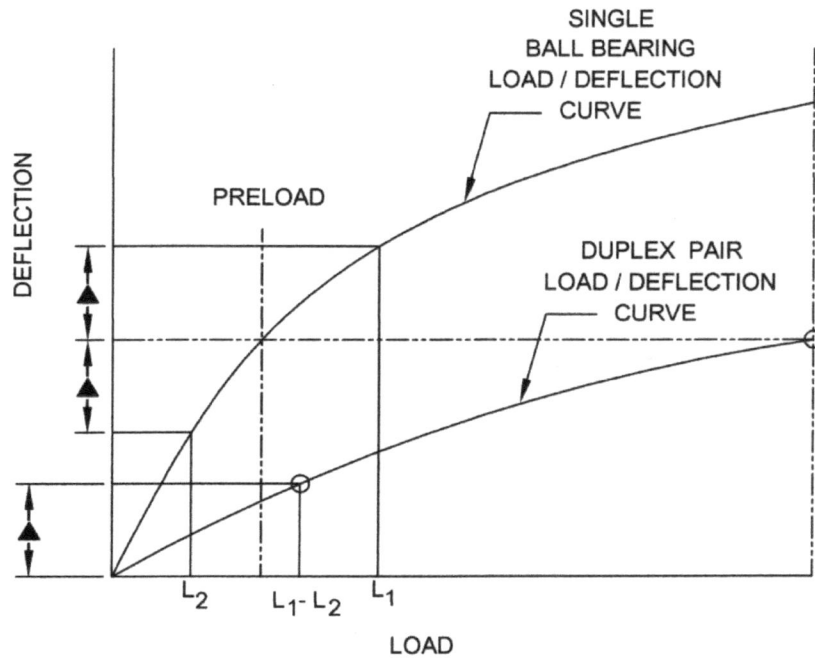

DETERMINING STIFFNESS OF BEARING PAIR

DISPLACE SHAFT BY DELTA
MEASURE L_1 & L_2
PLOT NEW STIFFNESS CURVE AS SHOWN

Figure 17 Determining Preloaded Stiffness

Preloading Methods

Spring preloading will always induce higher ball-bearing loads and will also require that a much higher preload be used if joint slop is to be avoided. The spring preloaded system must provide a near frictionless slip fit of the spring-loaded race. This is very difficult to assure. Remember the races are generally thin and will expand/contract in response to a preload. The deflection will cause a clamping action between the races and the shaft/housing. I don't believe that you can ever achieve reliable slip between races, shafts, and housings.

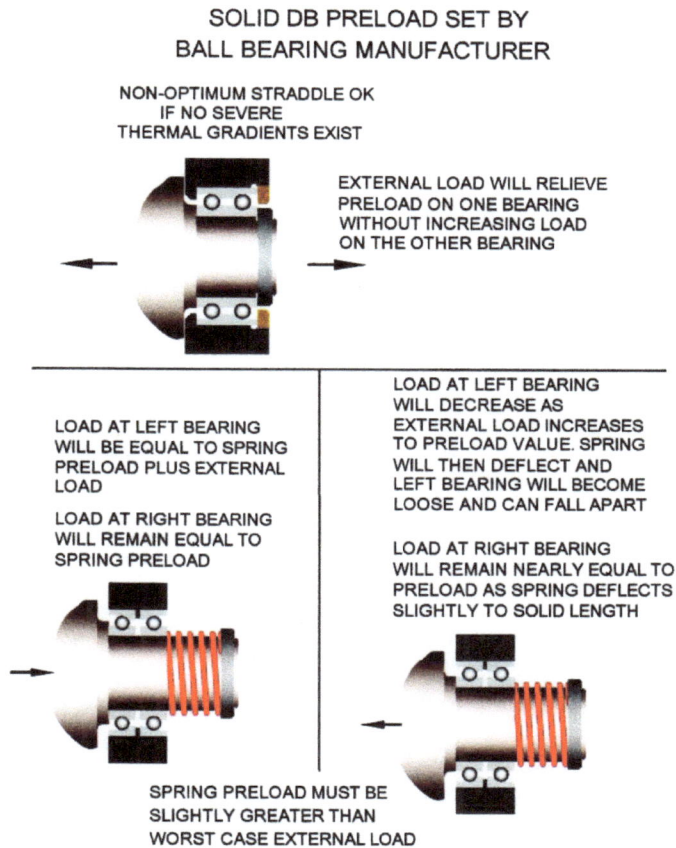

SOLID DB PRELOAD SET BY
BALL BEARING MANUFACTURER

NON-OPTIMUM STRADDLE OK
IF NO SEVERE
THERMAL GRADIENTS EXIST

EXTERNAL LOAD WILL RELIEVE
PRELOAD ON ONE BEARING
WITHOUT INCREASING LOAD
ON THE OTHER BEARING

LOAD AT LEFT BEARING
WILL BE EQUAL TO SPRING
PRELOAD PLUS EXTERNAL
LOAD

LOAD AT RIGHT BEARING
WILL REMAIN EQUAL TO
SPRING PRELOAD

LOAD AT LEFT BEARING
WILL DECREASE AS
EXTERNAL LOAD INCREASES
TO PRELOAD VALUE. SPRING
WILL THEN DEFLECT AND
LEFT BEARING WILL BECOME
LOOSE AND CAN FALL APART

LOAD AT RIGHT BEARING
WILL REMAIN NEARLY EQUAL TO
PRELOAD AS SPRING DEFLECTS
SLIGHTLY TO SOLID LENGTH

SPRING PRELOAD MUST BE
SLIGHTLY GREATER THAN
WORST CASE EXTERNAL LOAD

Figure 18 Preloading Methods

Diaphragms can be employed to avoid this problem; however, care must be taken to assure that the applied axial preload does not "roll" the diaphragm cross-section. A double diaphragm can prevent rolling, or a "special" diaphragm can be designed, as shown next. If the ball bearing cross-section is allowed to roll, the applied thrust load may cause the balls to override the bearing lip. This condition is known as "truncation" and causes higher contact stress (see Jones & Harris).

The purpose of next sketch is to show that a single spring diaphragm can be designed so that the bearing races will not roll due to the line of action of the preload.

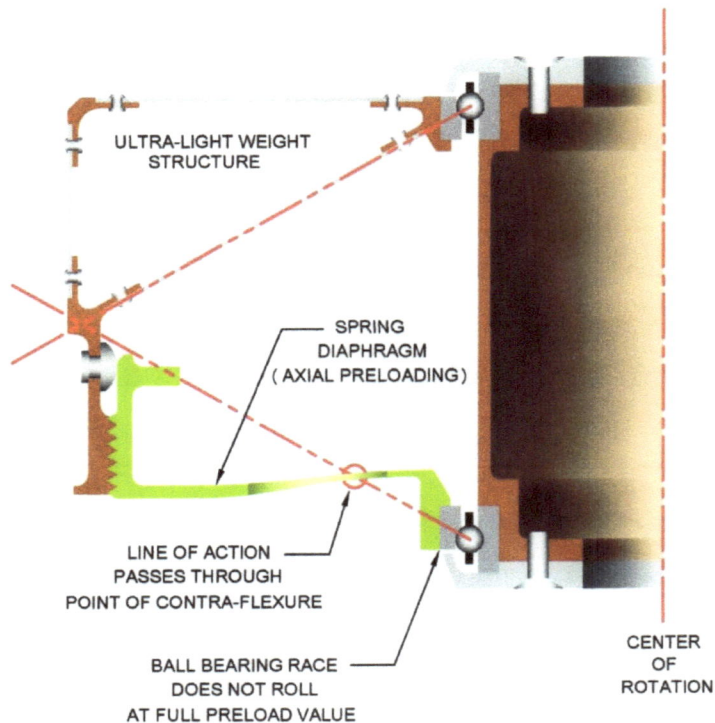

PRELOADING WITH A SINGLE SPRING DIAPHRAGM

Figure 19 Preloading with a Single Diaphragm

There is an additional item of discussion also included in the picture. An ultra light weight structure is shown. It represents the combining of precision machining and sheet metal technologies. I will discuss this a little later in this chapter.

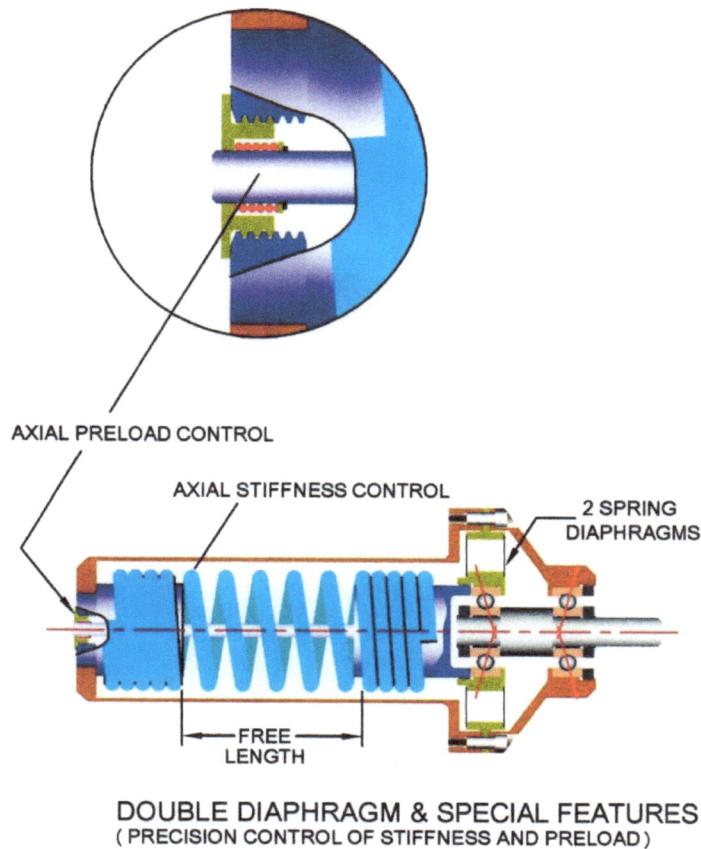

AXIAL PRELOAD CONTROL

AXIAL STIFFNESS CONTROL

2 SPRING
DIAPHRAGMS

FREE
LENGTH

DOUBLE DIAPHRAGM & SPECIAL FEATURES
(PRECISION CONTROL OF STIFFNESS AND PRELOAD)

Figure 20 Preload with a Double Diaphragm

The figure above shows a double diaphragm which allows axial motion. The purpose of this type of bearing mount is to provide extremely precise and independent control of bearing mounting stiffness and bearing preload. The inherent stiffness of the large blue spring produces the mounting stiffness of the ball bearing set. It is a frictionless axial support for the bearing pair. The double diaphragm is designed to be very compliant in the axial direction and has virtually no effect on system axial stiffness.

Preload of the bearing set is achieved independently with the small red spring at the left end of the device. The red spring is compressed to near solid length. The compression loading created by compressing the red spring stretches the large blue spring and is then reacted by compression loading of the ball bearing pair. This produces an extremely accurate DF preload of the bearing pair

48

Control of stiffness negates the effects of moderate thermal gradients and the control of preload assures that spin life time will meet calculated values because lubrication film thickness will match analysis predictions.

One additional special case of preloading is often useful: a pair of bearings can be mounted "face-to-face" (DF mounting)

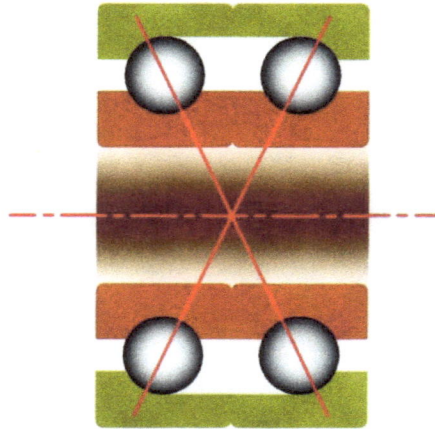

DF MOUNT WITH CONVERGING CONTACT ANGLES
(ZERO MOMENT CAPABILITY- ACTS LIKE A MONO-BALL)

Figure 21 Zero Moment Stiffness

It is possible to create a preloaded pivot similar to a mono-ball but with much lower friction. This type of preloading works well for devices that require only moderate load, speed, and life. The contact angle lines of actions must converge precisely to achieve an absolutely zero moment mount. While this is theoretically possible, it is not practical in the real world where load and dimensional changes cause the lines of action to shift. This is a neat trick, but it must be used with care.

Truncation

The next figure shows a loading case in which an extreme thrust load is applied to a ball bearing. The operating contact angle increases as the magnitude of the thrust load increases. If the thrust load is large enough, the ball contact area will over-ride the lip of the bearing race. This condition is called truncation and it results in a smaller contact area for a given load. The result is a higher contact stress. Truncation can result from a pure thrust load , a really vicious bending moment or the combination of both. Luckily the ball bearing analysis programs check for truncation and provide a warning if it occurs.

Some space programs have insisted that truncation not occur. This requires that larger ball bearings be used. And, the mass of the system is increased. However, there is an accepted technique for evaluating the effects of truncation. The existence of truncation does not have to invalidate a design.

Aerospace Corp. report TR-2001(8565)-4 provides a numerical method for evaluating truncation. You should refer to this report before you scrap a design.

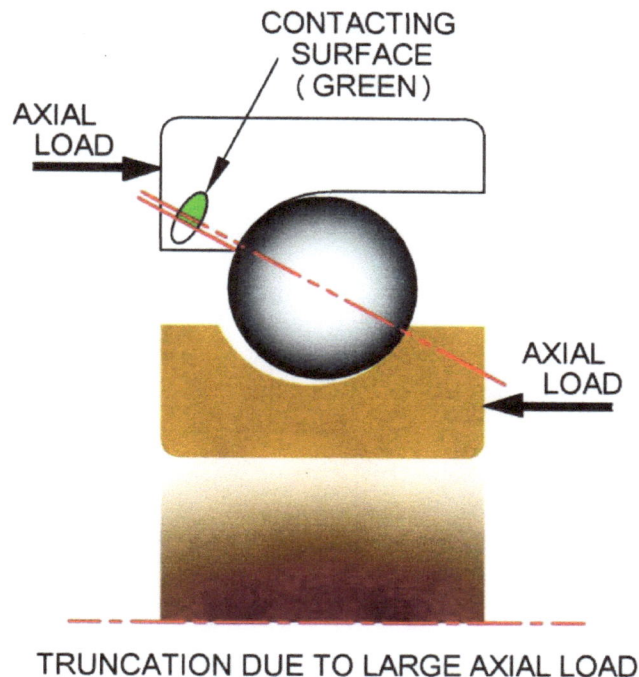

TRUNCATION DUE TO LARGE AXIAL LOAD

Figure 22 Definition of Truncation

Ultra Light Weight Support Structure

There is a trick which I have use very successfully several times. Occasionally, there is a need for a very light weight support for a ball bearing system. An example is shown below.

THIN GAGE SHEET METAL
RIVETED TO MACHINED RINGS
AND THEN FINAL CRITICAL BORES ARE MACHINED

LOAD LINE OF ACTION
IS ALIGNED WITH STRUCTURE

CENTER
OF
ROTATION

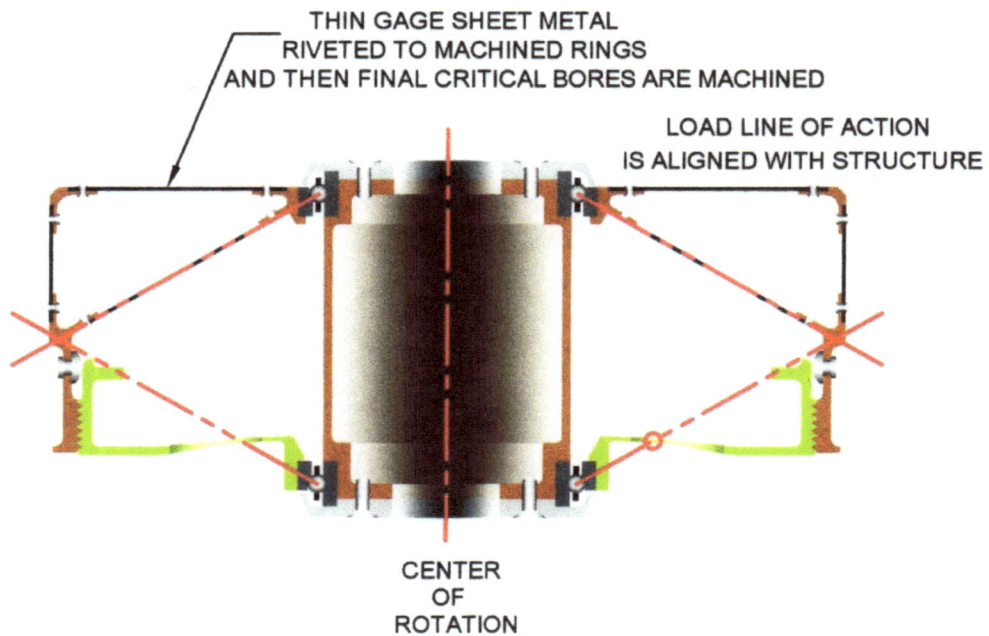

Figure 23 Ultra Light Weight Support Structure

The materials of choice would be steel ,titanium or beryllium sheet metal so that the structure thermal expansion characteristics match the ball bearing characteristics. The trick comes from a knowledge of sheet metal fabrication. I was lucky to have done substantial sheet metal design work early in my career. The folks who did that sort of work called themselves "tin benders" and they had many techniques to aid the process. Very few precision machinists know about "tin bending". The fields are very separate technologies.

There is a small device which any sheet metal fabricator knows about. It is a removable rivet called a "Cleco Clamp and, with its use, fabrication of ultra light structures is possible.

Figure 24 The Cleco Clamp

The Cleco Clamp (A Removable Rivet)

They can be installed and removed many times and, when installed, they preload the attached metal with a preload similar to a rivet. This returns a disassembled structure to its original alignment which is accurate enough that only a few thousand of an inch of extra material is needed for bearing bores and concentricity registration. Installation and removal of a Cleco is very easy using only a small hand tool.

Figure 25 Installation Tool for Clecos

The use of Clecos allows the rivet holes to be drilled and the structure to be thoroughly cleaned before rivets are installed. Some "blind rivets" will be necessary in order to allow closure of the structure. A blind rivet installs from one side only. No up-set head is require on the inside of the closed structure.

Chapter 5　　　　Gears and Gear Systems

Introduction and Source Information:

Gear technology in many ways is like ball-bearing technology. Lower quality, commercial gears are only a few "tenths" less accurate than high-precision aerospace gears.

I recommend that the section Understanding Precision (part of ball-bearing discussion) be reviewed before proceeding into Gear Design and Analysis.

Like ball bearings, gear design and analysis is best done with the use of computer programs, and a knowledge of gear geometry and terminology is required to use the program effectively. The following list of "source information" is provided to help the gear user.

Gear Design Source Information

There are many other "gear books," but I have found these sufficient to provide information for my gear design needs.

(1) Buckingham Gear Books "Revised Manual of Gear Design" (sections 1, 2 and 3)

"Analytical Mechanics of Gears"

"Design of Worm and Spiral Gears"

"Recess Action Gear Tables"

The original source for most other gear books

Available from: Buckingham Associates

591 Parker Hill Road

Springfield, VT 05156 (802) 885-5052

(2) "The Van Keuren Co. Handbook No. XX"

"Over-the-Pins" Gear Measuring System

Available from: The Van Keuren Co. Watertown, Mass

(3) "Precision Gearing Theory and Practice"

George W. Michalec

John Wiley & Sons, Inc.

The source for information on precision gearing

(4) "The Handbook of Practical Gear Design"

1st Edition 1984

Darle W. Dudley

McGraw-Hill Book Co.

The first edition contains a set of `programming information for gear analysis

(5) American Gear Manufacturers Standards

There is a very large group of gear standards published by the AGMA. The specific document numbers change frequently due to revisions. You can find listings for all the latest AGMA publication on the internet.

Two specific document titles to search out are:

"Design Guidelines for Aerospace Gearing" and

"Fundamental Rating Factors & Calculation Methods for Involute Spur and Helical Gears"

Computer Programs for Gear Design

There are a number of companies which sell gear design software. The primary problem with this material is cost. There are also several free programs, but be aware! You usually get what you pay for. The typical mechanism designer only occasionally does detail design of gears and this makes the cost of software important. I have developed my own gear design programs for spur gears. But, if you need more powerful software try names like: Universal Technical Services or KISSsoft. Check the internet.

Other Interesting Gear Information

(1) "Load/Life Curves for Gear and Cam Materials", Ralph A. Morrison, Machine Design
August 1, 1968

(2) "Wear Life of Aluminum Gears", A.H. MaschmeyerProduct Engineering

September 1956

(3) "Harmonic Drive -- A Factor in the Gear Industry", United Shoe Machinery Co.,October 28, 1962

AGMA 190.12, October 1962

(4) "Analysis of Harmonic Drive Reliability", C. Fredric Young/Ernest H. Scott

Harmonic Drive Division of USM

Special Gear Problems

Understanding Gear Errors

The next figure presents a simplified discussion of gear error generation. A very small error in run-out produces a large output position error. The actual problem is far more complicated, involving profile error, spacing error, lead angle variation, tooth thickness error, and backlash all, in addition to the run-out error discussed in the next figure. Also, each gear in the gear train exhibits similar errors. These errors will phase and sometimes add or subtract from each other. The actual input/output error plot of a complex gear system often shows a classical "beat" frequency. Chapter 4 of George Michalec's book, "Precision Gearing, Theory and Practice", discusses inherent gear errors in great detail. The simple analysis presented here provides a quick method for assessing the potential use of gearing in a precision system. But, read Michalec's work if you want to become really knowledgeable.

THE POSITION ERROR OF OUTPUT MOTION IS:
ANGULAR POSITION ERROR = e / R SIN 0
R = DRIVEN GEAR PITCH RADIUS
PEAK ANGULAR POSITION ERROR = e / R = TCE / 2R

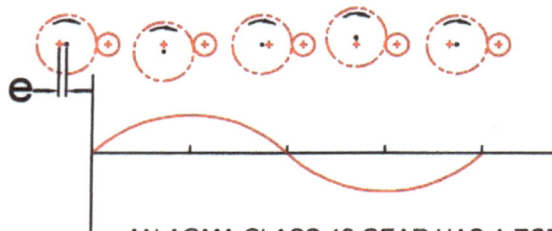

AN AGMA CLASS 13 GEAR HAS A TCE OF .0004
PEAK POSITION ERROR OF A 2.00 PITCH DIA GEAR WILL BE

E_{PEAK} = .0004 / 2.0 RADIANS = +/- 41.25 ARC SEC

CONCLUSION: PRECISION POSITIONING SYSTEMS SHOULD
SHOULD NOT USE GEARING AT OR NEAR THE OUTPUT.

Figure 26 Definition of Position Error

High-Frequency Tooth-to-Tooth Errors (TTEs)

Intuitively, a gear pair is thought to produce a precise amount of output motion for a specific amount of input motion. The ratio of input to output motions exactly equaling the "gear ratio." However, nature is not so kind.

In Figure 27, the slope of the "ideal" curve is the system gear ratio [θ_{in} / θ_{out} = gear ratio]. A closer look, reveals that the "actual" plot is a combination of a low frequency sine wave (the diametrical run-out) with a very much higher frequency sine wave (the individual tooth errors) superimposed upon it. The period of the high frequency error is equal to [360°/no. of teeth]. The slope of the instantaneous "actual" plot is negative for approximately one half of each sinusoidal cycle. The output is actually moving in the wrong direction!

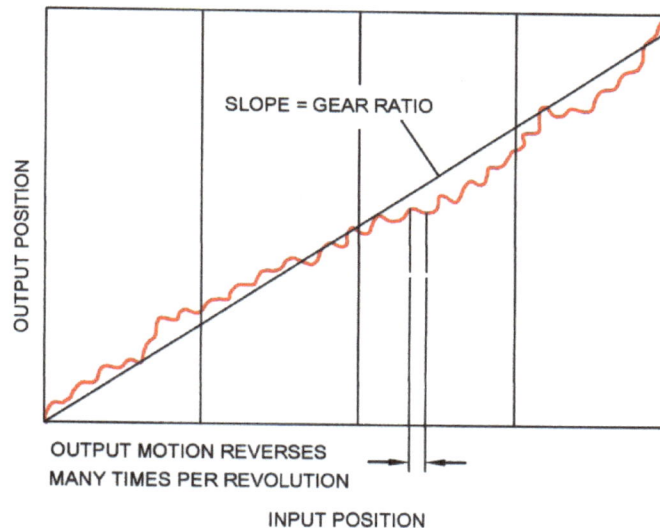

Figure 27 TTE High Frequency Errors

This effect becomes more pronounced in very high ratio systems because the ideal gear ratio curve is more nearly horizontal.

The effect is relatively repeatable (although temperature extremes may affect repeatability), and the majority of the error can be calibrated if a sufficiently accurate input-output measurement system is available. This represents time and money. Other less costly approaches should be considered. A band drive will totally eliminate the high frequency error, and it may be possible to maintain a positive drive.

However, the output motion must be smaller than one revolution so that the band can be secured to both the input shaft and output pulley.

A 128-tooth gear driven at 10 rpm will have a "tooth contact frequency" of:

$$\omega_{TTE} = 128 \left(\frac{cyc}{rev}\right) X \frac{1}{6} \left(\frac{rev}{sec}\right) X 2\pi \left(\frac{rad}{cyc}\right) = 134 \left(\frac{rad}{sec}\right) = 21.2HZ$$

It is important to consider the frequency at which the higher frequency tooth errors are occurring. In our example, the fundamental frequency for a 10 rpm output would be 21.2 Hz. This is definitely not a good neighborhood for motion reversals of large masses (low frequency structural vibration).

Deriving Worst-Case Torque Ripple

In the last two sections, position error and its frequency have been reviewed. This leads next to a discussion of the nearly instantaneous accelerations that must occur if output motion is to reverse periodically.

This section provides a simplified calculation of the "worst case" output acceleration which will occur. The acceleration is then applied to an arbitrary inertial mass to show that very large inertial torques can occur.

The following example will help to define the seriousness of the problem: We will call our mythical model "Doom Sat". The name's got a nice ring to it! Imagine hundreds of designers bending over their drawing boards, chuckling softly as they create "Doom-Sat". It will consist of two sections: (1) A stable platform, and (2) A rotatable platform with precise pointing accuracy requirements.

It will also probably have solar arrays and movable doors or covers. We chose to use a gearbox which is momentum compensated (see Chapter 15) to rotate the platform because accurate positioning is not required during periods of rotation.

We also place the appendage frequency well above the frequency of the gear box errors. We've covered the bases. Or have we?

If the torsional stiffness through the gearbox is very high and if the rotational control system employs dynamic braking (required to achieve accurate output positioning), the system will "stop on a dime." Settling time will be in a fraction of a second.

But what about those flexible appendages? Our torque ripple frequency was well below their natural frequency. The problem is that we have deflected the appendages slightly as our gearbox torque ripples through the system (momentum compensation can never be perfect in a geared system). The platform motion stops instantly. The deflected appendages then exchange momentum with the rigid two-body system, and each flexible element of the entire system continues to vibrate. By making the appendages stiff, we assured low damping and a very long settling time!

Gear drives can be used in positioning systems which require arc minute accuracies. But, the secondary effects such as torque ripple must be evaluated.

The error in tooth contact generates torque ripple.

$$\textbf{High Freq Position Error} = \frac{\textbf{TTE}}{\textbf{2R}}(\sin \theta) = \frac{\textbf{TTE}}{\textbf{2R}}(\sin \omega t)$$

A 128-tooth gear driven at 10 rpm will have a "tooth contact frequency" of :

$$\omega_{TTE} = 128 \left(\frac{cyc}{rev}\right) X \frac{1}{6}\left(\frac{rev}{sec}\right) X 2\pi \left(\frac{rad}{cyc}\right) = 134 \left(\frac{rad}{sec}\right)$$

If the driven gear is 2.0 in. in diameter and AGMA class 13 :

$$\textbf{Output Acceleration} = \pm \left(\frac{\textbf{TTE}}{\textbf{2R}}\right)\omega^2 = \pm \frac{.0002}{2.0}(134)^2 = \pm 1.8 \frac{rad}{sec^2}$$

And, (for a 1.0 slug-ft^2 output inertia),Generated torque ripple = ±1.8 ft-lb

Very large torque ripple can be generated by very small dimensional errors.

Next, let's look at a case where the "speed" of the error is much greater than 10 rpm.

The harmonic drive provides a special case. A size 20 (2.0 pitch diameter) harmonic drive will have a peak position error of 2.0 arc minutes or 0.00058 rad and the error frequency will be twice per input revolution because of the 2 lobe wave generator.

If, as in the previous example, the output speed is 10 rpm and the gear ratio is 100:1, the forcing frequency will be:

$$\omega_{input=} 2 \ x100x \ \frac{1}{6}\left(\frac{rev}{sec}\right) x \ 2\pi \left(\frac{rad}{rev}\right) = 209 \left(\frac{rad}{sec}\right)$$

and (for a 1.0 slug-ft2 output inertia), Generated torque ripple = ±25.3 ft-lb

$$\textbf{Output Acceleration} = \pm.00058 \textbf{ rad x} \left(209 \left(\frac{rad}{sec}\right)\right)^2 = \pm 25.3 \frac{rad}{sec^2}$$

Conclusion: The harmonic drive is significantly less accurate and produces far more torque ripple than simple precision spur gear pairs.

Important Characteristics of Gear Systems

All new geared actuators should be tested to generate a plot of output shaft mechanical hysteresis (see figure below). This single plot contains the friction, backlash and spring rate characteristics of the actuator. The data is fundamental to system-level analysis. Typical test method is to apply a maximum load in one direction and to lower the load in increments through zero load and out to maximum load in the opposite direction then reduce the load in the same increments through zero and back out to the original starting load. The test load must be applied and removed very smoothly. The test is self-checking. If the measured "loop" does not close, you haven't done the test correctly. Discussion in Chapter 14 (BDC motor performance calculations) shows why it is fundamentally important to generate this information.

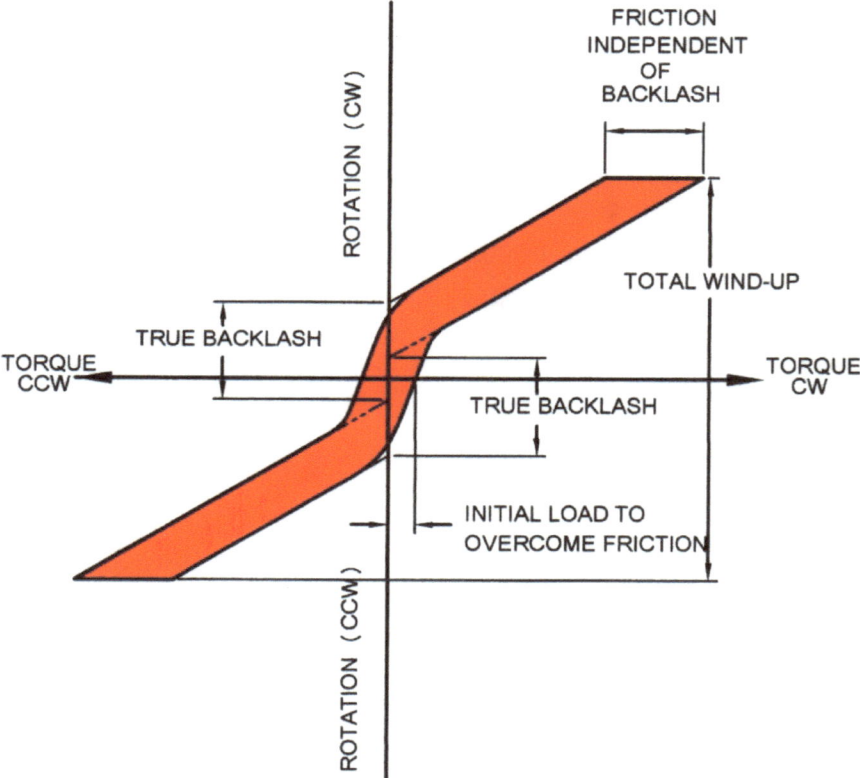

Figure 28 Mechanical Hysteresis Loop

Another important test parameter is input shaft friction versus input speed. I have found that gear box losses can best be defined as a two part loss. (1) The first part is a "no load" drag torque measured over the operating speed range. And, (2) an operating efficiency number based upon an estimate of the operating efficiency of the gear box. This data should include testing at cold extremes also.

Reflecting Gear System Stiffness

The torsional stiffness of a gear drive is reflected by the square of the gear ratio:

$$K_{out} = \frac{T_{out}}{\theta_{out}}$$

$$T_{out} = N\ (T_{in})$$

$$K_{in} = \frac{T_{in}}{\theta_{in}}$$

$$\therefore\ K_{in} = \frac{1}{N}\ x\ \frac{T_{out}}{N(\theta_{out})} = \frac{1}{N^2}\ \frac{T_{out}}{\theta_{out}}$$

$$K_{out} = N^2\ K_{in}$$

Things to learn about Gears

My intent in this document is to discuss items which are not well explained in the "Classical Literature". I also try to provide you with the names of items which I believe are "Classics" with regard to the field of Mechanisms Design.

This body of literature contains very good answers to the following questions:

(1) What is involute tooth profile modification and when do you use it?

Answer: See Buckingham's "Manual of Gear Design" Section 2, pg 52 through 55.

(2) How is recess action and approach action changed?

Answer: see answer to question (1).

(3) Is heavily recessed action always good?

Answer: No! If the driving gear becomes the driven gear (as in dynamic braking), you get full approach action.

(4) Can pure rolling motion ever be achieved with involute gear pairs?

Answer: No!

(5) Is there any other gear tooth form which can provide pure rolling motion?

Answer: Yes! The cycloidal tooth profile will produce pure rolling action.

(6) Is it important to protect gear systems?

Answer: (read Chapter 17, titled "Protection").

(7) What is gear tooth contact ratio and why is it important?

Answer: See Buckingham's "Manual of Gear Design" Section 2, pg 32. It is defined as (mp) and represents the number of teeth sharing load in a working gear mesh.

(8 What is the significance of Helical Gears to contact ratio?

Answer: Helical Gear pairs will have higher contact ratios.

(9) Is the backlash specification for a gear pair affected by the motor / driver?

Answer: Yes!, Any gear system which acts as a driver and a brake must have minimized backlash. The electric car guys found this out the hard way.

Chapter 6   Transmitting Motion Without Gears

Introduction:

A Discussion of Motion Transmission where Gears are not the best solution.

(1) Friction Drives

(2) Metallic Band Drives

(3) Timing Belts

Friction Drives:

The friction-drive system is a flight proven device. (See Figure 29). It provides very smooth, long-life performance. The recommended friction material is polyurethane (Adriprene L-100) or equivalent procured to MIL-R-3065. The friction drive is not a positive drive. The instantaneous gear ratio is proportional to the instantaneous torque transmitted; however, the friction drive is still usable in very high accuracy systems provided the position is sensed beyond the friction interface (at the output). The torsional stiffness of a friction drive is a function of the thickness of the polyurethane coating. If the friction drive is located near the high-speed end of a drive, its contribution to overall compliance will be small (remember, stiffness reflects as the square of the gear ratio). Wear is minimal well beyond a million or more wheel revs.

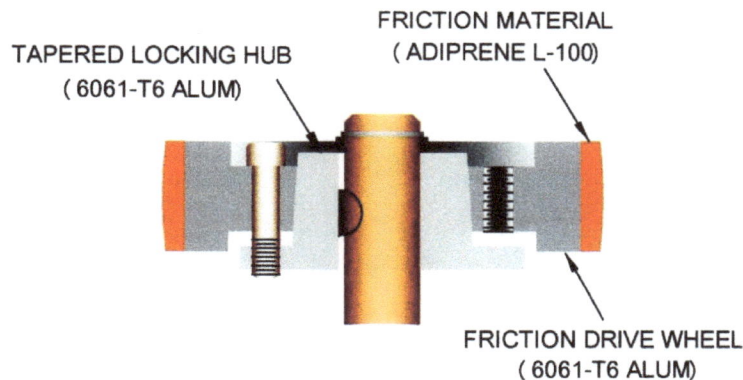

Figure 29 The Friction Drive Wheel

Drive rim must be coated to improve coefficient of friction. Magnesium should be coated with DOW 17 anodic coating. Aluminum should be coated with a sulfuric acid anodize. The achievable coefficient of friction is 0.9 or better.

Material Specification for Friction Material

The requirements called out for control of the polyurethane elastomer are as follows:

Molded urethane conforming to MIL-R-3065 with properties and procedures per MIL-STD-417, SC 830-3A1, F2, K1, 100 lb/in/w minimum peel strength. Amber color, outgas 1.5 hr at 180°F in a vacuum of 5 mm Hg immediately after cure.

(1) Code callout "SC" indicates oil-resistant, low-volume-swell type of material.

(2) 830 indicates a shore "A" harness of 80 ± 5 and a minimum tensile strength of 3000 psi.

(3) 3 indicates that the material shall have a minimum elongation of 300%.

(4) A1 is resistance to heat aging (70 hr at 212°F).

(5) F2 is low-temperature brittleness of -67°F.

(6) K1 indicates adhesion to metal with the bond made during cure (2 hr at 212°F).

(7) Z1 indicates special requirements over and above the requirements of MIL-R-3065, these requirements are: 100 lbs/in./w peel strength, to be out-gassed 1.5 hrs. at 180°F in a vacuum of 5 mm Hg immediately after cure.

(8) Further control of the polyurethane processing is achieved by requirements imposed on the vendor of the molded elastomer for control of batch compounding and physical test data of each batch of material.

Actual Test Results

	REQUIRED	OBTAINED
DUROMETER HARDNESS, SHORE A	80 ± 5	85
TENSILE STRENGTH (PSI)	3000 (MIN)	4320
ULTIMATE ELONGATION (%)	300	430
TEAR STRENGTH (LB/IN) THICKNESS	---	---
HEAT AGED 70 HR @ 212°F	50 % (MAX)	28 %
HARDNESS CHANGE (%)	+ 15 MAX	± 0
TENSILE CHANGE (%)	-15	+30
ELONGATION CHANGE (%)	-35	+9
COMPRESSION SET AFTER 22HR @ 158°F	50 % (MAX)	28 %
VOLUME CHANGE (%)	0 TO +120	+21
F2	PASS	PASS
K1 (LB / IN)	100 MIN	185 (R)
Z1	ADRIPRENE L-100 POLYURETHANE	PASS

Figure 30 Friction Material Specification

Gear Ratio Variation

The gear ratio of any friction drive will change whenever the transmitted torque changes. The effect is caused by the stretching of the elastomeric interface which occurs any time that torque is being transmitted. This is not a slippage at the contacting surfaces. The effect is very repeatable and can be easily determined by counting driver/driven relative rotation under load at speed.

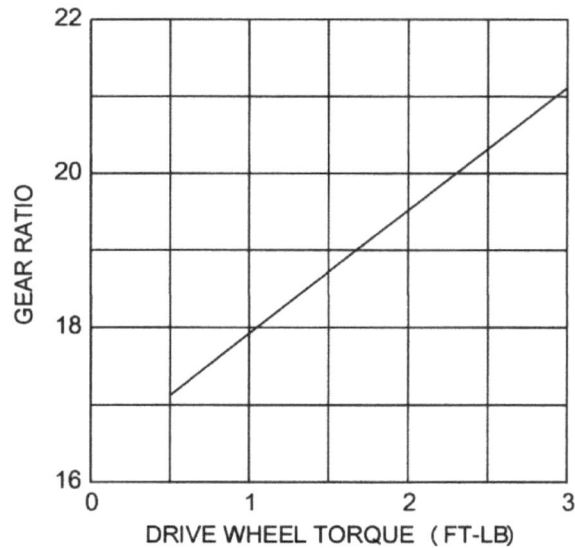

Figure 31 Gear Ratio Variation

The friction drive applications which have been developed used brush or brushless motors. If you plan to use a stepper motor / friction drive, you should carefully evaluate the effect on gear ratio.

Torsional Stiffness of a Friction Drive

The torsional stiffness of a friction drive can be estimated as follows:

(assume E= 695 lb/in^2)

A = Contact Ellipse Area   r = Radius of Coated Wheel

G= Shear Modulus (Approx 1/3 of E)   L= Thickness of Elastomer

$1/K_{(linear)} = L/AG$

$K_{(rotation)} = r^2 [K_{(linear)}]$

$$F_n = \frac{1}{2\pi} \sqrt[2]{K_r/I}$$

A two foot diameter wheel with an inertia of 1.0 slug ft^2 and a 1/8 elastomer tire would have a Torsional Stiffness of 5.56x10^4 in-lb/radian and a natural frequency of 10.8 HZ

See: ASME paper 84-DET-100 for a more detailed analysis.

Metallic Band Drives

The metallic band drive can provide a smooth, high stiffness, positive drive for limited rotation applications. There are perforated metallic drive bands. However their life characteristics are unknown and it would be expected that long life lubrication of such systems would be very difficult to achieve. The band drives shown in this section are tested configurations. They have demonstrated millions of revs/inches of travel with only moderate wear. The band drive is at least as clean as any equivalent gear drive/rack and pinion.

The metallic band drive has been used for many long-duration deployment applications. There are certain applications where the metallic band is uniquely suited. Historically, Metallic bands are also usable at much colder temperatures than friction drives or positive drive belts.

Figure 32 Dual Band Drive System

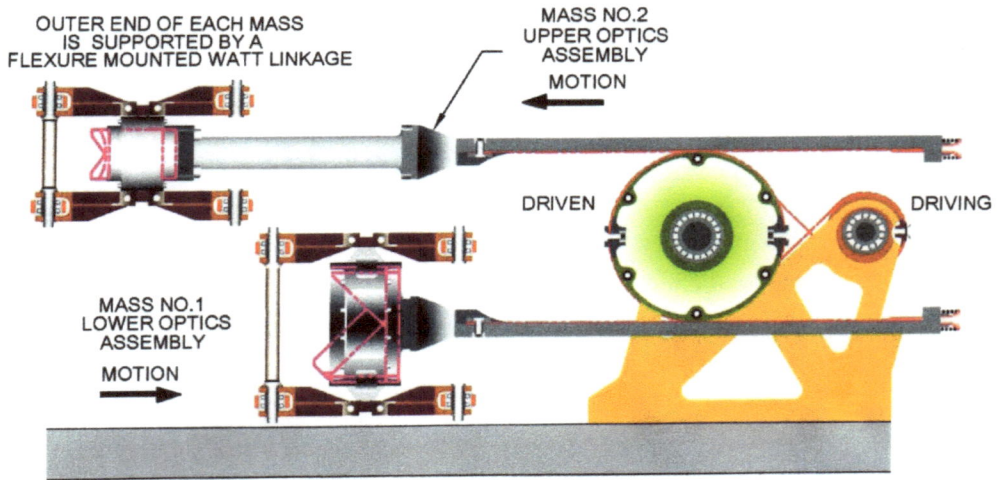

Figure 33 Side View of Dual Band Drive

OUTER END OF EACH MASS
IS SUPPORTED BY A
FLEXURE MOUNTED WATT LINKAGE

MASS NO.2
UPPER OPTICS
ASSEMBLY

MOTION

DRIVEN

DRIVING

MASS NO.1
LOWER OPTICS
ASSEMBLY

MOTION

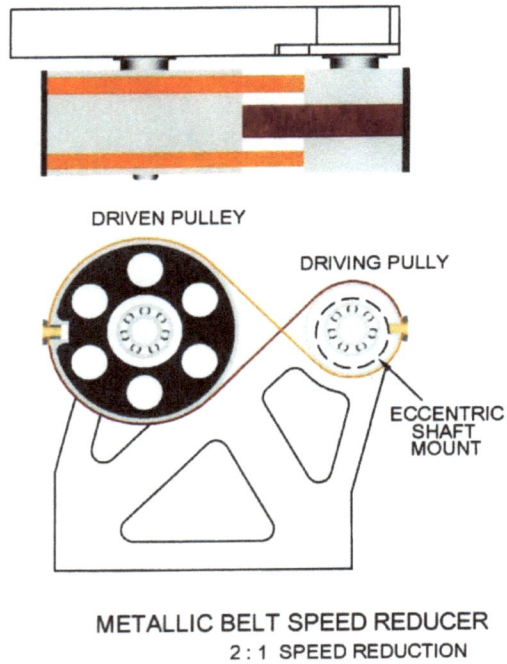

DRIVEN PULLEY

DRIVING PULLY

ECCENTRIC
SHAFT
MOUNT

METALLIC BELT SPEED REDUCER
2 : 1 SPEED REDUCTION

Figure 34 Ratio Band Drive

A Band Drive System as shown in the next figure can be used at cyrogenic temperatures to produce long life linear and rotary motion. The supporting ball bearings can be thermally isolated in a warmer environment and grease lubricated to provide a long operating life. The band tensioning system shown below will not cause loading of the support ball bearings.

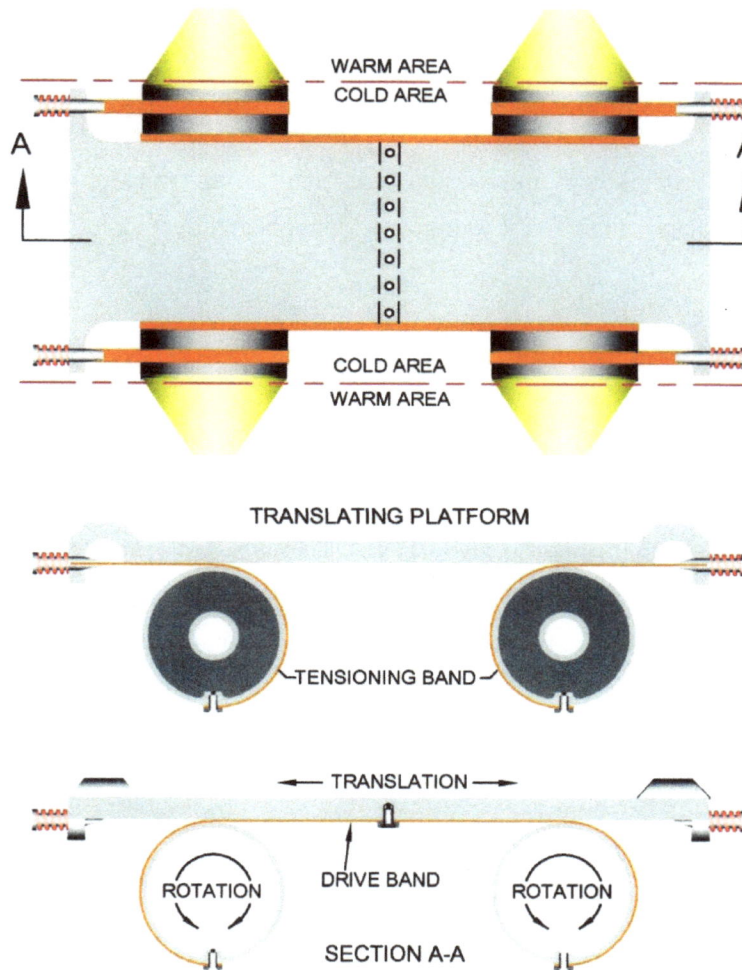

Figure 35 Linear Motion in an Ultra Cold Environment

Recommended Materials for Drive Bands

The flexure stress required to bend a flat band over a radius is equal to: $STRESS_{FLEXURE} = \frac{Ec}{R}$

Two metallic materials are available in strip form with lengths of several thousand inches: Elgiloy is a nickel-cobalt alloy: F_{tu} = 368,000 lb/in^2 , E = 29x10^6 lb/in^2

Be-Cu is a copper- beryllium alloy: F_{tu} = 175,000 lb/in^2 , E = 19x10^6 lb/in^2

A third possibility is titanium strip but available length is uncertain.

Titanium (13V-11Cr-3Al): F_{tu} = 250,000 lb/in^2 , E = 16x10^6 lb/in^2

Deployment Rate Limiters

The Magnetometer Booms on the Galileo and Cassini spacecrafts were stored energy deployment devices which used a viscous damper and a deployable metallic band lanyard to limit the rate of boom deployment. The Proceedings of the 19TH Aerospace Mechanisms Symposium contains a paper which discusses this subject.

Simultaneous Deployment and Retraction

Band drives can also provide special deployment functions. A single drive system can deploy a telescoping boom structure by drawing in a metallic lanyard while simultaneously paying out a second spring tensioned lanyard which maintains structural stability of the deploying mass. Two pulleys would be linked together with a torsional spring preload (negator spring). The pulleys rotate in the same direction. One of the pulleys draws in a metallic lanyard to cause the deployment to occur while the other pulley pays out a tensioned metallic lanyard to stabilize the deploying boom. The payout pulley is only attached to the drive actuator through the negator spring coupling the two pulleys. Therefore, the payout pulley can windup or unwind as the deployment progresses assuring a nearly constant lanyard tension. This wind/unwind feature compensates for the changing payout / take-up rates caused by the number of raps of lanyard material on each pulley (the lanyard working radius varies as material is added / removed. A differential wind-up must occur during the first half of deployment and beyond deployment midpoint the windup will reverse so that the pulleys will return to the same relative rotational positions which existed at the start of deployment. Obviously, the empty pulley spool should be as large a diameter as possible to minimize the payout/take-up rate differences.

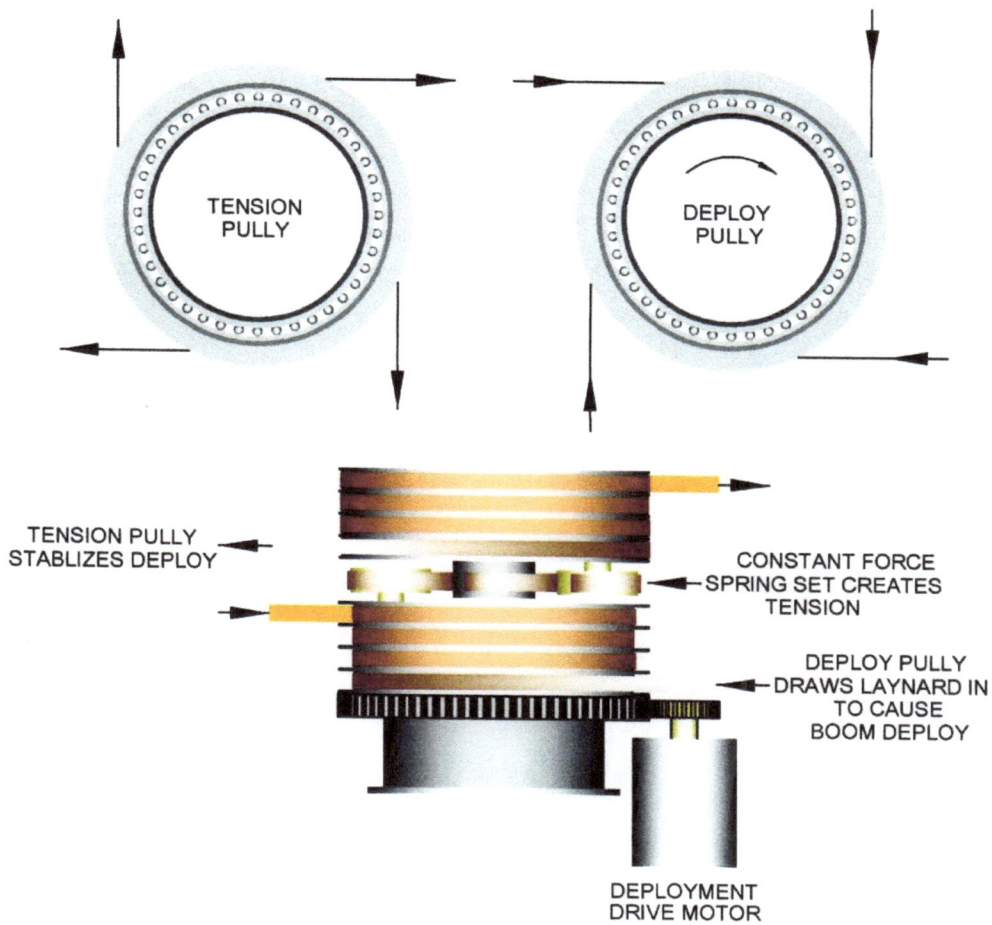

TENSION
PULLY

DEPLOY
PULLY

TENSION PULLY
STABLIZES DEPLOY

CONSTANT FORCE
SPRING SET CREATES
TENSION

DEPLOY PULLY
DRAWS LAYNARD IN
TO CAUSE
BOOM DEPLOY

DEPLOYMENT
DRIVE MOTOR

Figure 36 Simultaneous Deployment and Retraction

Positive Drive Belts:

Positive drive belts have been used in space but only to a very limited extent. The positive drive belt provides smooth, positive, continuous motion. However, belt wear debris is a real problem in long-life applications.

It is usually necessary to tension the positive drive belt using an auxiliary tensioning idler pulley. This adds extra functional components and reduces reliability.

Emergency disengagement of the belt drive system is a real problem (see "Protective Devices"). It is possible to mechanically decouple the drive motor but the belt and tensioning idlers remain attached to the operating system.

Figure 37 Commercial Positive Drive Belt

Timing belts have several standard pitch sizes. Standard drive pulleys and tensioning pulleys are also available as catalog items Check out the information available on-line.

Helically wound tension members
are the secret to timing belt strength,
long life and resistance to elongation.

Figure 38 Construction Details - Drive Belts

Source Information – Drive Belts

Goodyear Tire and Rubber Co.

Lincoln MFG Division

Lincoln, Nebraska 68501

Emerson Power Transmission Corp

Morse Industrial

Ithaca, New York 14850

Stock Drive Products

New Hyde Park, New York 11040

(Mini-Pitch Series)

PIC Design

Middlebury, CT 06762

Winfred M. Berg Inc.

East Rockaway, L.I., NY 11518

Problems with Belt Drives

(A) Contamination
 (B) Inhibits Redundancy
 (C) Temperature Sensitivity

Chapter 7   Spring Elements

Introduction:

The most basic equations of spring design are presented here. Much more information is available in the referenced source material. Any designer/engineer who frequently uses springs should, as a minimum, own copies of the following material:

"Mechanical Springs," A.M. Wahl

McGraw-Hill (1963)

This is probably the single best source for spring design information ("a great read"). He begins with the basics of spring design (Parts I, II, and III) and then in Part IV, he addresses spring theory.

"Design Handbook, Springs and Custom Metal Parts,"

Associated Spring Corporation, Bristol, CN 06010

This design handbook contains much of the same information as Wahl's book, but in an easier-to-use format.

MIL-STD-29A "Springs, Mechanical, Drawing Requirements for"

This document is a good source for cross-reference purposes.

A Few Tips Include:

(1) Don't forget to use corrected stress values.
(2) De-rate working stress for high temp applications (MIL-STD29A)
(3) Avoid resonance effects and surging (Wahl p. 294)
(4) Remember, high-strain materials make the best springs
(5) Remember, a buckled column (The Elastica) is a nearly constant force spring
(6) For helical springs, design for no yield at solid height. Then use "cold-set" to obtain maximum performance.
(7) Remember that compressing a helical spring will cause the ends to rotate and the outside diameter to expand

High Strain

The selection of a material for use in designing a spring element is greatly aided by the idea of "High Strain Capability":

$$\text{Strain} = \frac{\text{Tensile Strength}}{\text{Modulus of Elasticity}}$$

If you want to store the maximum energy, use materials with the highest possible tensile strength coupled with the lowest possible Modulus of Elasticity.

Spring Materials Operated in Bending (Beams and Columns)

$$\text{Example (Steel) Utl Strain} = \frac{250,000 \frac{lb}{in^2}}{30 \times 10^6 \frac{lb}{in^2}} = .83\%$$

$$\text{Example (Titanium) Utl Strain} = \frac{250,000 \frac{lb}{in^2}}{16 \times 10^6 \frac{lb}{in^2}} = 1.56\%$$

$$\text{Example (S Glass Epoxy) Utl Strain} = \frac{250,000 \frac{lb}{in^2}}{7.2 \times 10^6 \frac{lb}{in^2}} = 3.47\%$$

Spring Materials Operated in Torsion (Helical Springs)

$$\text{Example (Steel) Utl Strain} = \frac{100,000 \frac{lb}{in^2}}{10 \times 10^6 \frac{lb}{in^2}} = 1.00\%$$

$$\text{Example (Titanium) Utl Strain} = \frac{100,000 \frac{lb}{in^2}}{7 \times 10^6 \frac{lb}{in^2}} = 1.43\%$$

(S-GLASS EPOXY)   Not Applicable Because it is a uni-directional laminated material which should not be used in torsion.

Special Materials:

The previously mentioned "design" source books contain much valuable data on common spring materials but there are many newer materials of great value:

"Titanium, Cold Worked 13V-11Cu-3Al Wire and Strip"

This is a special long lead material

Cold worked round wire aged at 800°F for 10 hours

F_{tu} = 250 to 300 Ksi for wire diameter of .064 inch or less

F_{tu} = 240 to 290 Ksi for wire diameter of .065 inch to .099 inch

F_{tu} = 230 to 280 Ksi for wire diameter of .100 inch to .159 inch

F_{tu} = 220 to 270 Ksi for wire diameter of .160 inch to .224 inch

F_{tu} = 210 to 260 Ksi for wire diameter of .225 inch or greater

Tensile Modulus (E) = 15.0 x10^6 lb/In^2

Shear Modulus (G) = 6.2 x10^6 lb/In^2

"Elgiloy, the Cobalt-Nickel Alloy"

Available from Elgiloy Co., Elgin, IL 60120

Cold drawn and aged

F_{tu} = 280 Ksi (min) for wire dia of .060 inch to .120 inch

Tensile Modulus (E) = 27.5 x 10^6 lbs/In^2

Shear Modulus (G) = 11.2 x 10^6 lbs/in^2

"N-S Spring Wire"

National-Standard Co.

N-S Wire Div, Niles, MI 49120

(specifically regarding super alloy wire)

"Titanium Beta C Alloy 3-8-6-4-4"

(per AMS 4957)

This is a readily available titanium material used by spring manufacturers

Source Material for Stiffness & Natural Frequency Equations

"Vibration Theory and Application", William T. Thomson

Prentice-Hall (1965)

(See figure 101 of that book)

"Shock & Vibration Handbook", Cyril M. Harris & Charles E. Crede

MCGraw-Hill (1961)

(See figure 102, 103 & 104 of that book)

Source Material for Data of Deflecting Structures

"Handbook of Formulas For Stress & Strain", Frederick Ungar Publishing Co. (1976)

"Formulas for Stress & Strain", Roark & Young, MCGraw-Hill (1975)

Stiffness Relationships

The stiffness characteristics for Bending (EI/L), Torsion (JG/L) and Tension / Compression (AE/L) are very simple:

However, the classical helically wound spring which performs the same function as the tension rod / column appears to have a very different set of functional parameters. This is because the material in the helical spring is actually operating as a torsion rod!

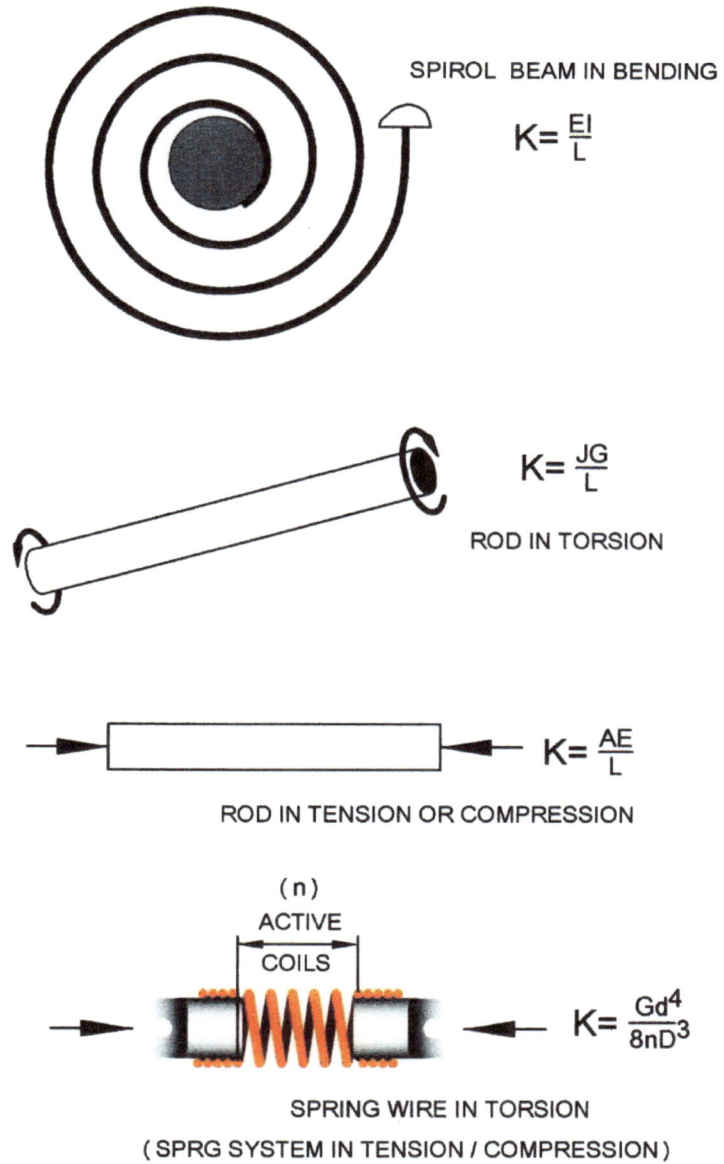

SPIROL BEAM IN BENDING

$$K= \frac{EI}{L}$$

$$K= \frac{JG}{L}$$

ROD IN TORSION

$$K= \frac{AE}{L}$$

ROD IN TENSION OR COMPRESSION

(n)
ACTIVE
COILS

$$K= \frac{Gd^4}{8nD^3}$$

SPRING WIRE IN TORSION
(SPRG SYSTEM IN TENSION / COMPRESSION)

Figure 39 Stiffness of Helical Springs

The next figure shows how the parameters of the stiffness equations change when the application of loading changes:

TENSION / COMP

$$K = \frac{Gd^4}{8nD^3}$$

LATERAL

SEE: HARRIS & CREDE
EQ (34.10 & 34.11)
FIGURE (34.22)

TORSION

$$K = \frac{Ed^4}{32\, nD}$$

BENDING

$$K = \frac{Ed^4}{32\, nD} \left(\frac{1}{1 + \frac{E}{2G}} \right)$$

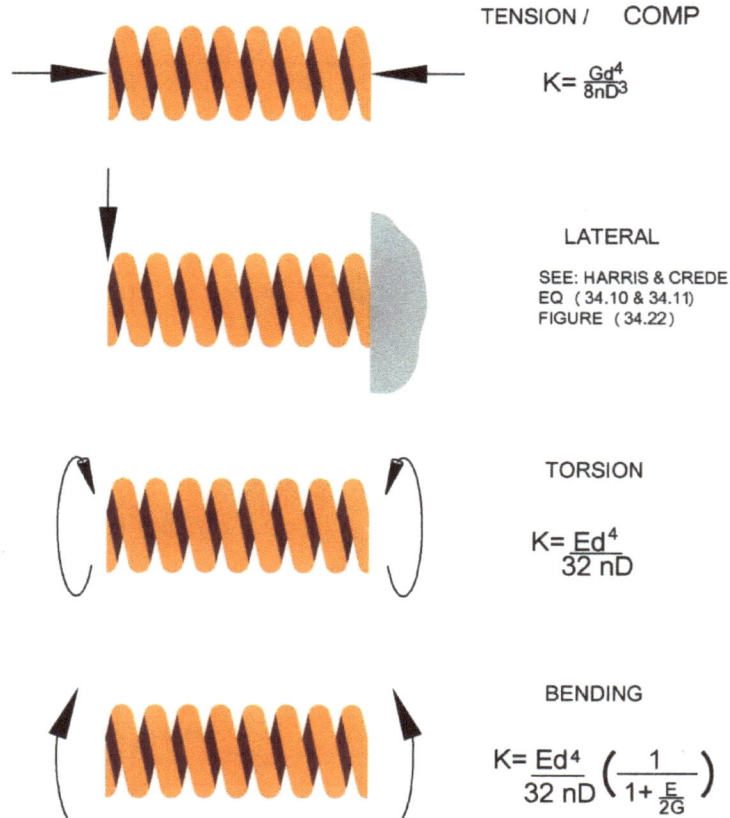

Figure 40 Stiffness Equations

Designing Helical Springs

Typically, the two most important parameters for a helical spring are: (1) load capacity and (2) deflection. A simple way to quickly "size" a spring is described as follows.

Start by selecting a material for the spring. This provides you with an allowable working shear stress. Use a conservatively low allowable stress because a stress correction factor (K) will be calculated once the wire size and mean spring diameter are known. The ratio of Mean Spring Diameter (D) / Wire Diameter (d) is called the spring index (c).

c = D / d

The stress correction factor (K) is:

$$K = \frac{4c-1}{4c-4} + \frac{0.615}{c}$$

Usually the volume available for the spring is known. So, a guess can be made at the spring diameter. Use a diameter less than the maximum available volume because (D) is a mean diameter not the spring outside diameter. Next, use the following equation to calculate a wire diameter:

$$\textbf{Uncorrected Shear Stress } (\tau) = \frac{8PD}{\pi d^3}$$

(P) =the desired spring load. A deflection per coil (δ) can then be calculated:

$$\frac{\textbf{Deflection}}{\textbf{Coil}}(\delta) = \frac{Gd^4}{8nD^3}$$

(G) is the Shear Modulus of the selected spring material

(n) is the number of active coils and is equal to one .

Knowing the deflection per coil, calculate the number of active coils necessary to produce the desired total spring deflection. Remember, the spring will probably be partially compressed to start with and will need extra active coils to account for initial deflection plus working deflection.

These initial calculated parameters can then be used to recalculate final parameters which use a properly corrected shear stress.

Practical Considerations

Note that the shear stress is very sensitive to minor variations of the wire diameter (d) and the deflection is very sensitive to both wire diameter (d) and spring diameter (D).

The final selection of a wire size will be influenced by the cost and availability of that specific wire size. Spring manufacturers have many wire sizes "in stock". However, the available "in stock" wire will probably not be the same exact size which you initially calculate. If you are lucky enough to work for a company which will allow you to contact the spring manufacturer directly, during the design phase, before you "release" your design to purchasing, you can avoid a redesign by simply asking a specific spring manufacturer for his available wire sizes. Then design your spring to a specific available wire size. Of course, this requires that the springs actually be procured from the contacted supplier. No body, including procurement organizations likes to be told "where to go"! A way around this problem is to find the wire and place an advanced purchase order for the wire only. If the purchasing group understands what is going on, they will be much more likely to agree to place the spring order with a specific company (a single source procurement). It becomes a win-win situation for everyone.

Special Springs

Bi-Stable Springs

It is possible for a spring manufacturer to produce a "bi-stable" flat spring by controlling the residual stress pattern in the sheet stock material.

Many years ago the Associated Spring Corporation (ASC) produced two bi-stable spring configurations: (1) The "Tru-Trac" continuous strip material and (2) The "Flip-Flop" disc. These products are missing from the more recent ASC catalogs. But a good starting point for exploring these devices would be the Associated Spring Corp.

**Figure 42 Flip-Flop
Bi-Stable Spring**

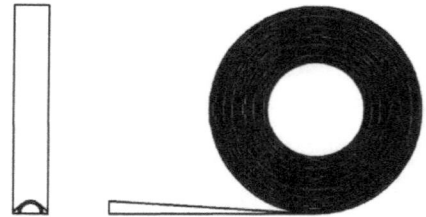

**Figure 41 True-Track
Measuring Tape**

Initially, the disc is curved along the X axis.
when the disc is deflected to its "other" stable position,
the axis of curvature moves to the Y axis and the curvature reverses.

81

Ring Springs

CONTACT: Ringfeder Corporation, Westwood, NJ 07675

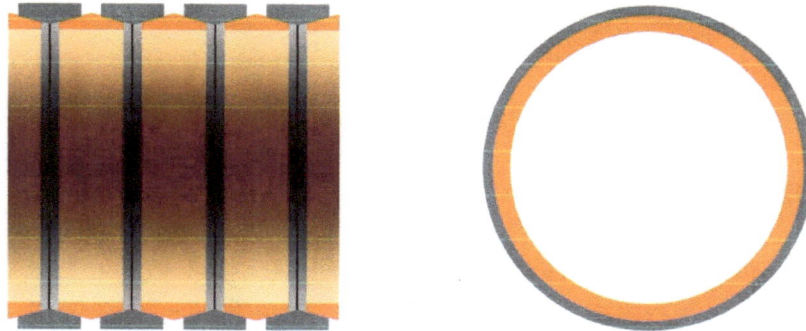

Figure 43 Ring Spring Set

The Ring Spring provides excellent energy absorption.

The travel and stiffness are easily modified by increasing or decreasing the number of rings.

Zero Twist Springs

A machined spring with reverse coils will not experience end-rotation when it is compressed.

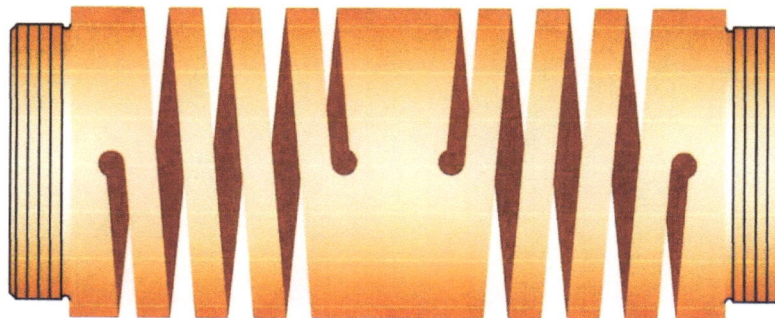

Figure 44 Zero Twist Spring

Constant Force Springs

(1) Neg'ator® Constant Force Springs   AMETEK Hunter Spring Division, Hatfield, PN 19440

(2) A Buckled Column (The Elastica)

There is a finite solution for the deflection of a buckled column.

Information about the "Elastica" can be found in:

"Theory of Elastic Stability", S. Timoshenko, Dover Press 2009

An E-Book copy is available: (www.doverpublications.com)

The maximum allowable deflection is limited by the column flexure stress.

$$S_{flexure} = \frac{Ec}{R}$$

E = Tensile Modulus

c = distance from neutral axis to outer most fiber

R = minimum radius of curvature of buckled beam

α	P/Pcr
0°	1.000
20°	1.015
40°	1.063
60°	1.152
80°	1.293

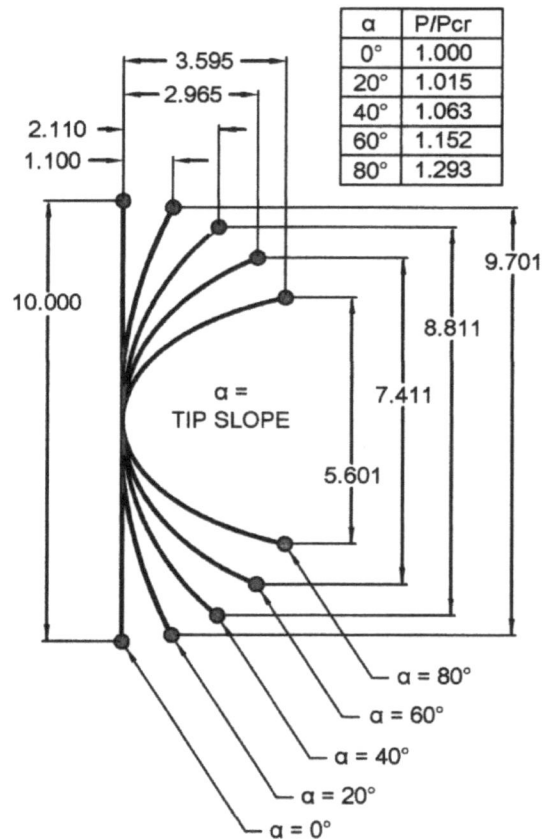

Figure 45 The Elastica

Special Problems for Springs

Expansion of Spring Diameter (D) during Loading

End rotation prevented:

$$\Delta D = 0.05 \left[\frac{p^2 - d^2}{D} \right]$$

Ends free to unwind;

$$\Delta D = 0.01 \left[\frac{p^2 - 0.8pd - 0.2d^2}{D} \right]$$

Mean Spring Diameter (D)

Coil pitch at Free Length (p)

Wire Diameter (d)

Cold Setting of Helical Springs

This technique (also known as Presetting or Scragging) is used to achieve greater load capacity without the danger of yielding the finished spring at solid height. It allows you to get the maximum performance from a wire sample (You won't have to design to minimum values of F_{tu} / F_{ty}).

Length is left on the unfinished coiled spring and the spring is then compressed to solid height. Any yielding which occurs is compensated when the spring ends are finished after the cold setting . The physical effects of the cold set are described in detail in ("Wald", section 5-3).

Fine Tuning the Spring Rate of Helical Springs

The earlier section "Practical Considerations" contained a discussion of a springs sensitivity to even minor changes of wire size or spring diameter. This characteristic can be troublesome but It can also be useful.

It is very difficult to achieve a precise spring rate. Earlier, we noted that the spring diameter actually expands as the spring is compressed. We also noted that the magnitude of the diametric expansion is affected by the rotational fixity of the ends of the spring. It is easy to understand why a "precise spring rate" is hard to achieve. You can measure the spring rate of any existing spring.

 But how do you modify it?

Well, it turns out that there is a way, if you pick the right spring type. Any "square wire" spring can be modified after manufacture to "fine tune" the spring rate.

$$K = \frac{P}{\delta} = \left[\frac{a^2}{D^3}\right]\left[\frac{b^2\,G}{n\gamma}\right]$$

Where: P = Applied Load

δ = Deflection @ load (P)

a = (see Figure)

b = (see Figure)

D = D$_{mean}$ (see Figure)

n = number of active coils

γ = (from Wahl Fig 10.6)

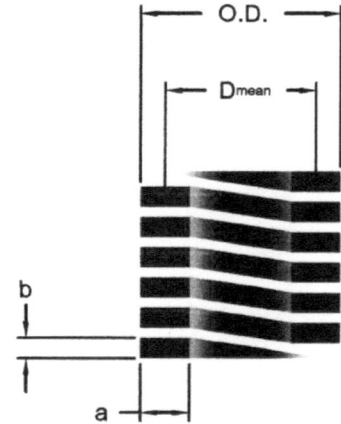

Figure 46 Square Wire Spring

If we remove (Δ) material from the O.D. surface (O.D. is reduced by 2Δ), then

a$_{final}$ = (a - Δ) and D$_{final}$ = (D$_{mean}$ - Δ)

The stiffness equation above indicates that: $K = \left[\frac{a^2}{D^3}\right] X$

(X is a group of parameters which are not altered when the O.D. is machined) :

$$\left[K_{Final} = \frac{(a-\Delta)^2}{(D-\Delta)^3}\right] X$$

If we assign values as follows:

a = 0.1 inch, D = 1.0 inch, Δ = .005 inch (reduces O.D. by 0.010 inches)

We can then evaluate the change in spring rate as follows:

$$K_{initial} = \left[\frac{a^2}{D^3}\right] \qquad\qquad K_{final} = \left[\frac{(a-\Delta)^2}{(D-\Delta)^3}\right]$$

$$K_{initial} = 0.01 \qquad K_{final} = \left[\frac{(0.1-.005)^2}{(1-0.005)^3}\right] = \frac{(0.095)^2}{(.995)^3} = .00916$$

$$\% \text{ REDUCTION OF } K = \frac{(0.01-0.00916)}{0.01} \text{ X } 100 = 8.4\%$$

Clearly, a final grind of the spring O.D. can alter the O.D. by much less than .005 inch. If the depth of cut was .0005 inch instead, a % reduction of only 0.84% could be achieved!

☺ !!!

Relaxation of Springs

You just have to watch those lazy little devils every minute! Mechanisms may be stored for years and it is important that any heavily loaded springs not lose force while stored. There is very limited data available regarding room temperature spring relaxation. If you must survive years of storage consider designing to a lower working stress. Available data indicates that relaxation will occur early in the storage period so it would make sense to obtain a production lot spring and store it under load (much like cold setting) and then occasionally unload the test spring and measure its free length. Any loss of free length would indicate relaxation. This test also confirms that the materials and processing of the spring were not faulty.

"Relaxation of Helical Springs at Room Temperature," Melvin C. Vagle, Jr., Metal Progress, Feb 1965

"Stress Relaxation of Spring Materials," Hanna, Chang, Steckel; Proceedings of the 32nd Aerospace Mechanisms Symposium

End Fixity of Columns and Beams

The equation for the critical buckling load (P) of a long slender column is as follows:

$$P_{critical} = C \left[\frac{\pi^2 EI}{L^2} \right]$$

The term (C) is the value for end fixity of the column.

Text books such as those referenced in the paragraph titled " Source Material for Stiffness & Natural Frequency Equations" specify a range of values for (C) from:

C = 1/4 for (one fixed end & one free end)

        to

C = 4 for (both ends fixed)

This is a factor of 16 variation of the fixity value. The beam stiffness equations shown in (Chapter 8) also indicate the same sensitivity to end fixity that columns exhibit. For most structure design this characteristic is not a concern of the same magnitude as it is for mechanisms. Classical structures would never be designed to operate at or beyond the critical buckling load. However, a mechanism (a moving structure) relies on operation beyond critical buckling (the elastica).

Any structure which uses beam bending or column buckling to achieve a predictable motion must have very careful attention paid to the design of the end fittings. Friction is almost never the mechanism engineers friend. It can be a killer in mechanisms where structure must buckle predictably.

Chapter 8   Spring Systems and Vibration

The discussion presented here applies to systems containing classical springs (Chapter 7) or Flexures (Chapter 9). However, constant force "springs" such as an elastically buckled column or a negator spring do not apply.

Determining Natural Frequency:

The equations for natural frequency generally take the following form:

$$F_n \text{ (Cycles/Sec)} = \frac{1}{2\pi} \sqrt{\frac{\text{stiffness}}{\text{mass or inertia}}}$$

A determination of stiffness is fundamentally important to calculating the natural frequency of any spring/mass system. The following examples as well as examples shown in the chapter titled "Spring Elements" provide methods for calculating stiffness.

$$K_{parallel} = \left[\frac{(A + B)^2}{\dfrac{A^2}{K_2} + \dfrac{B^2}{K_1}} \right]$$

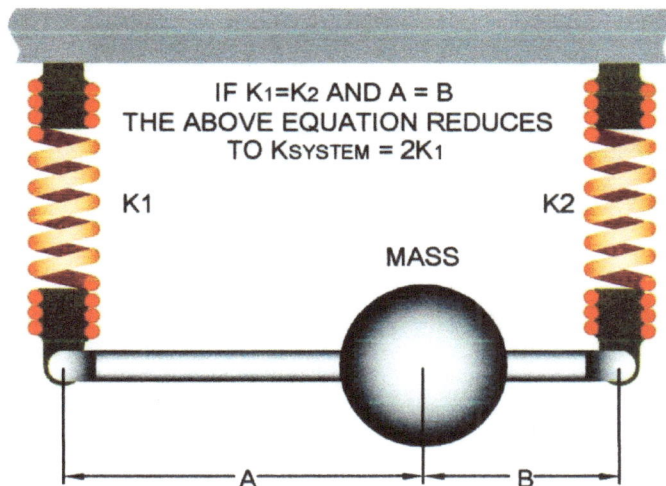

IF $K_1 = K_2$ AND A = B
THE ABOVE EQUATION REDUCES
TO $K_{SYSTEM} = 2K_1$

Figure 47 Parallel Springs

$$K_{series} = \frac{1}{\left(\frac{1}{K_1}\right) + \left(\frac{1}{K_2}\right)}$$

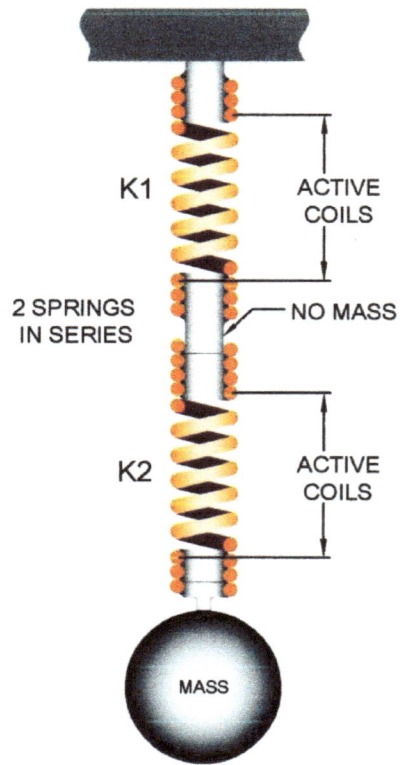

Figure 48 Series Springs

Also, the equations for calculating natural frequency are included as follows:

$$f_n = \frac{1}{2\pi} \frac{A}{B} \sqrt{\frac{K}{M}}$$

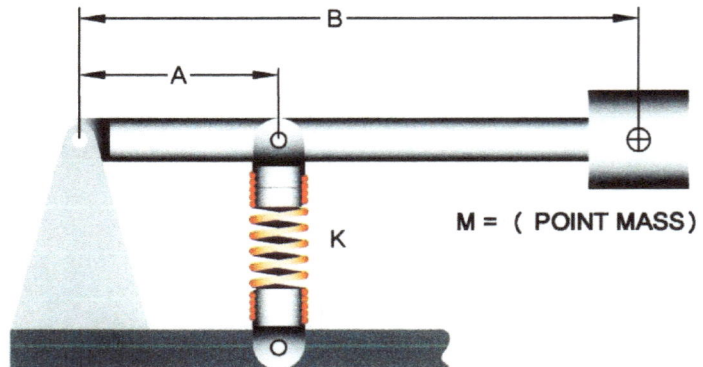

Figure 49 Cantilever Loading

$$f_n = \frac{1}{2\pi}\sqrt{\frac{K}{M}}$$

$$f_n = \frac{1}{2\pi}\sqrt{\frac{K}{\left(M + \frac{m}{3}\right)}}$$

π

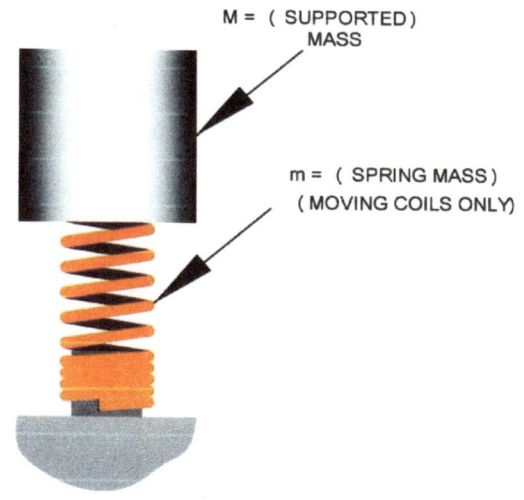

M = (SUPPORTED) MASS

m = (SPRING MASS) (MOVING COILS ONLY)

Figure 50 Simple Spring Mass

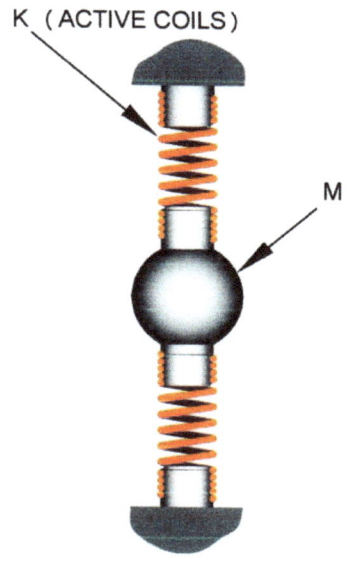

K (ACTIVE COILS)

M

Figure 51 Series Springs

(no spring mass included)

$$f_n = \frac{1}{2\Pi}\sqrt{\frac{2K}{M}}$$

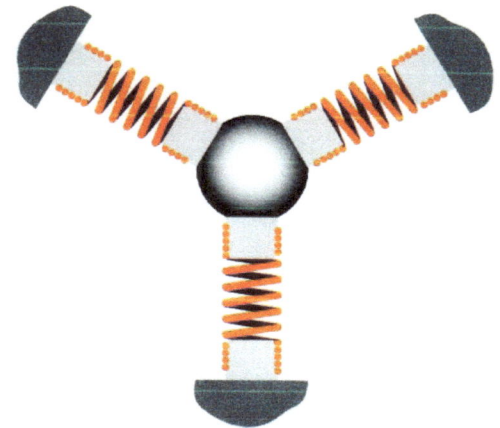

Figure 52 Three Spring Suspension

(includes spring mass)

$$f_n = \frac{1}{2\pi}\sqrt[2]{\frac{\frac{3}{2}K}{M + \left(\frac{m}{3}\right)}}$$

Note how the stiffness and mass

terms change as fixity changes!

$$f_n = \frac{1}{2\pi} \sqrt{\frac{3EI}{L^3 (M + .23m)}}$$

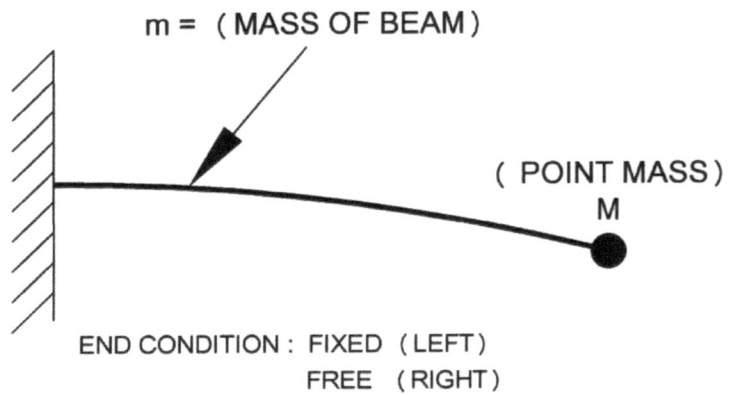

m = (MASS OF BEAM)

(POINT MASS)
M

END CONDITION : FIXED (LEFT)
FREE (RIGHT)

$$f_n = \frac{1}{2\pi} \sqrt{\frac{48EI}{L^3 (M + .5m)}}$$

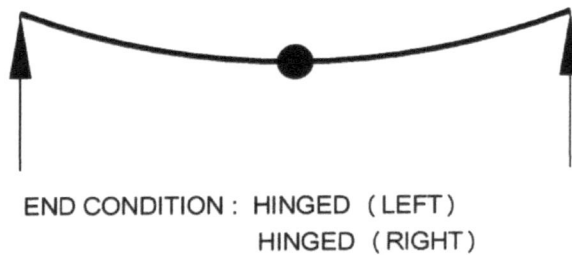

END CONDITION : HINGED (LEFT)
HINGED (RIGHT)

$$f_n = \frac{1}{2\pi} \sqrt{\frac{192\, EI}{L^3 (M + .375m)}}$$

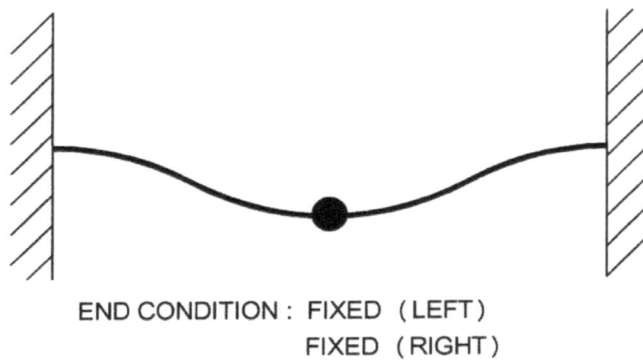

END CONDITION : FIXED (LEFT)
FIXED (RIGHT)

Figure 53 Beam Natural Frequencies

Special Spring Suspension (Iso-Elasticity)

The three element spring suspension shown in figure (52 & 54) has a special property. This arrangement will provide a two dimensional support which, for small deflections, will have identical stiffness in any direction in that plane. It is also possible to make the suspension a very effective thermal isolator if the spring elements have very low thermal conductivity such as fiberglass bands instead of metallic springs. Proper positioned, four of these suspensions can produce a three dimensional, isoelastic, thermally isolated support. It is possible to obtain a desired vibration response and desired thermal conductivity for any three dimensionally supported object.

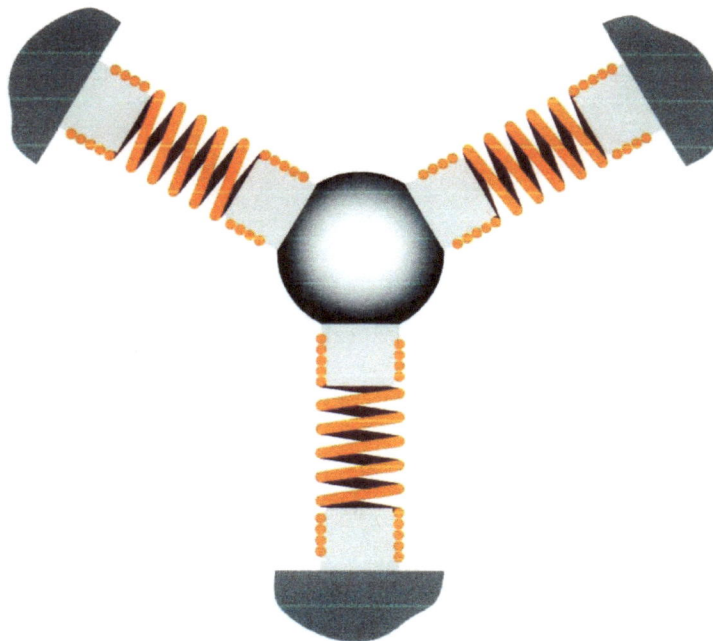

Figure 54 The Isoelsatic Suspension

Relationship of Frequency, Deflection and Loading

Now, we can use natural frequency to learn a great deal about a vibrating system:

Relating load, frequency and displacement begins with the simple description of instantaneous displacement in a vibrating system:

Displacement = Peak Displacement (Sin ωt)

Where ω is the system natural frequency (rad/sec).

Likewise, we can define velocity and acceleration:

Velocity = Peak Displacement x (ω) Cos ωt

Acceleration = - Peak Displacement x $ω^2$ Sin ωt

This final relationship contains the terms that we have been looking for:

(1) Acceleration, (2) Displacement and (3) Frequency. Next, things get really interesting when we convert the equation to specific recognizable units of (G's), Inches (o-p) and (Hz).and set Sin/Cos functions to their maximum values of 1.0. I will let you have that fun. The final answer is very simple and very useful:

DISPLACEMENT (Inches) (0 to Peak) = 9.8 (G's) / $(Hz)^2$

DISPLACEMENT (Inches) (0 to Peak) ≈ 10 (G's) / $(Hz)^2$ (Approx.)

So? Big Deal!!!   Yes! It really is!

Would you like to estimate the natural frequency of a sagging structure. Measure the sag and you have your answer!!!

 Assume: Sag = 0.1 inch

G = 1.0 (on earth)   So: f_n = 10 hertz (cyc/sec)

Or, would you like to know how much clearance to allow around a vibrating object.

If you can estimate the peak applied G force and if you can estimate the natural frequency of that object, you have your answer!!!

Assume: Applied g's = 150 g's (peak landing load)

Natural Freq = 30 hz

So: Displacement (zero-to-peak) = 1.67 inches

If you make this estimate early in the design process it becomes apparent that some form of launch restraint will be necessary to limit deflection to a much smaller number!

Assume: Applied g's = 150 g's (landing load)

Natural Freq = 122 hz (with restraint system)

So: Displacement (zero-to-peak) = 0.10 inches

And, you figured all this out without your PC !

Damping (Did They Teach You This One!):

If you excite any complex mechanical system, it will settle back into a stationary state at a rate determined by its inherent internal damping. But, once again nature plays tricks. Most complex structures are composed of numerous elements that rub together and that rubbing is the source of most damping. If you carefully measure the decaying vibration of any complex mechanical system, you will notice that the frequency of vibration shifts to higher frequencies (the system gets stiffer) as the amplitude of the vibration decreases. And the rate of amplitude decay slows noticeably (damping goes away). This characteristic is the result of various moving elements within the system settling out (locking together) at different times. The resulting reduction of damping occurs because fewer and fewer elements rub together.

Friction Damping

If you are required to achieve an absolutely stationary condition quickly, it will require some extra source of damping in the system. I found that light coulomb friction does a great job of eliminating the last energy from a vibrating system. Imagine a small caliper brake attached to and continuously engaging the rotatable portion of a pointing platform. The very light drag would not be noticeable during platform position changes. But, it would gobble up the last residual energy in the system and greatly improve settling time. The torque available to accelerate a massive system exceeds the light drag torque by orders of magnitude. High system torsional stiffness prevents significant pointing error due to the very light drag. I have developed devices like this and have been able to achieve 1.0 to 1.5 cycle damping after the last braking pulse from the active control system. A system with 10 Hz final ring-out becomes absolutely motionless in less than 0.15 seconds.

You can also Out-Smart Backlash

I have also been able to use coulomb friction to stabilize low cost pointing systems (systems with significant backlash). The Galileo Probe Relay Antenna used a Dual Drive Actuator (see Chapter 18) to point the antenna as it communicated with the Probe entering Jupiter's atmosphere. The actuator had a few degrees of backlash. However, we negated this by placing a friction band across the rotating interface. And, then we commanded only in one direction as the antenna tracked the Probe. A 3 foot diameter reflector was attached to a structural boom. And, that boom attached to the pointing actuator. The coulomb friction in the system prevented the antenna/boom combination from bouncing off the gear box compliance. The system remained stable as it tracked the Probe. During Dynamic Qualification Tests, shakers were mounted to the deployed antenna/boom in an attempt to excite them about the rotational axis. It proved impossible to excite that mode because of the coulomb friction. The friction material was Delrin AF against aluminum. This low friction combination prevented problems with stick-slip (see Chapter 11 for more information).

Special Spring Systems for Storing Energy

There are both linear and rotary mechanisms concepts for storing very large amounts of kinetic energy with a very light weight device. The "high strain" unidirectional s-glass epoxy would be the material of choice.

Potential Problems

(1) Any mechanism which relies on beams or columns to store energy must have carefully controlled end fixity of the deflecting elements (see discussion in the Spring Elements Section).

(2) The direction of buckling should be determinate. This can be achieved by "pre-buckling the elements or by application of a slightly eccentric load.

The linear and rotary spring stops shown in the next two figures only store energy. They will return virtually all of the stored energy if their return motion is not inhibited. They make great push-off springs, but need extra features to be "bumper stops".

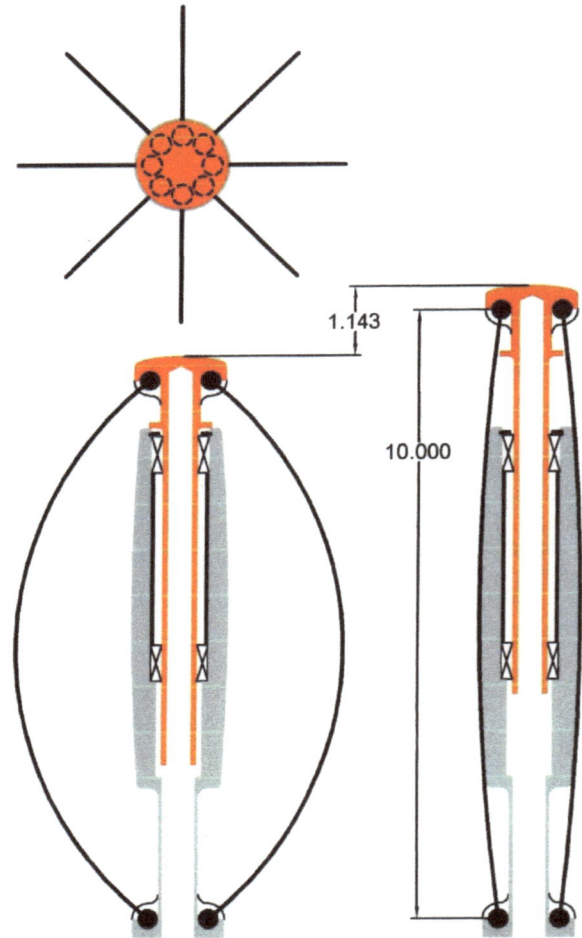

Figure 55 Nearly Constant Force Spring

The device shown below is a concept for a rotary mechanism to store large amounts of spring energy. One set of rods would buckle for CW rotation and the other set would buckle for CCW rotation. The non-buckled rods would float in their slots as the opposite set of rods buckled.

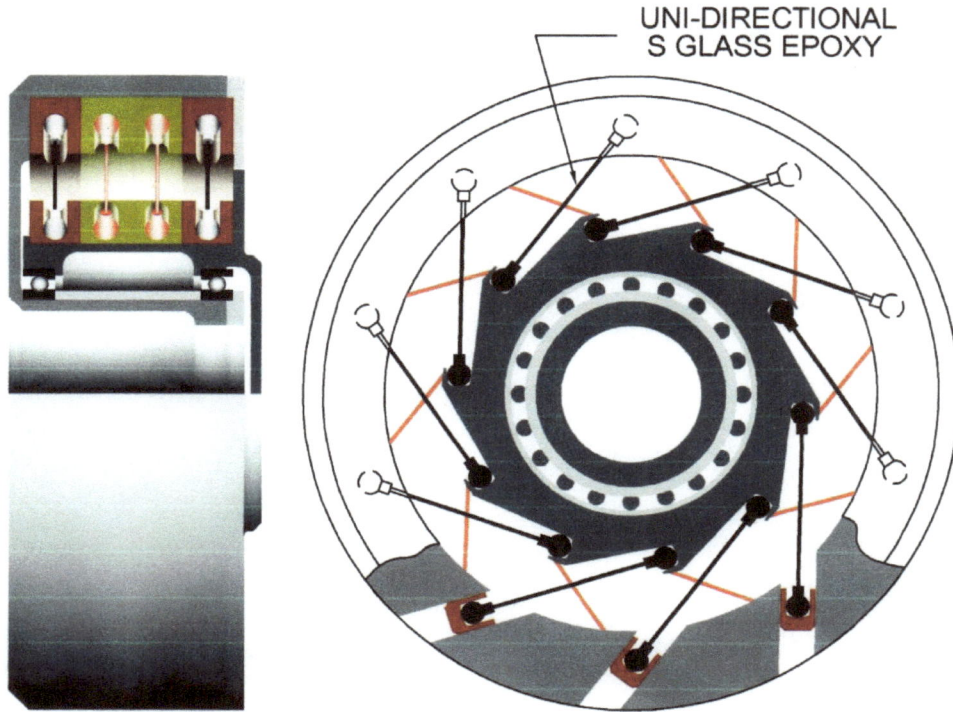

Figure 56 Nearly Constant Torque Rotary Bumper

The Dangers of Stored Energy in Spring Structures

There are several types of deployable masts which have been used very successfully in space. The three legged "Astro- Mast" and the four legged "Fast Mast" are representative of this class of buckled structures. These structures stow in a very compact package size and they want to "get long" again. All the buckled elements desire to return their stored energy to the deploying mast. Some type of mechanical damper must be used to absorb the stored spring energy and limit the rate of deployment.

There was a short coil-able mast used for the camera mast on the Mars Pathfinder Mission. No deployment damper was used. The final kinetic energy in the deploying components was rotational and the mast tip simply rotated through lock-up and began to re-stow. This technique was successful because the tip mass was small and the mast length was short.

There was an interesting failure of a "folding strut" mast many years ago. The folding struts were of a double lenticular shape (see Figure 57). The two opposing sides were seam welded along both edges to increase torsional strength of the strut. The struts were the column members in each bay of a very long multi bay mast system. It was easily recognized that the folding process for each strut stored energy and a deployment rate limiting damper was supposed to absorb that energy. However, no one recognized that a second component of spring energy also existed. The strut cross-section was elastically flattened to allow the strut to fold. The flattening energy was returned to the mast almost instantaneously at strut lock-up. This put a huge axial load spike into all struts at the same time. The five bay, test mast became a basket of parts instantly.

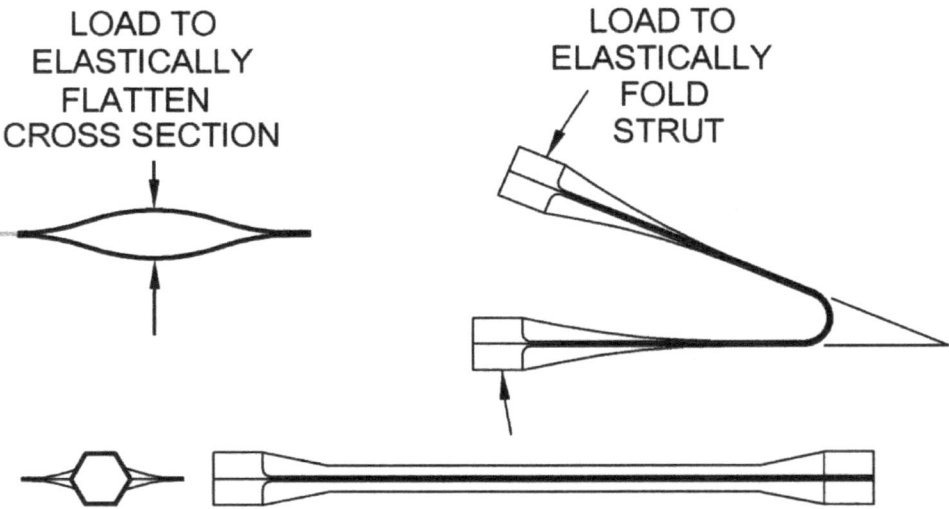

Figure 57 The Folding Strut

Chapter 9   Flexures and Flex Pivots

Introduction to Flexures

Flexures can provide very low-friction suspension systems for linear and rotary motion. The flexure concept is very simple. However, the math associated with flexure analysis involves messy 2nd order differential equations for beam bending.

The work done by F.S. Eastman at the University of Washington forms the basis for virtually all other work (Bulletin No. 86, 1935).

Another noteworthy paper authored by H. Troeger (1962) contains the mathematical solution for center shift in flex pivots. (Lucas Aerospace)

And a third paper, by Warren D. Weinstein (1965), describes among other things the tri-flex pivot, which is capable of much greater rotation than commercial flex pivots.

All of these items, plus many others, are included in the references at the end of this section.

Flexure Concepts

1. One Blade Flexures

2. Two-Blade Flexures

3. Cross-Strip Pivot

4. Cross-Band Drive

5. Roller and Rack (also see "band drives")

6. Y-Cross Pivot

7. Parallel-Motion Link

8. Straight Line Motion Flexures

9. Thermal Isolator

10 Universal Joint (light duty)

11. Shaft Coupling (high torque capacity)

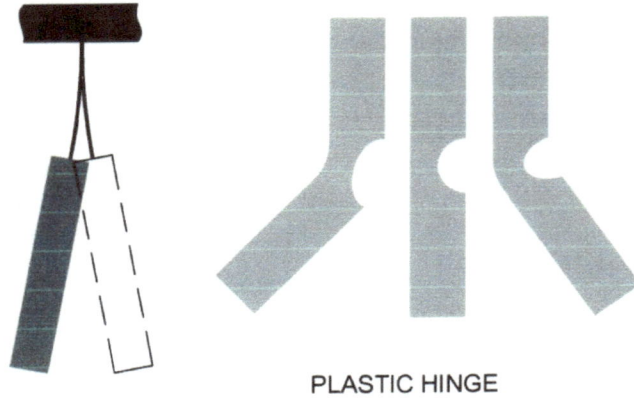

PLASTIC HINGE

Figure 58 One Blade Flexure

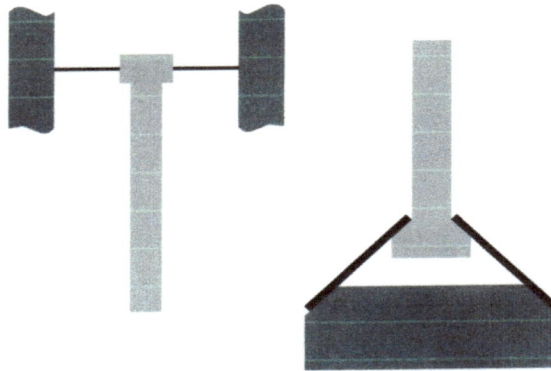

Figure 59 Two Blade Flexure

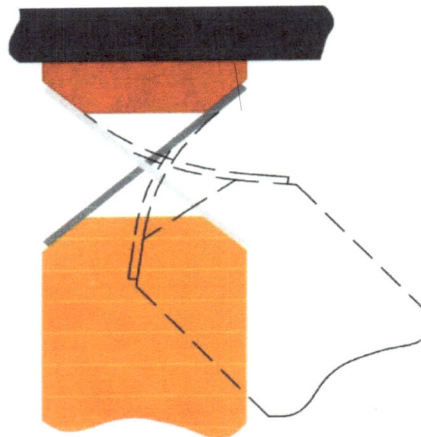

Figure 60 Cross Strip Pivot

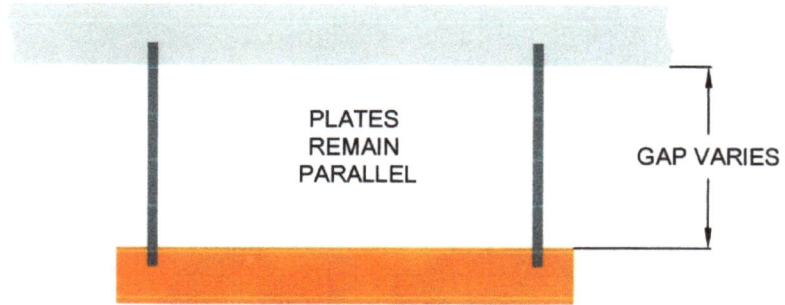

Figure 61 Non-Planer Parallel Motion

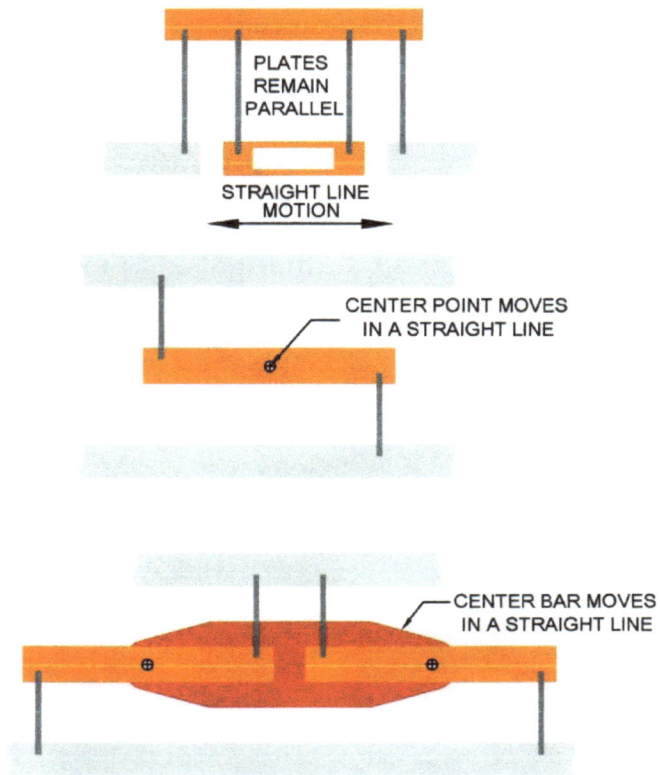

Figure 62 Planer Straight Line Motion

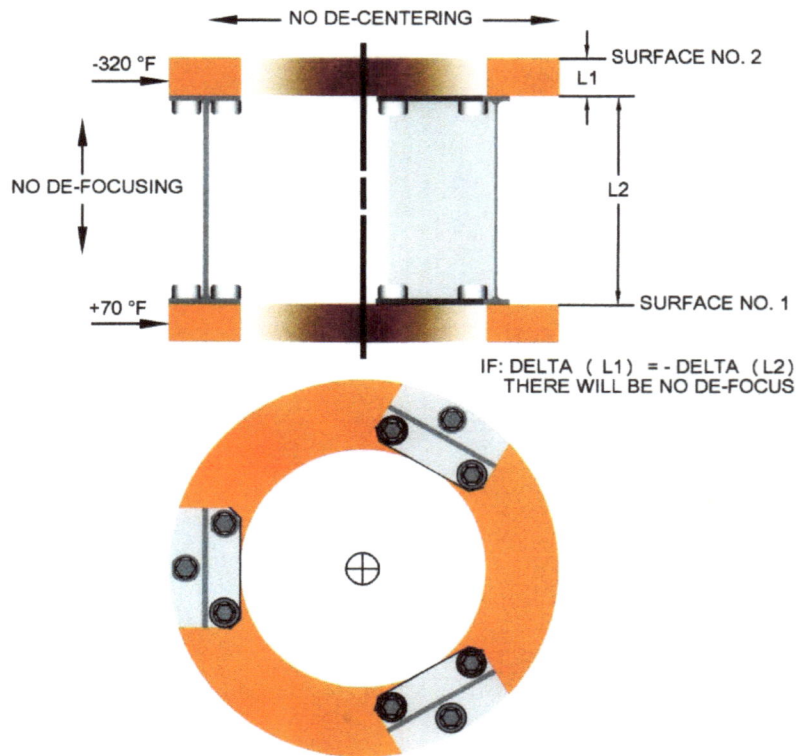

NO DE-CENTERING

-320 °F

SURFACE NO. 2

L1

NO DE-FOCUSING

L2

+70 °F

SURFACE NO. 1

IF: DELTA (L1) = - DELTA (L2)
THERE WILL BE NO DE-FOCUS

Figure 63 Athermalized Flexure Mount

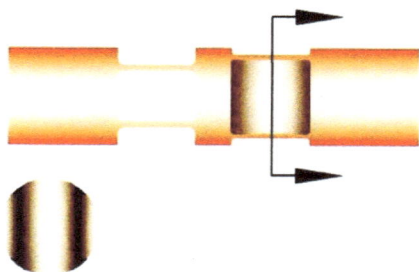

**Figure 64 Oldham Coupling
U-Joint**

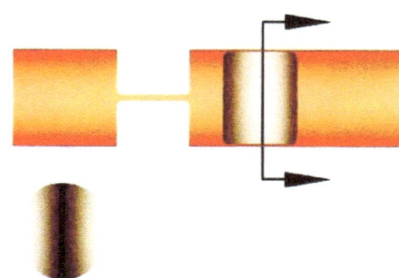

Figure 65 Light Duty U-Joint

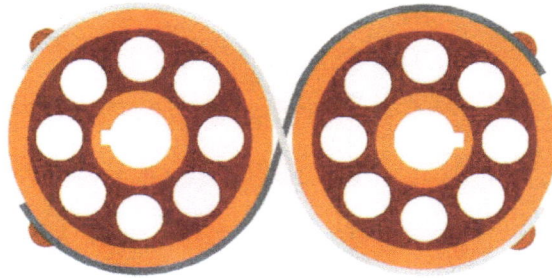

Figure 66 Cross Band Drive

Figure 67 Roller and Rack

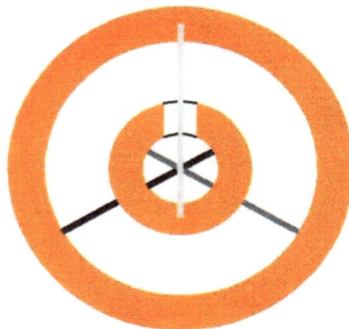

Figure 68 Y-Cross Pivot

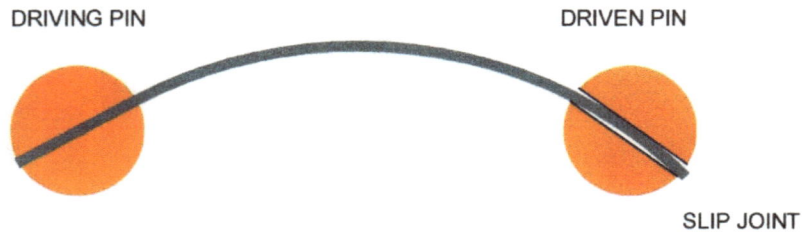

Figure 69 Flexure Creates Rotation

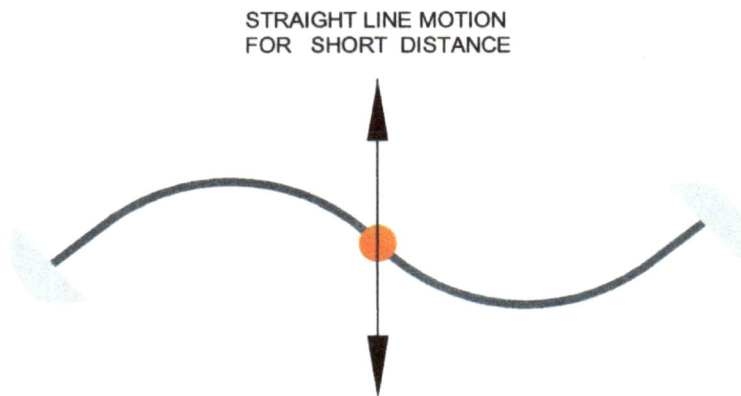

Figure 70 Sine Spring

Commercial Flex Pivots

The Free-Flex Pivot is a cross strip type flexure. There have been many successful applications. There are a large number of "off-the-shelf" sizes available. However, the cross strip flexure has some limitations which must be understood.

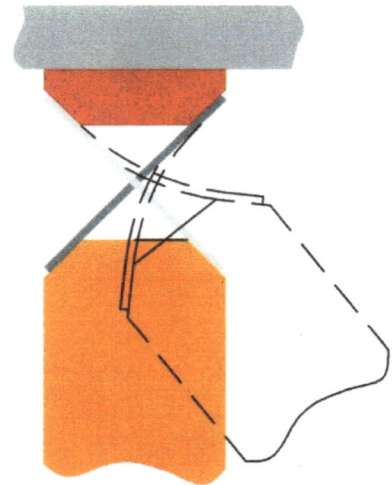

Figure 71 Origin of Free Flex Pivot

Things to Know

The load carrying capability of this device is only moderate. External loads in the plane of rotation must be reacted as column loading internal to the device.

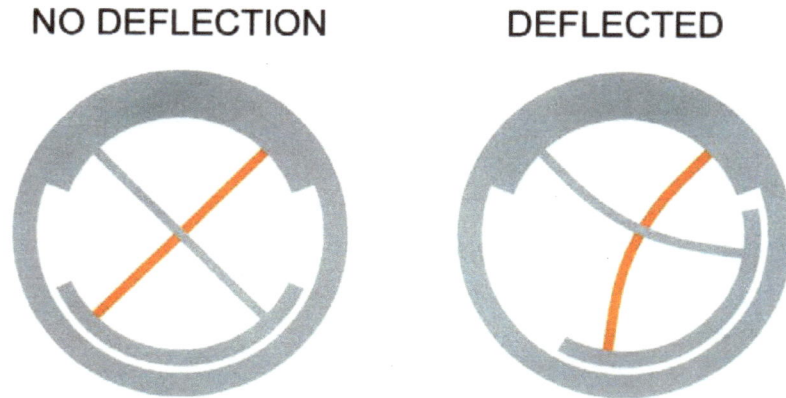

NO DEFLECTION   DEFLECTED

Figure 72 Deflections of a Free-Flex Pivot

These commercial flex pivots should be used with the knowledge that a significant number of failures have been experienced when the brazed version is subjected to vibration and large deflections . Remember that a buckled column (the Elastica) is a constant force spring. which can not react loads higher than the buckling load. It is possible to make one piece units (no brazed joints) using wire cut EDM.

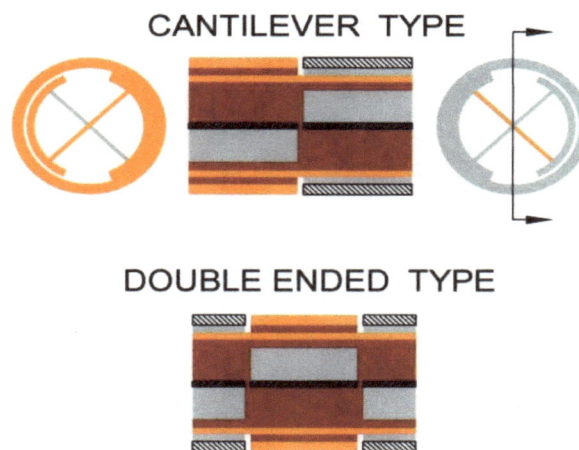

CANTILEVER TYPE

DOUBLE ENDED TYPE

Figure 73 Free-Flex Configurations

Tri-Flex Pivots

This concept uses a series of modular tensioned bands to produce very large rotation angles. The large rotation is possible because the tensioned band is guided and the radius of curvature of the guided band is selected to prevent excessive bending stress.

$$\textbf{Band Stress} = \frac{\textbf{P}}{\textbf{A}} + \frac{\textbf{EC}}{\textbf{R}}$$

Where:

P = Band Tension

A = Band Cross-Section Area

E = Band Tensile Modulus

C = 1/2 of Band Thickness

R = Band Curvature Radius

Accuracy and Rotational Stiffness of Tri-Flex Pivots

A total of six band modules is required to obtain a stable structural configuration. The stiffness and band preload of each module must match exactly in order to obtain a "centered" configuration (the inner spindle wants to roll up on a band and the other band sets operating at +/- 120° must prevent this). Center shift will occur if even minor band/spring stiffness differences exist. This concept should only be used if low pointing accuracy is acceptable.

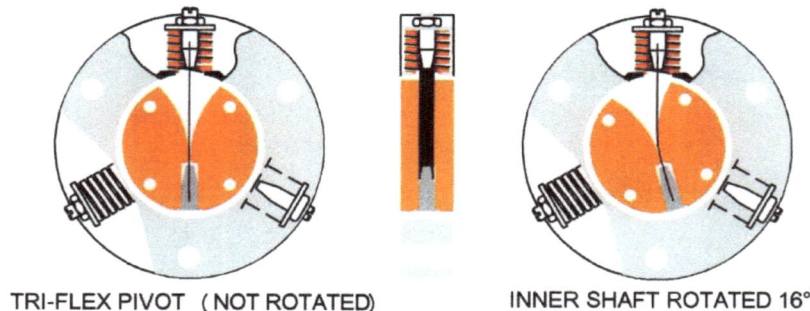

TRI-FLEX PIVOT (NOT ROTATED)   INNER SHAFT ROTATED 16°

Figure 74 Tri-Flex Pivot

JPL Wire Cut Pivots

Engineers at the Jet Propulsion Lab have developed two flexure configurations that are machined as "one piece" units by using wire EDM (wire cut electrical discharge machining). These flexure configurations are called: (1) The Trefoil and (2) The Hexafoil. More data can be obtained from NASA. See NASA Tech Briefs NPO-20228 and NPO-21154 for more information.

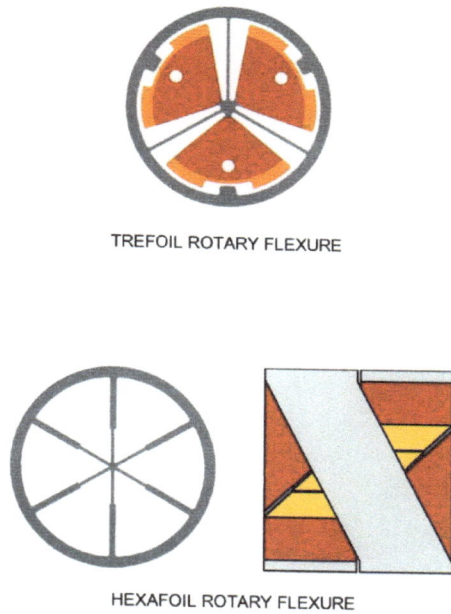

TREFOIL ROTARY FLEXURE

HEXAFOIL ROTARY FLEXURE

Figure 75 JPL Wire Cut Pivots

Figure 76 CSEM High Accuracy Pivot

Source Information for Flexure Design

Eastman, F.S., Flexural Pivots to Replace Knife Edges in Ball Bearings, Engineering Experimental Station Bulletin No. 86, University of Washington, Seattle, 1935.

Eastman, F.S., Design of Flexural Pivots, Journal of Aeronautical Sciences, 5:16-21, Nov 1937.

Eastman, F.S., The Unique Properties of Flexural Pivots, The Trend in Engineering, University of Washington, Seattle, 12 (1), 1960.

Wittrick, W.H., The Theory of Symmetrical Crossed Flexure Pivots, Department of Aeronautical Engineering, University of Sydney, Australia, 1948.

Thorp, A.G., II, Flexure Pivot Design, Product Engineering, Feb 1953.

Troeger, H., Considerations in the Application of Flexural Pivots, Automatic Control, 17 (4):41-46, No. 1962.

Weinstein, W.D., Flexure-Pivot Bearing (Part 1), Machine Design, Jun 10, 1965.

Weinstein, W.D., Flexure-Pivot Bearing (Part 2), Machine Design, Jul 8, 1965.

Paros, J.M. and L. Weisbord, How to Design Flexure Hinges, Machine Design, Nov 25, 1965.

Seelig, F., Flexural Pivots for Space Applications, Third Aerospace Mechanisms Symposium, Jet Propulsion Laboratories, Pasadena, May 1968.

Seelig, F., Effectively Using Flexural Pivots, ASME Design Engineering Conference and Show, May 11-14, 1970.

Wilkes, D.F., Rolamite: A New Mechanical Design Concept, SC-RR-67-656, Sandia Laboratories, Oct 1967.

Henein, Simon , Flexure Pivot for Aerospace Mechanisms, CSEM Presentation

Chapter 10   Threaded Devices

Terminology and Performance Calculations:

LEAD: The axial advance of one (single) thread for one screw rev.

STARTS: The number of individual threads on a screw.

> Think of an old phonograph record! How many grooves?

> Answer? Two, one on each side!

THREAD PITCH: The lead (in.) divided by the number of starts also equals the axial distance between adjacent threads.

You can determine the number of starts on any screw by viewing the end of the screw.

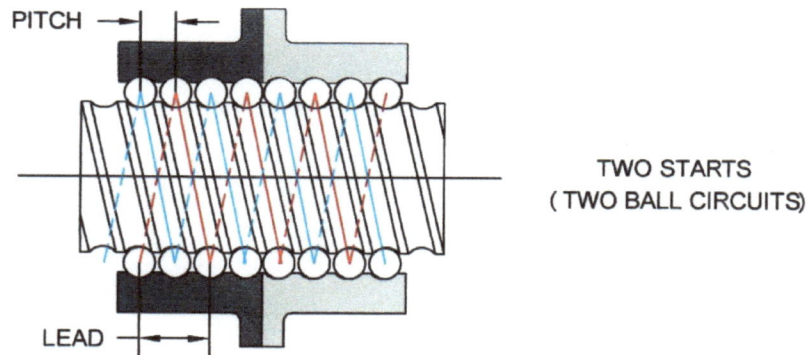

Figure 77 Multi-Start Threads

Friction always opposes the work being done and is specified as an "efficiency" less than one .

$$\textbf{Axial Force Produced (lbs)} = \frac{2\pi}{\textbf{Lead(in)}} \textbf{ (Input Torq)(inlb) (Eff)}$$

$$\textbf{Torque Produced (inlb)} = \frac{\textbf{Lead (in)}}{2\pi} \textbf{ (Axial Force) (lbs) (Eff)}$$

Concentricity Control

The thread design standards shown below indicate that significant clearance exists between mating threads. You can't use threads to accurately control concentricity. A separate set of precision register diameters must be provided.

Thread Types & Standards:

Thread Form Standards;
NATIONAL BUREAU OF STANDARDS
HANDBOOK H28

ALLOWS VERY LARGE UNI-DIRECTIONAL AXIAL LOADS
WITHOUT GENERATING LARGE RADIAL LOADS
FIGURE 19 SHOWS A BUTTRESS THREAD APPLICATION

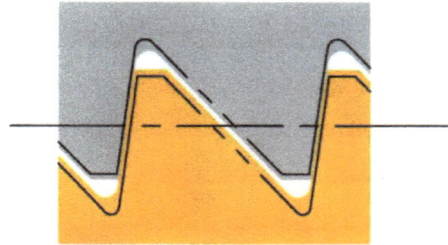

Figure 78 Buttress Thread Form

Very high load capacity in one direction

It Even Includes "Funny" Threads

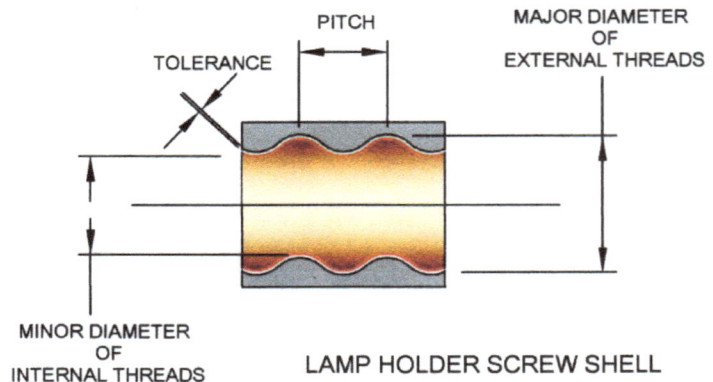

PITCH

MAJOR DIAMETER
OF
EXTERNAL THREADS

TOLERANCE

MINOR DIAMETER
OF
INTERNAL THREADS

LAMP HOLDER SCREW SHELL

Figure 79 The Light Bulb Thread

Do you recognize this one?   It's a Light Bulb thread

Types of Threaded Devices:

Configuration Information and Supplier Data

Acme Threaded Screw

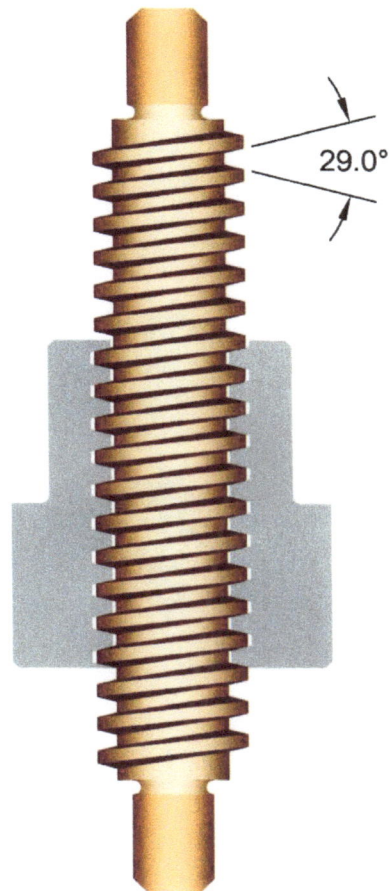

Roll Nuts

Re-circulating Ball Screw

Re-circulating Roller Screw

Re-circulating Planetary
Rollers Screw

Special Screws

      Very High Leads

      Multiple Starts

      Motor Mikes

Acme Thread Screw

Figure 80 Acme Thread Screw

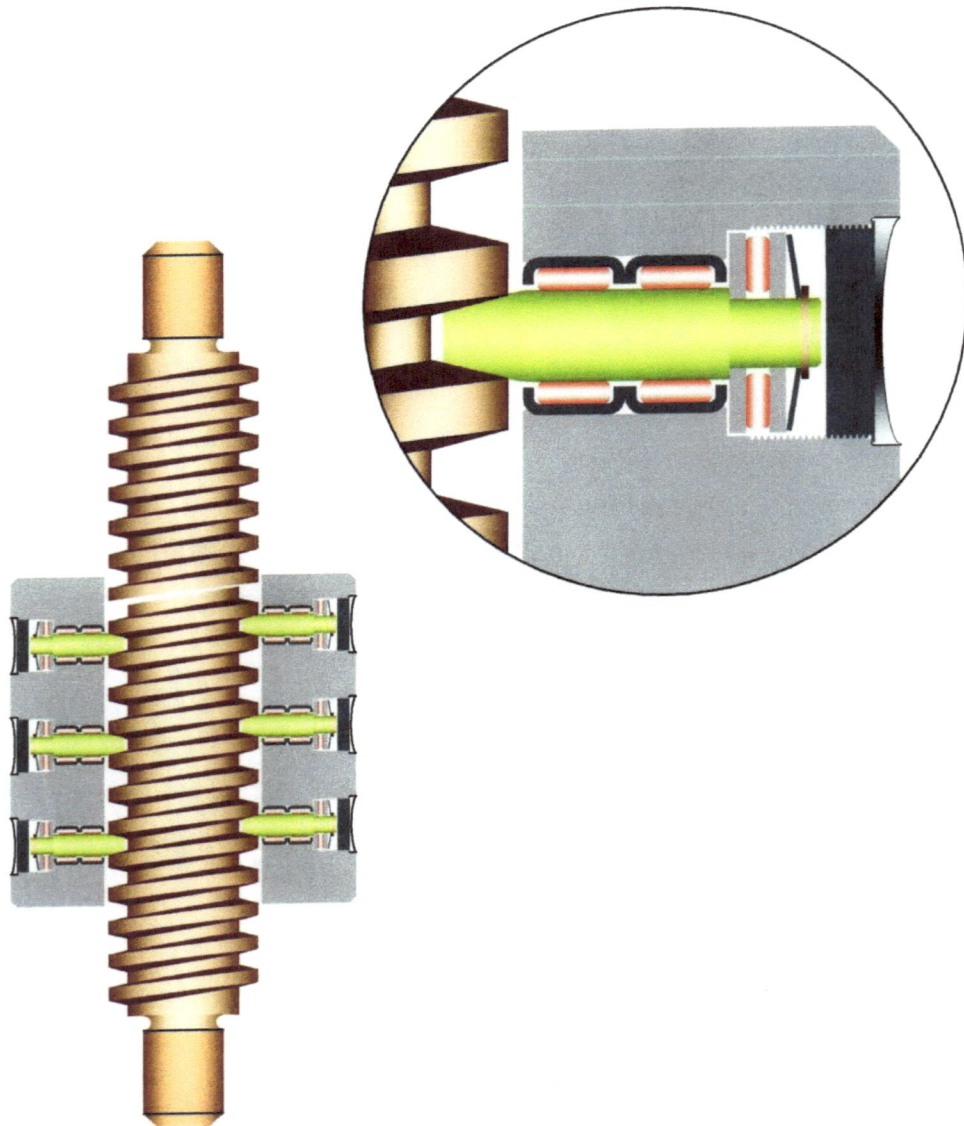

Figure 81 The Roll Nut- Norco Inc.

Re-circulating Ball Screw

A ball screw is a mechanical driver that converts either torque to thrust, or thrust to torque. It is used wherever accuracy or high efficiency is required. The low friction obtainable with a ball screw drive makes possible very small increments of motion. However, this high efficiency can also create a coupling of drive produced vibration and driven system natural frequency.

A ball screw assembly consists of a screw and nut, each with matching helical grooves, and balls that roll in these grooves between the nut and the screw. Rotation of one member translates the other. The balls travel at half the speed of the grooves and exit at the trailing end of the nut. A return tube picks up the balls at the trailing end of the nut and re-circulates them into the leading end, thus keeping the train of bearing balls continuous in motion. (see Figure 82).

Ball screws are most commonly used to convert torque to thrust by:

(1). Rotating the screw to drive the nut along the screw.
(2). Rotating the nut to drive the screw axially through the nut.

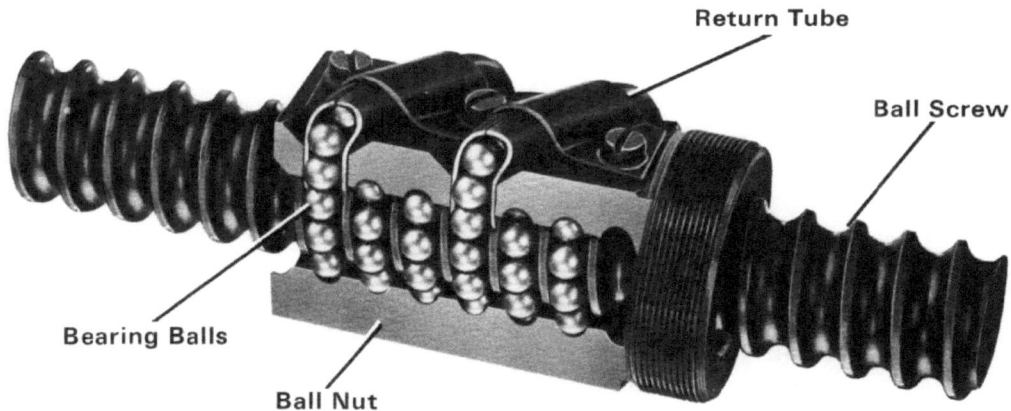

Figure 82 Recirculating Ball Screw

Roller Screw

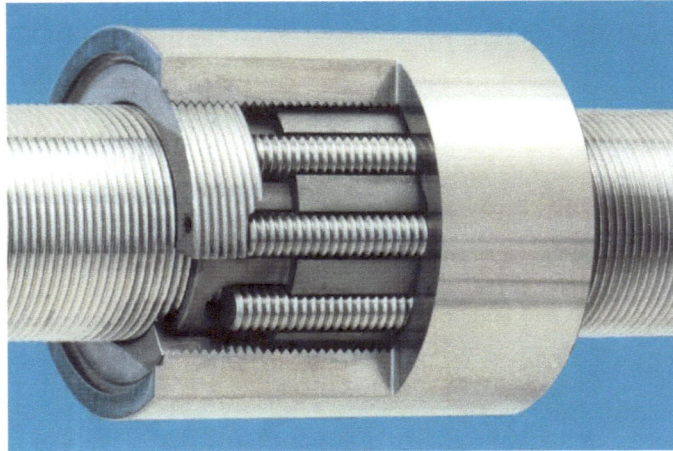

Figure 83 Roller Screw

Good Characteristics:

 1-mm lead on screws from 8- to 50-mm diameter.

 Fine resolution.

 High load capacity.

 Cylindrical nuts with play or preloaded.

Bad Characteristics

 Multiple Rollers are not synchronized and may not load share.

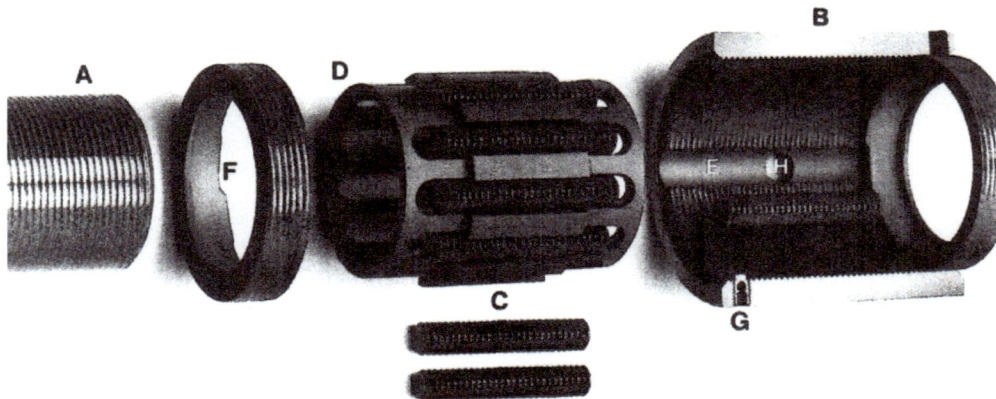

Figure 84 Roller Screw Internal Details

Planetary Roller Screw

The planetary roller screw is the only high-efficiency screw in which the motion of the rolling elements is controlled at all times: It is the most reliable high-efficiency screw. Externally, the Roller Screw and the

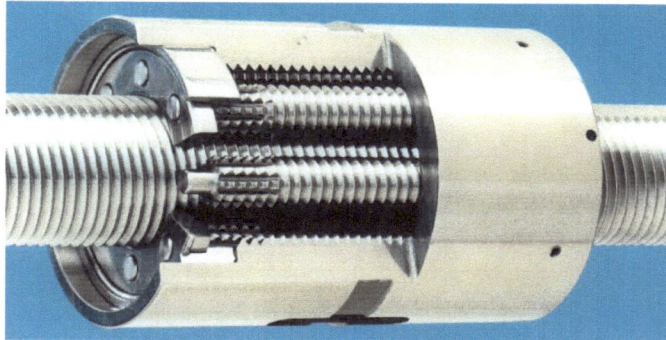

Figure 85 Planetary Roller Screw

Planetary Roller Screw look identical. However, the internal details of the Planetary unit shows a very significant difference! The planetary unit has a set of "planetary gears" which force all rollers to work together.

Each end of each roller has gear teeth machined into it. The planet pinions each mesh with a ring gear (H) which maintains pinion positions relative to each other. The planetary gear is a timing mechanism that

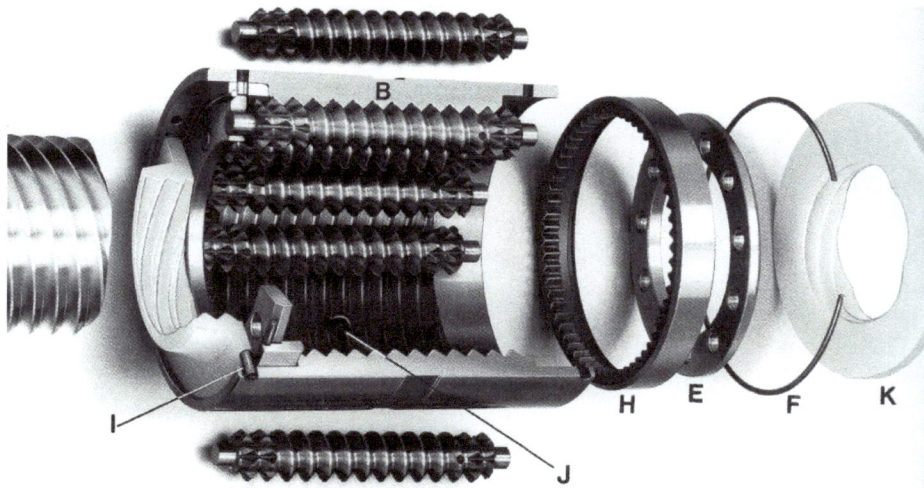

Figure 86 Internal Details- Planetary Roller Screw

assures correct rolling motion. If something tries to stop the rolling motion, such as poor lubrication, the gears drive the rollers round and ensure correct functioning.

Planetary roller screws are characterized by

    Very high load-carrying capacity.

    Very long life.

    High rotational speed and long lead permits linear speed up to 60 m/minute.

    Planetary timing mechanism permits high acceleration (up to 7000 rad /sec^2).

Special Screws

Kirk Motion

Figure 88 Very High Lead Screw

PART NO.	LEAD	SCREW OD
ZBC6120	1.200	3/8
ZBC6100	1.000	3/8
ZBC7050	.500	7/16
ZBC7025	.250	7/16
ZBC7012	.125	7/16

Figure 87 Available Sizes and Leads

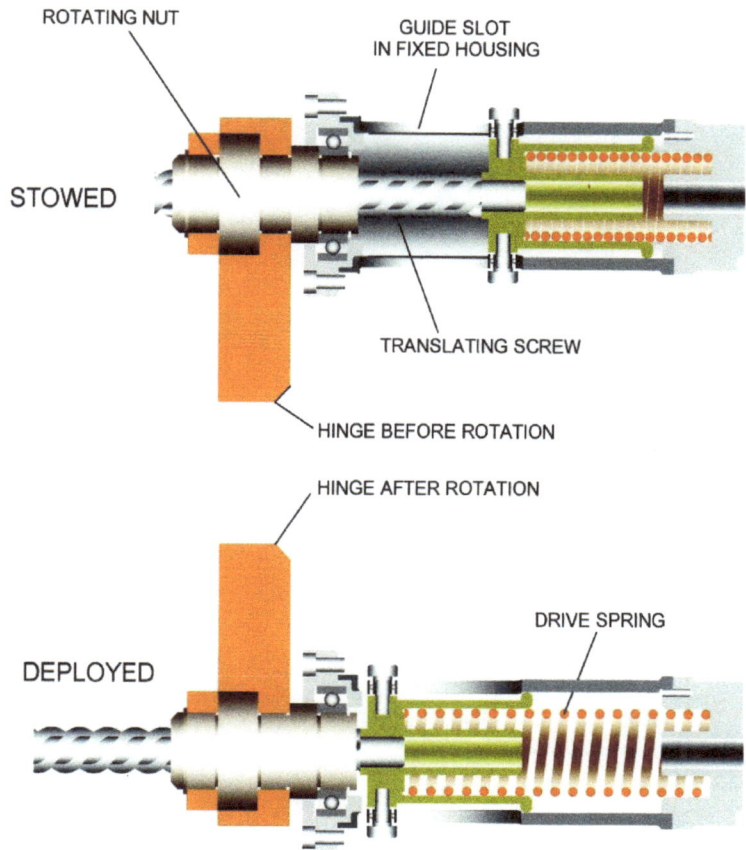

ROTATING NUT

GUIDE SLOT
IN FIXED HOUSING

STOWED

TRANSLATING SCREW

HINGE BEFORE ROTATION

HINGE AFTER ROTATION

DEPLOYED

DRIVE SPRING

Figure 89 Convert Linear Motion to Rotation

Motor Mike Actuators

Motor Mike® is the size and shape of a conventional manual micrometer drive, but has a built-in miniature DC motor and 485:1 precision gear-head. Motor Mike contains a fine-pitch spindle that rotates in a precision-threaded nut, providing resolution of 0.01 µm.

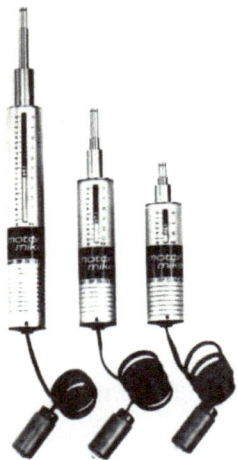

Figure 90 The Motor Mike

116

Special Screw Characteristics:

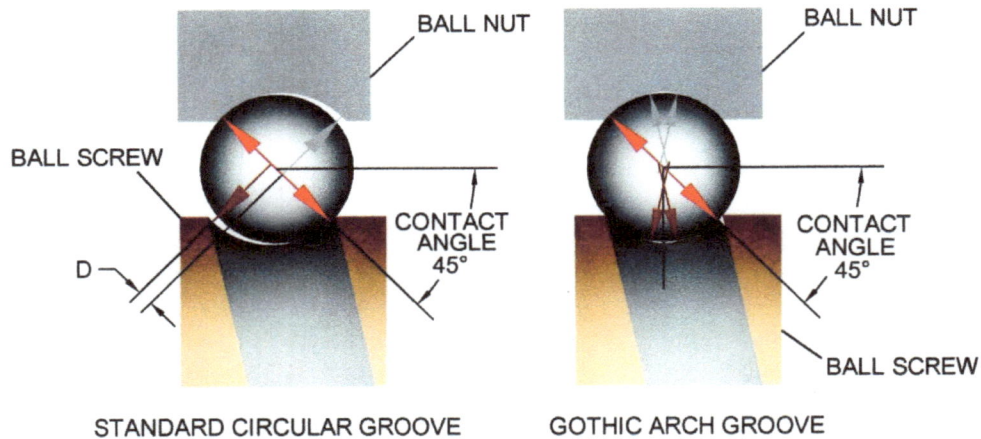

Figure 91 Ball-Race Conformity

There are two types of ball grooves: (1) Circular Grooves and (2) Gothic Arch Grooves.

$$D = f_o + f_i - 1$$

$$f_o \text{ (outer race curvature)} = \frac{\text{outer race radius}}{\text{ball diameter}}$$

$$f_i \text{ (inner race curvature)} = \frac{\text{inner race radius}}{\text{ball diameter}}$$

Typically, the race curvature (also called conformity) is selected by the manufacturer and is approximately (.55) and is also referred to as 55% conformity.

These same equations apply for ball bearing design (see Chapter 4). The special gothic arch design is intended to minimize backlash and is similar to the technique used to make X-Type (Four Point Contact) ball bearings. I do not recommend this type of groove design unless there is some over-riding need for it. The multiple contacting surfaces are subject to sliding contact, lubricant depletion, and rapid wear.

This happens because the high operating contact angle causes a significant velocity variation across the contacting surfaces. The contact surface is an ellipse. This causes an additional spinning motion of the ball. Remember, the linear velocity at any point on the ellipse is equal to: $V = R\omega$. And, R varies because of the plane of contact is a slope due to the contact angle.

Preloaded Ball Bearings in a Nut Assembly

There must be some clearance between the balls and the groove if the balls are to roll freely. The clearance causes looseness (backlash) between the screw and the nut When torque is applied, this play is taken up, and the balls ride at an angle of approximately 45° in the side of the groove toward the load reaction point.

Preloading is always used where maximum axial stiffness is required, as in numerically controlled machine tools. It minimizes deflection in the system under an operating load. Axial movement resulting from race deflection is nonlinear (unequal) for equal changes in load; the initial deflection from the first unit of applied load is larger than that for the successive similar increments of load. Preloading a nut assembly introduces this initial deflection in the direction opposite to that of the load. When the operating load is applied, the preload is relieved on one group of grooves and the other group carries the working load

It is possible but not generally desirable to minimize backlash by specifying a noncircular groove and then selecting the ball size for tight fit. A preferable method of eliminating backlash is to preload the ball nut. A preload is an internal load established by making one group of grooves work in opposition to another within the nut assembly. The preload serves to keep the balls as closely as possible at the contact angle of 45° with the groove.

The preload produces an offload point (the point where preload is lost) as shown in (Figure 91). However, in long life space applications friction torque or lubricant related failure modes may dictate a much lower preload than (P). (see Chapter 18). The value of 1/3 P clearly provides an upper bound for preloading. This gives optimum conditions of stiffness, drag torque, and life. Higher preloading shortens life, because the balls are always operating under a high load, whether the tool is producing work or not, yet does not add significantly to stiffness. Preloading can be applied to a single nut, or to two nuts used together. The operating characteristics of a single integral preloaded nut are about the same as those of the double preloaded nuts, but preload cannot be readily adjusted. Internal preloading saves space; in addition, cost savings may also be realized in certain sizes and quantities but these benefits are usually not the driving concern for Space Mechanisms which suffer from short development schedules.

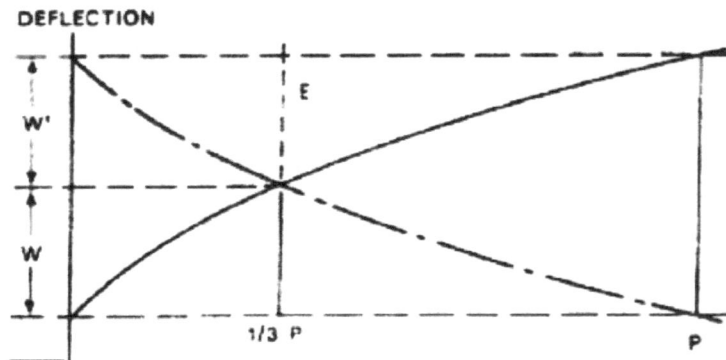

Figure 92 Off Load verses Preload

An integral preloaded nut combines two or more circuits in a single housing. The spacing between the circuits or groups of circuits is shortened or increased slightly to load the circuits in opposition to each other. One circuit or group takes the load when the load is moved in one direction; the other circuit or group takes over when the load is moved in the opposite direction, thus eliminating backlash. Each circuit or group must be capable of carrying the maximum operating load in the direction of motion for the life required. When the load is reversed, the nut shifts and the balls ride on the opposite side of the groove at the same 45° angle. This is a much fancier way than simply preloading two nuts together but it can save serious volume if that is critical.

The integral preload technique can't be easily modified. If you get it wrong the first time and schedule is critical you have "bought the farm". I prefer to preload two nuts together in order to eliminate backlash.

Preloading with Two Nuts

The next two figures show two ways to produce a preload with two nuts. The first method creates a nut/screw combination which has a low moment stiffness and the second method produces maximum moment stiffness.

PRELOAD FORCES

THIS PRELOAD METHOD
PRODUCES A MINIMUM
MOMENT STIFFNESS

45.00000°

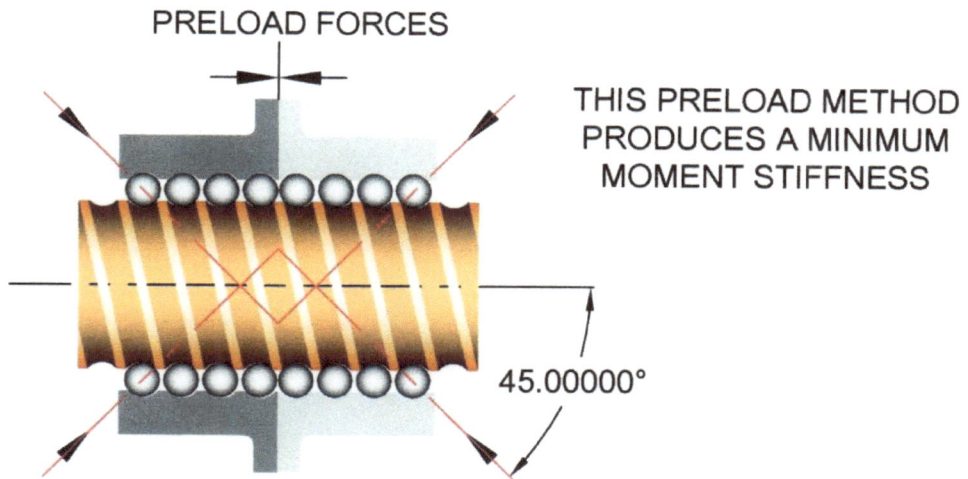

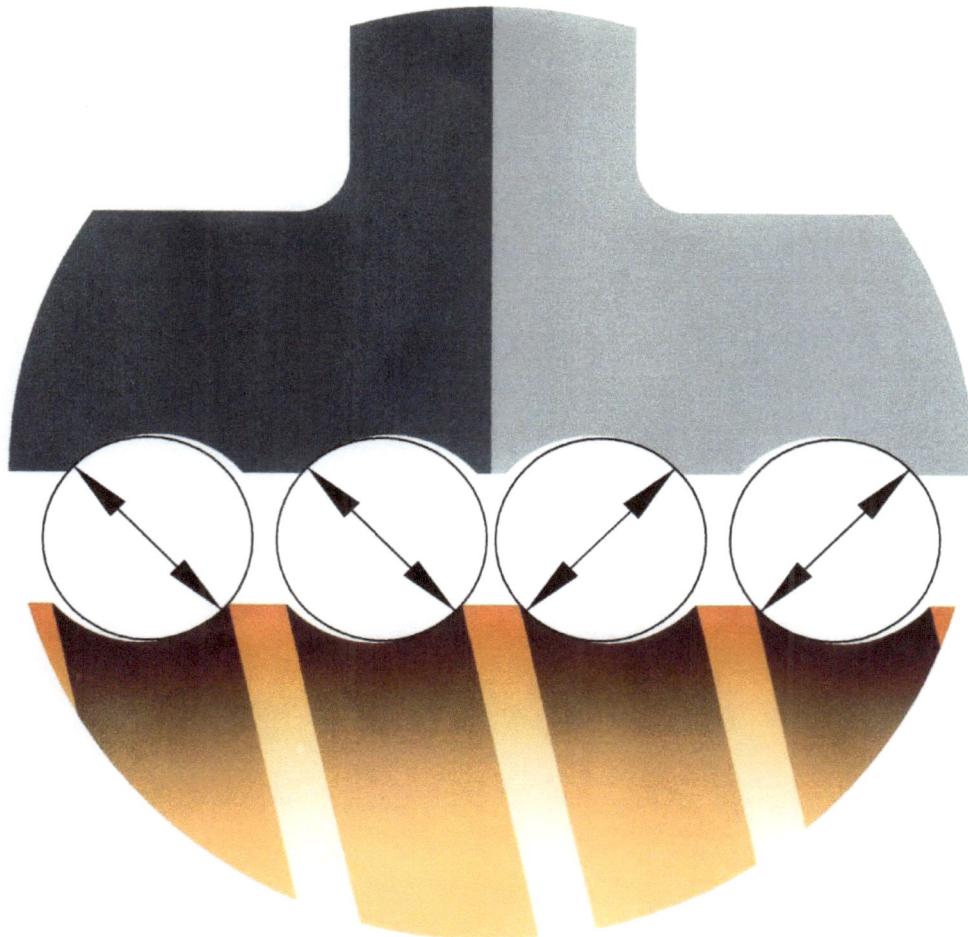

Figure 93 Minimum Moment Stiffness

120

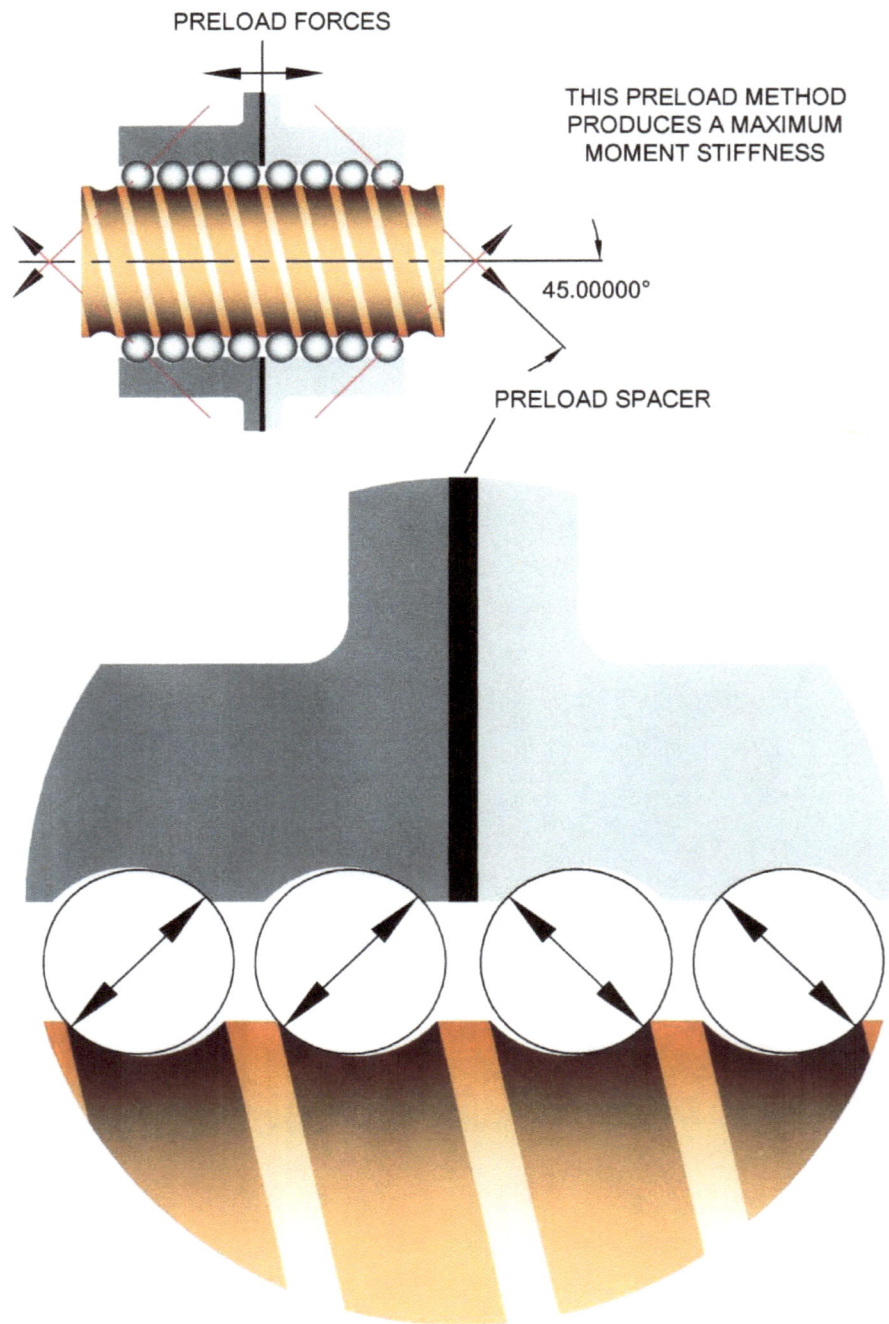

PRELOAD FORCES

THIS PRELOAD METHOD
PRODUCES A MAXIMUM
MOMENT STIFFNESS

45.00000°

PRELOAD SPACER

Figure 94 Maximum Moment Stiffness

121

Limitation on Ball Quantity

A single ball circuit should never have more than approximately 200 balls The exact limitation has substantial fuzz on it. Fewer, larger balls are always better! Let see? Oh, I didn't tell you why. When you try to push too many balls through a single circuit, intermittent jamming will occur. This is definitely not good! Using spacer balls can sometimes reduce or eliminate the jamming.

Differential Thread Devices

One revolution of driven gear produces only .00056 inches of output linear motion.

One percent of a revolution of drive gear (3.6°) is possible. And, .000056 inches of output linear motion would be produced.

An additional order of magnitude motion decrease is possible but gear errors (position errors) will begin to limit fineness of motion increments. Also, thread backlash must be carefully controlled.

Clearly, micron size motion increments are possible if a design is carefully thought out.

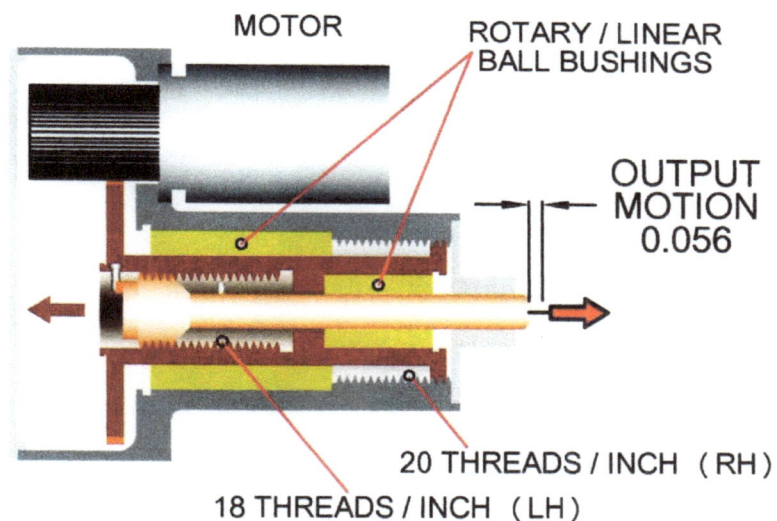

Figure 95 Differential Threads for Small Motions

The Linear Harmonic Drive

Concept for Extremely Fine Motion Increments

Combined with Very High Axial Force/Stiffness Capability

Total output motion = .025 inches

Travel increment = 7.31 microinches / Input degree

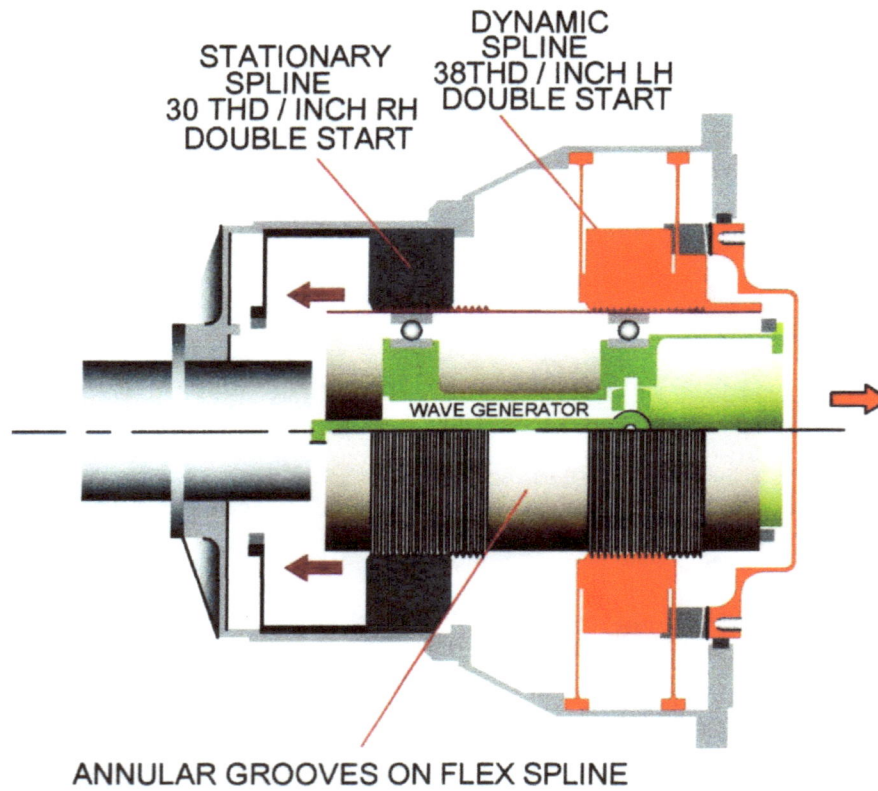

Figure 96 Linear Motion with Harmonic Drive Technology

Chapter 11   Damper Technology

Introduction:

Damping devices have three primary spacecraft functions to perform. (1) They can stabilize spacecraft attitude. (2) They can limit the rate of deployment of spacecraft appendages and (3) they can limit structural vibrations.

Even America's first successful space satellite, Explorer I, suffered attitude stability problems. Explorer I encountered an attitude control problem involving spin dynamics and nutation. The spacecraft was spin stabilized in order to maintain a known attitude. However, the technology of spinning spacecraft was in its infancy in 1957. A problem now known as wobble amplification occurred. The spacecraft began its orbital life with a spin about the spacecraft's long axis, but quickly began to wobble and eventually ended in a flat spin with the long axis in the spin plane.

If you would like to know more about this, see a report written in 1958 at JPL:

"Vehicle Motions as Inferred from Radio Signal Strength Records," External Publication No. 551, Jet Propulsion Lab, Cal Tech, Pasadena, CA Sept 5, 1958.

Spin Stabilization and Attitude Control:

Ball-in-Tube Dampers

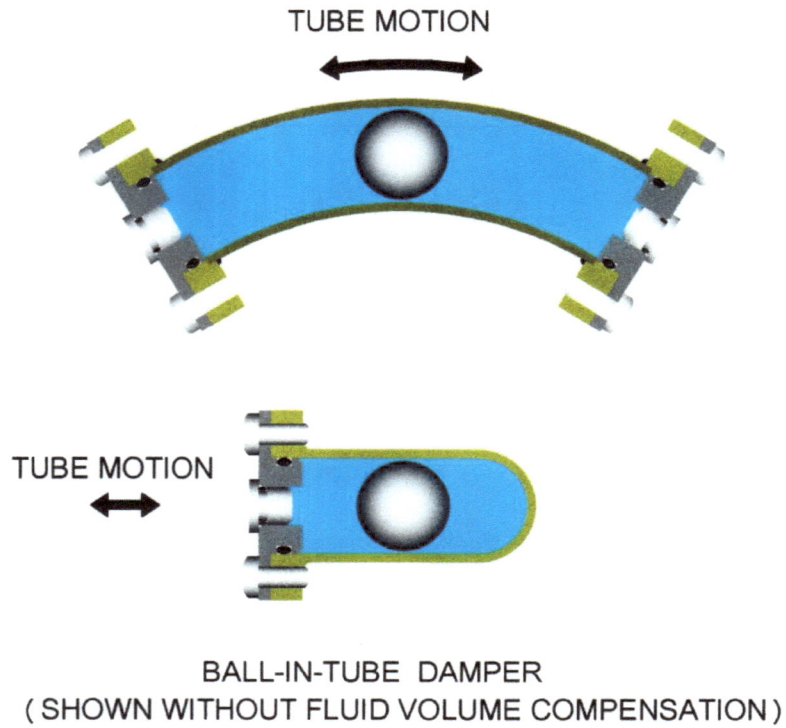

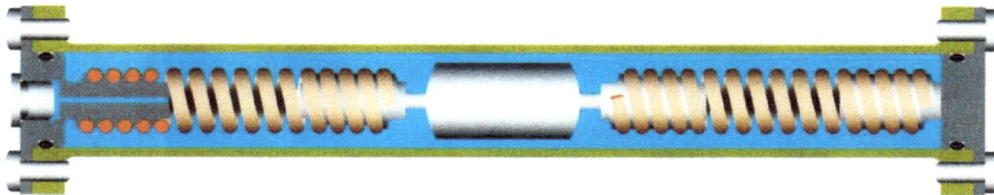

TUBE MOTION

TUBE MOTION

BALL-IN-TUBE DAMPER
(SHOWN WITHOUT FLUID VOLUME COMPENSATION)

MASS WITH TUNABLE NATURAL FREQUENCY

Figure 97 Ball-In-Tube Dampers

Pendulum Type Wobble Dampers

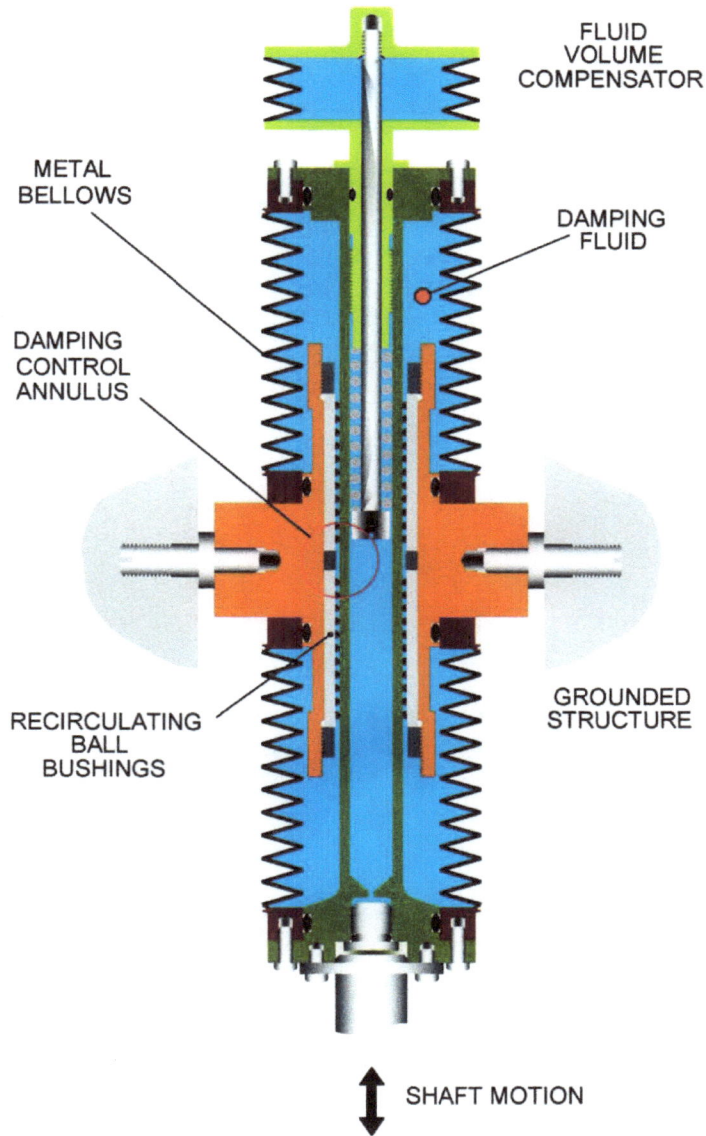

FLUID VOLUME COMPENSATOR

METAL BELLOWS

DAMPING FLUID

DAMPING CONTROL ANNULUS

RECIRCULATING BALL BUSHINGS

GROUNDED STRUCTURE

SHAFT MOTION

LINEAR VERY LOW FRICTION DAMPER
(SHOWN AT MIDPOINT OF TRAVEL)

Figure 98 Fluid Filled Metal Bellows

Deployment Dampers:

A common mechanisms problem encountered during spacecraft design is the control of the rate of deployment of appendages, panels, and booms. JPL has developed, qualified, and flown many of these dampers since 1970. The two types of dampers include a limited-rotation vane damper and a continuous-rotation shear damper.

Rotary Vane Dampers

JPL developed the rotary-vane damper in the late 1960s. It is a limited rotation unit producing rotary damping by squeezing silicone fluid through a diametrical gap. The piston (vane) produces pressure against the fluid. This type of damper is capable of very large damping constants.

These dampers have found wide usage at JPL and throughout the aerospace industry. The proceedings of the 10th AMS includes a paper: "Viscous Rotary Vane Actuator/Damper". Since that paper was written, the rotary-vane damper has been used on Voyager, Galileo, and Cassini.

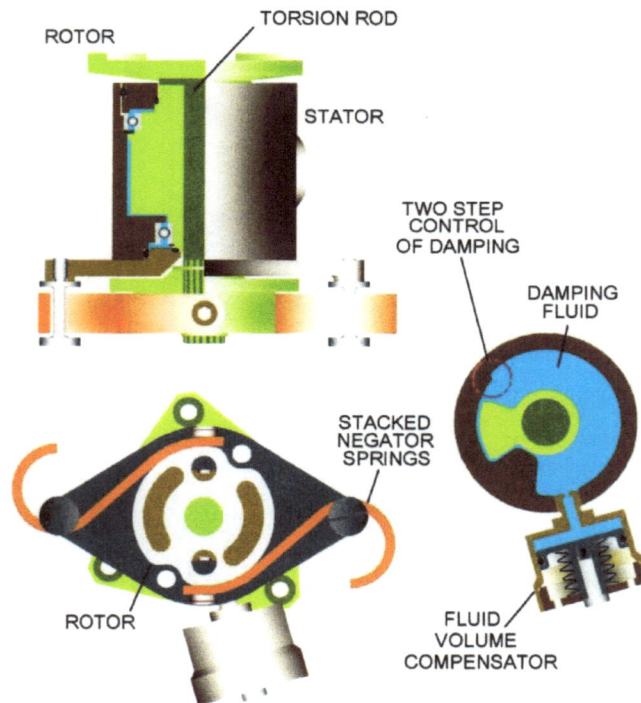

ROTARY VANE DAMPER
(SHOWN FULLY DEPLOYED)

Figure 99 Vane Damper (Fully Deployed)

Linear Piston Dampers

A linear damper was developed for deployment rate control of the Galileo science boom. Damping is achieved by shearing a medium-viscosity silicone fluid between a housing and piston. This type of damper, like the rotary vane damper, is capable of producing large damping constants. The design of linear piston dampers is discussed in detail in the following AMS paper:

"Nutation Damper System";

 Donald R. Sevilla, Jet Propulsion Laboratory, Pasadena,

CA; Seventeenth AMS, 1983.

MEDIUM
VISCOSITY
SILICONE
FLUID
(50K Cs)

PISTON

FLUID
VOLUME
COMPENSATOR

| EVACUATED |
| METAL |
| BELLOWS |

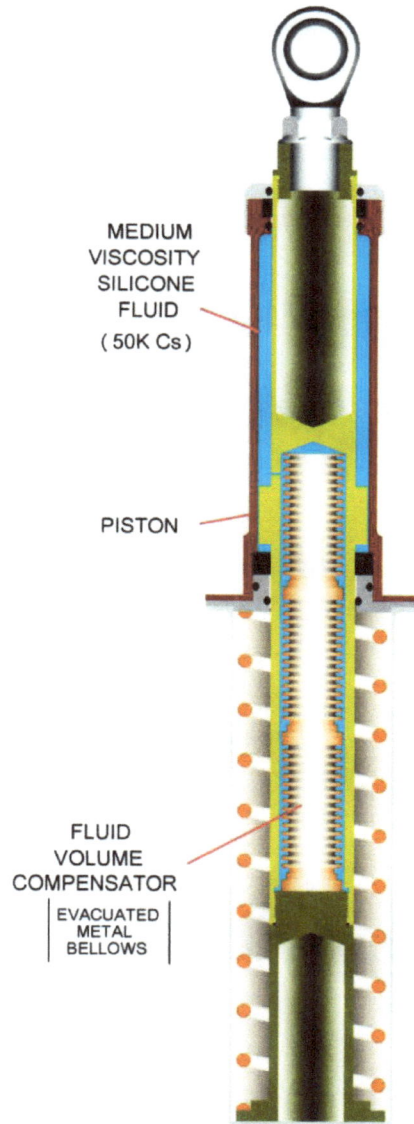

**Figure 100 Piston Damper
0-Ring Seals**

Shear Dampers

A continuous-rotation damper was developed for deployment rate control of the Voyager magnetometer boom. Similar rate limiters have been used on Galileo and Cassini for mag-boom deployment rate control. Damping is achieved by shearing a high-viscosity silicone fluid between a housing and drum. The design of rotary shear dampers is discussed in detail in the following AMS paper:

"Galileo Spacecraft Magnetometer Boom";
 Packard, D.T. and Benton, M.D., Jet Propulsion Laboratory, Pasadena, CA; Nineteenth AMS, NASA CP-2371

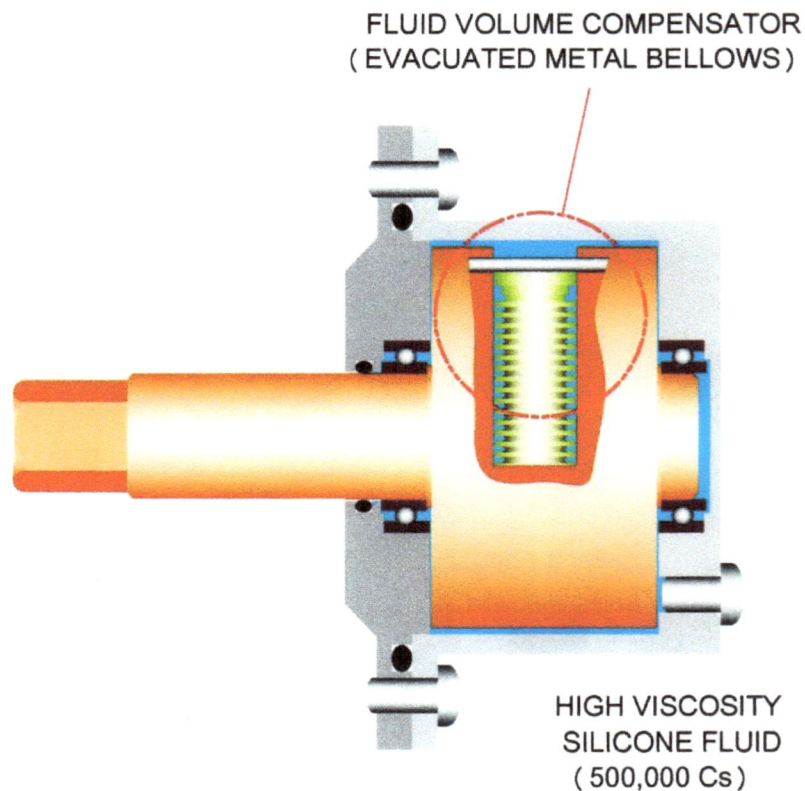

FLUID VOLUME COMPENSATOR
(EVACUATED METAL BELLOWS)

HIGH VISCOSITY
SILICONE FLUID
(500,000 Cs)

Figure 101 Rotary Shear Damper

Structural Damping

Fluid-damped structures can provide very effective damping. The effect can provide vibration control and rapid settling time. JPL developed "greasy-tube dampers" in the mid 1960s and more recently damping struts have become commercially available.

Performance estimates for the damping struts suggest that near "one hop" damping is achievable. I have some experience with this technology. My experience indicates that the fluid damping alone will not achieve "one hop" performance. You will need a very small amount of coulomb (dry) friction acting in parallel with the fluid damper. I have achieved "one hop" damping of a massive (3HZ) object which rotated at six degrees per second. The system became absolutely stationary within 1.5 seconds of the last control system breaking pulse. However, a very low friction drag brake was needed to produce this performance.

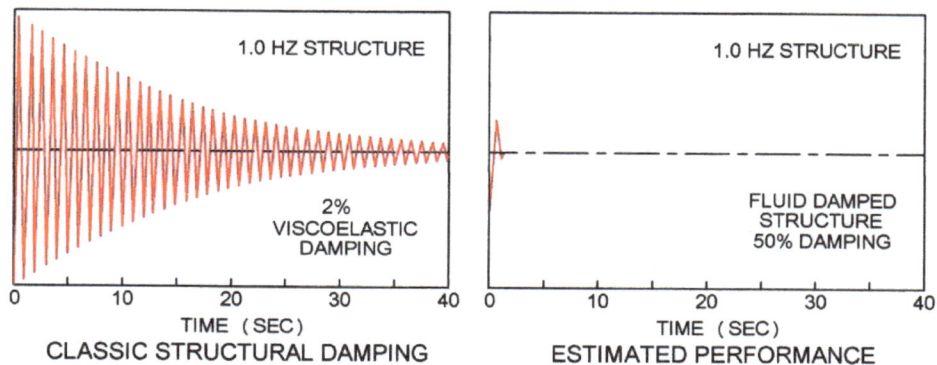

Figure 102 Structural Damping

The Nutation Damping System on the Galileo spacecraft presented the reverse problem. We wanted the 40 foot long Science Boom / Mag Boom combination to rotate about the inboard hinge line so that nutations of the spinning spacecraft could be eliminated. All moving elements in the system were either flexure mounted or supported by lightly loaded, liquid lubricated rolling element ball bearings. We were able to confirm hinge motion down to hinge torque levels below 2.5 inch ounces.

The Greasy Tube Damper (Linear Shear Damper)

JPL, during the mid 1960s, faced a problem that was more or less unique to interplanetary exploration. The design constraints associated with the very lightweight interplanetary spacecraft configurations such as Ranger and Mariner caused JPL to incorporate structural damper designs. Very neat configurations were developed. One example was a 10-lb antenna structure provided with near-critical damping using a 0.125-lb greasy-tube damper.

Two outstanding reports on damper design and development were produced:

"Development of a Point Damper for the Ranger Solar Panels," M. Gayman, NASA/JPL Tech Rpt No. 32-793.

"Mariner-IV Structural Dampers," P.T. Lyman, First AMS AD 638 916.

The first paper derives the basic equations for two damper classes, the low-friction, bellows-type nutation damper (later used on Galileo) and the linear dashpot (also used on Galileo). The second paper provides a very important piece of missing information on the relationship of dynamic viscosity to fluid-shear rate. This relationship yields the "apparent viscosity." The paper also presents the basic equations necessary to design a greasy tube damper. Damping in the greasy tube damper is achieved by shearing a thin film of very high-viscosity silicone fluid between two thin-walled concentric tubes.

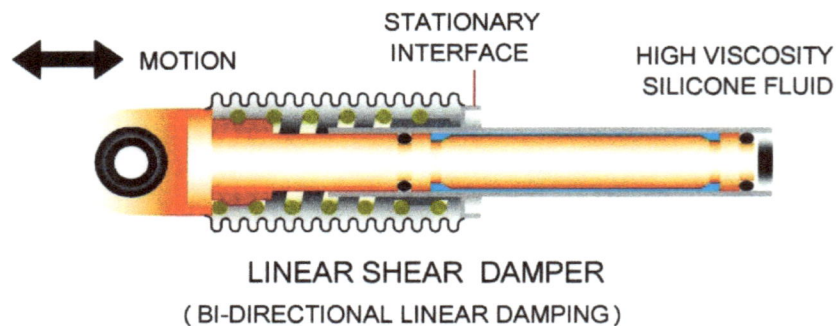

Figure 103 Linear Shear Damper (Greasy Tube Damper)

Honeywell D-Strut

The D-strut provides damping by pumping a column of fluid through a long, circular passage. This form of damping is defined by the Hagen-Poiseville formula. Damping occurs because the outer tube axial stiffness is less than the inner tube stiffness. The damping fluid transfers through the long tube as the "strut" is stretched and compressed.

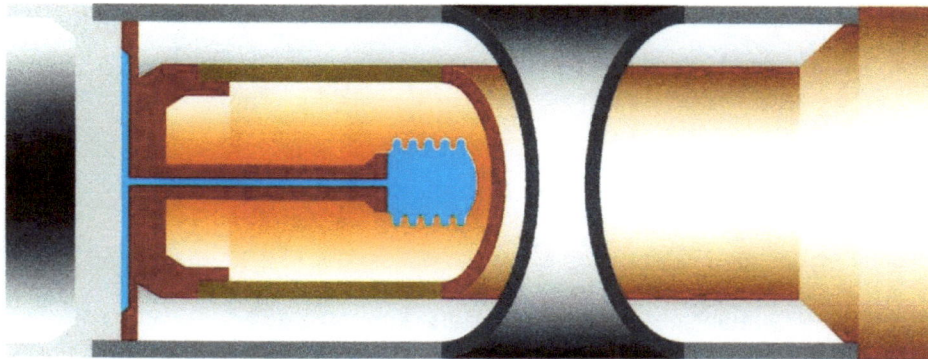

Figure 104 The D-Strut

Characteristics of Damping Fluids

The damping fluid selected for use in all of these dampers is silicone fluid (methyl-polysiloxane). The fluid has been sold commercially as Dow Corning 200,210 and 510 with the usual chose being the 210 fluid because it has been available in kinematic viscosity ranges from near zero to 500,000 centistokes. The wide operating temperature range and very low out-gassing characteristics of these fluids also make them the right choice.

However, there are a few thing you need to know before you work with these fluids:

(1) Special cleaning procedures are recommended.

(2) The silicone fluids must be vacuum out-gassed at high temperature before filling dampers.

(3) Dampers must be pressure filled in a vacuum . This is achieved by forcing the high viscosity fluid into the evacuated damper using a custom filling device which operates remotely in the vacuum chamber.

(4) The operating viscosity of the fluid is dependent upon the fluid shear rate.

(5) High fluid shear rates cause temporary hysteresis loops to form.

Effects of Fluid Shear Rate

Data for Dow Corning 210 Silicone fluid with a nominal 500,000 cs viscosity.

$$\textbf{Kinematic Viscosity } (v) = 1.58 \times 10^6 \left(\frac{V}{\Delta}\right)^{-\frac{1}{2}} \textbf{ centistokes}$$

$$\textbf{Dynamic Viscosity } (\mu) = .223 \left(\frac{V}{\Delta}\right)^{-\frac{1}{2}} \textbf{ lbsec/in}^2$$

Where: V = velocity across the fluid gap and Δ = width of fluid gap

These equations apply for shear rates equal to or greater than 10.

Data from: "Mariner-IV Structural Dampers," P.T. Lyman, First AMS.

Terminology of Viscosity

The terminology associated with fluid viscosity is very messy. It is beneficial to begin a discussion of fluid damping by defining the standard measures of viscosity. The term viscosity alone is not sufficient because viscosity may be dynamic viscosity or kinematic viscosity.

$$\textbf{Dynamic Viscosity } (\mu) \; (1.0 \text{ poise}) = 2.089 \times 10^{-3} \text{ (lb sec)}/(\text{ft}^2)$$

$$\textbf{Kinematic Viscosity } (v) \; (1.0 \text{ stoke}) = 1.0 \; \frac{\text{cm}^2}{\text{sec}}$$

$$\textbf{Kinematic Viscosity (v) (1.0 centistoke)} = .01 \frac{\textbf{cm}^2}{\textbf{sec}}$$

Kinematic viscosity (v) x Density (ρ) = Dynamic viscosity (μ)

ρ silicone fluid = 0.035 lb/in3

$$\mu \left(\frac{\textbf{lb sec}}{\textbf{in}^2} \right) = \textbf{v (centistokes)x (.00293)}$$

Occasionally the term "Saybolt Seconds is used. It is a measure of kinematic viscosity as shown below:

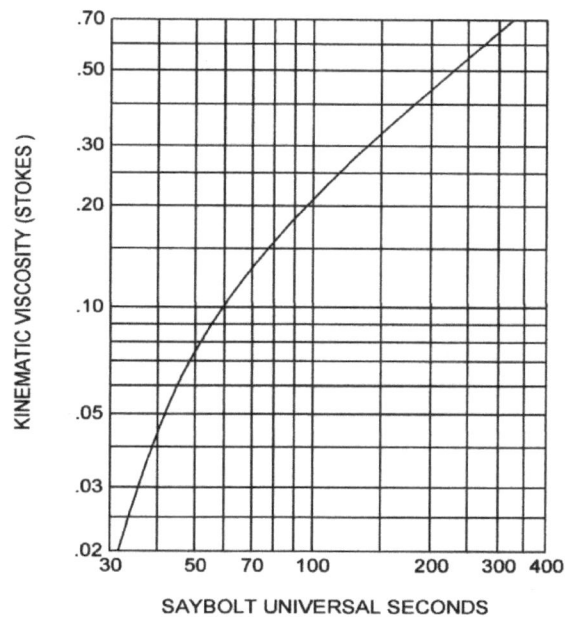

Figure 105 Viscosity Relationships

Another term, reyns, is also used to describe dynamic viscosity.

1.0 reyn = 1.0 lb sec / in2

GEE!   Isn' this FUN!!

Non-Newtonian Behavior

The figure shows several peculiarities of the silicone damping fluids. The "strange" characteristics can be used or avoided depending on the desired performance.

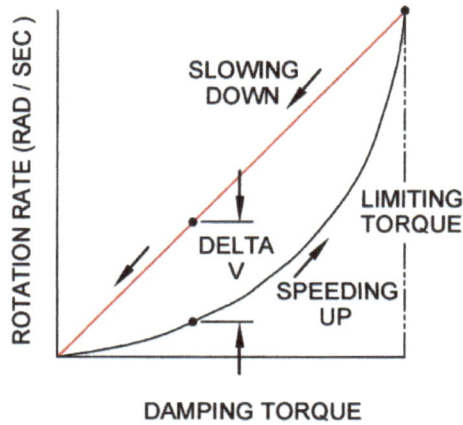

Figure 106 The Fluid Hysteresis Loop

The Voyager mag boom rate limiter encountered a loop at shear rate of 411 sec^{-1}.

The fluid shear rate is not linear; there is a limit beyond which drag torque will not increase. A temporary hysteresis loop forms at very high shear rates. Shear rates greater than the limiting torque do not produce additional damping. At very high shear rates all viscosity grades have the same "apparent" shear rate and the damper becomes insensitive to temperature changes.

"Flow Characteristics of Organopoly-Siloxane Fluids and Greases"
Ind & Engr Chem., Ind. Ed., Dec 1950, Vol 42, No. 12

"Consistency and Temperature of Oils & Printing Inks at High Shearing Stresses"
Ind & Engr Chem., Ind. Ed., 40, 272, 1948.

Temperature-Volume Compensation

The silicone damping fluids have a volumetric coefficient of thermal expansion of 0.00096 cc/cc (°C). These fluids are also incompressible. These two characteristics make temperature-volume compensation a must when significant fluid volume is used and/or when a wide operating temperature is required.

The figures show two different approaches used for JPL damper volume compensation. The rotary vane dampers have a spring-loaded piston which maintains a positive pressure but also moves in response to volumetric changes of the damping fluid. The second compensation technique involves an evacuated and sealed metal bellows. The bellows is located in the fluid cavity of rotary shear dampers or linear dampers. The bellows length expands or contracts to compensate fluid volume changes. And, it also maintains a positive pressure on the fluid. Commercial dampers most often lack temperature-volume compensation and this results in bubble formation and possible overpressure / leakage. I personally would not use an "uncompensated" damper regardless of how many fools had flown it!

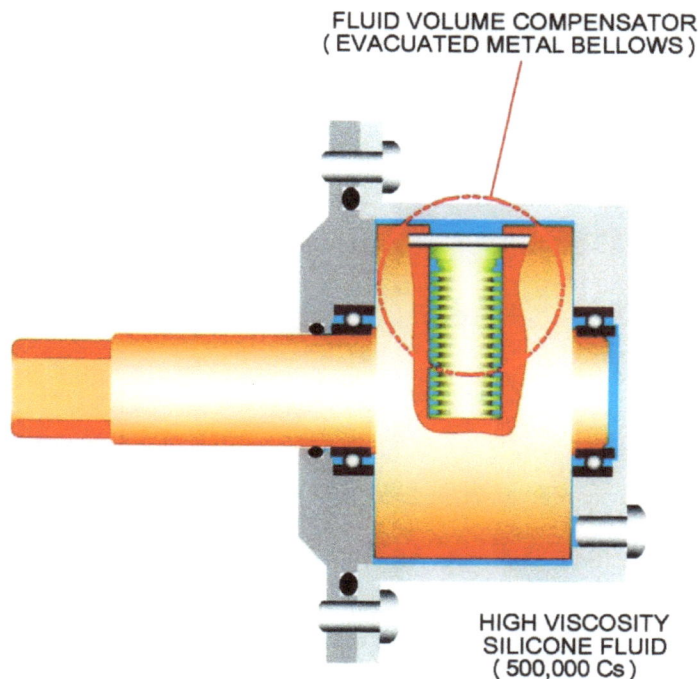

FLUID VOLUME COMPENSATOR
(EVACUATED METAL BELLOWS)

HIGH VISCOSITY
SILICONE FLUID
(500,000 Cs)

Figure 107 Temperature Compensation

Sample Calculation (Evacuated Bellows)

Bellows P/N 10035052 (VGR mag-boom rate limiter)

Fluid volume 4.703 cc @ 24°C

Bellows height @ (1) atmos @ 24°C = 0.795 in.

Bellows min height 0.565 in. @ 123 psi

Bellows max (constrained) height = 1.094 in.

Travel = 0.529 in. = ±0.264 in.

Mean height @ filling 1.094 - 0.264 = 0.83 in.

Bellow effective cross-section area = 0.0495 in^2

Δh = 0.83 - 0.795 = 0.035

Equivalent volume change = 0.035 x 0.0495 x 16.39 cc/in^3 = 0.28 cc

$$\Delta T = \frac{0.028}{0.00096 \times 4.703} = 6.3 \text{ deg C}$$

Fill instruction: Fill @ 18°C (65°F)

Δ vol = 0.264 x 0.0495 x 16.39 = 0.214 cc

Δ temp = 0.214/ (.00096 x 4.675) = ±47°C

T $_{max}$ = + 150 deg F.   T $_{min}$ = - 20 deg F

Performance Equations

Ball - in - Tube Damper

An explanation of the analysis for Ball-in-Tube Dampers is contained in the following group of reports:

Auelmann, R.R., and Lane, P.T., "Design and Analysis of Ball-in-Tube Nutation Dampers," Proceedings of Symposium on Attitude Stabilization and Control of Dual-Spin Spacecraft, TR-0158(3307-01)-16. Aerospace Corporation, Los Angeles, Calif., Nov. 1967.

Auelmann, R.R., and Lane, P.T., "Design and Analysis of Ball-in-Tube Nutation Dampers," Proceedings: Symposium on Attitude Stabilization and Control of Dual Spin Spacecraft, Aerospace Corp., El Segundo, Calif., Aug. 1967, AF Report No. SAMSO-TR-68-191, U.S. Air Force, Washington, D.C., Nov. 1967.

Bauer, A.B., and Du Puis, R.A., "Fluid Drag on a Sphere Rolling in a Tube," J. Appl. Mech., Preprint 67-APM-18, 1967.

Bellows Damper & Piston Damper

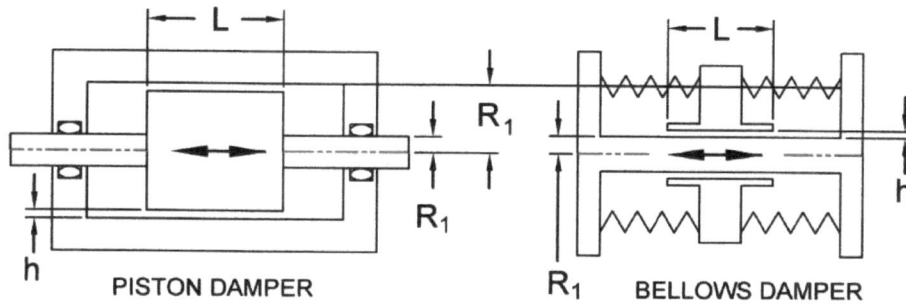

Figure 108 Dimensions Affecting Damping (Linear Dampers)

$$v = \frac{Fh^3}{6\pi\mu LB}$$

$$B = \left\{ \left(R_2 - \frac{h}{2}\right)^2 - (R_1)^2 \right\} \times \left\{ \frac{[(R_2)^2 - (R_1)^2]}{\left(R_2 - \frac{h}{2}\right)} - h \right\}$$

V = Linear velocity   (in./sec)

F = Damping force   (lb)

h = Fluid gap width (in.)

μ = Dynamic Viscosity (lb sec / in2)

The Damping Coefficient (lb-sec/in) = C

$$C = \frac{F}{v} = \frac{6\pi\mu LB}{h^3}$$

Rotary Shear Damper

Rotary Shear Dampers are continuous rotation dampers which use very small amounts of very viscous silicone fluids.

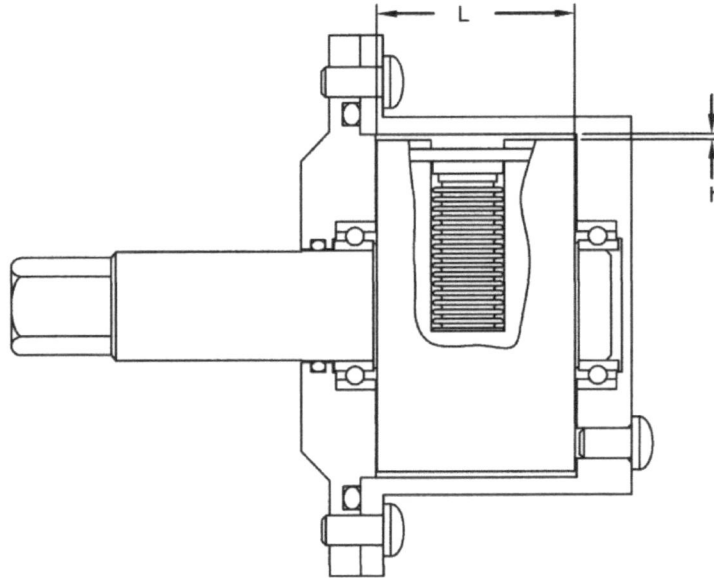

**Figure 109 Dimensions Affecting Damping
(Rotary Dampers**

$$T = \frac{\pi\, L\, \mu\, \Omega\, D^3}{4\, h}$$

T = Torque (in lb)

L = Rotor Width (in)

μ = Apparent Dynamic Viscosity (lb sec / ft2)

Ω = Rotor Speed (rad /sec)

D = mean Diameter of Fluid Gap (inches)

h = Fluid Gap Width (inches)

$$\mu = .223 \left(\frac{D}{2h}\right)^{-\frac{1}{2}}$$

For DC210 Silicone Fluid (500,000 cs):

Shear Damped Deployment Rate Limiter

$$\text{Deploy Velocity } (V_D) = \frac{F_D\, R^2\, 4h}{\pi\, \mu\, L\, D^3}$$

F_D (Deployment Force) = T (applied Torque) / R

R = Lanyard Radius

Ω = VD / R

Note that the lanyard radius (R^2) varies as it pays out. If you need a nearly constant deployment rate (V_D), the pulley diameter must be as large as possible.

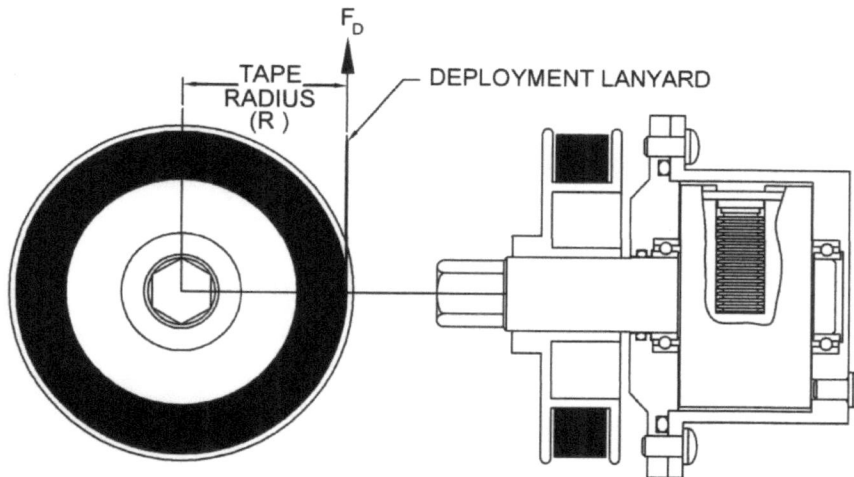

Figure 110 Shear Damper as a Deployment Rate Limiter

Rotary Vane Damper

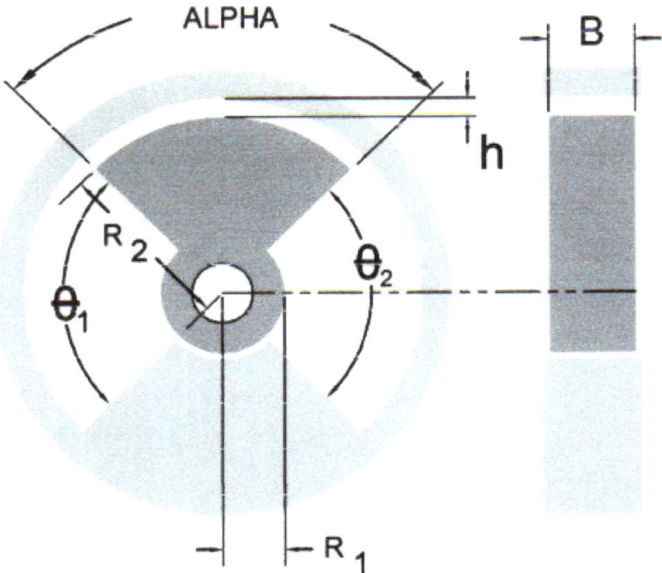

**Figure 111 Dimensions Affecting Damping
(Rotary Vane Dampers)**

$$T = \frac{3\,\mu\,[(R_2)^2 - (R_1)^2]^2\,B\,L\,\omega}{h^3}$$

$$\omega = \frac{\theta}{t}$$

$$L = R_2\,\alpha$$

T = Torque (in.-lb)

R2= Outer radius (in.)

R1 = Inner radius (in.)

B= Rotor width (in.)

L = Arc Length of clearance path (in.)

ω =Rotation speed (rad/sec)

h =Outer fluid gap (in.)

μ = Dynamic viscosity (lb-sec / in2)

t = Time (sec)

α= Rotor Angle (rad)

$$\text{Total Rotation } (\theta) = \theta_1 + \theta_2$$

$$\text{Fluid Gap } (h) = \sqrt[3]{\frac{3\mu[(R_2)^2 - (R_1)^2]^2 \, B \, R_2 \, \alpha\theta}{T\, t}}$$

$$\text{Internal Pressure } (\Delta P) = \frac{2T}{[(R_2)^2 - (R_1)^2]B}$$

Linear Shear Damper

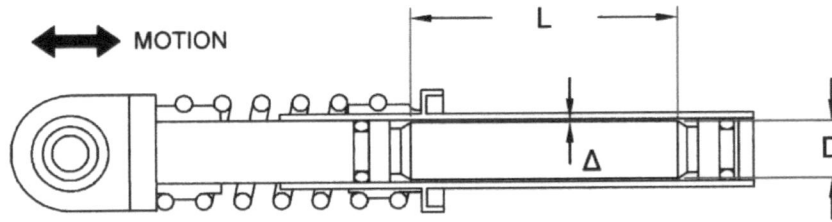

Figure 112 Dimensions Affecting Damping (Greasy Tubes)

$$F = \mu \left(\frac{V}{\Delta}\right) \pi D L$$

F = Damping force at velocity (v) (lbs)

V = Linear velocity (in./sec)

Δ = Radial clearance between tubes (in.)

D = Mean diameter of annulus (in.)

L = Eff length of piston (in.)

μ = Apparent Dynamic Viscosity (lb-sec/in2)

For 500,000 centistoke DC210 fluid :

$$\text{Dynamic Viscosity } (\mu) = .223 \left(\frac{V}{\Delta}\right)^{-\frac{1}{2}} \frac{\text{lbsec}}{\text{in}^2}$$

$$\text{For: } \frac{V}{\Delta} \geq 10$$

143

Damping Through a Small Diameter Orifice

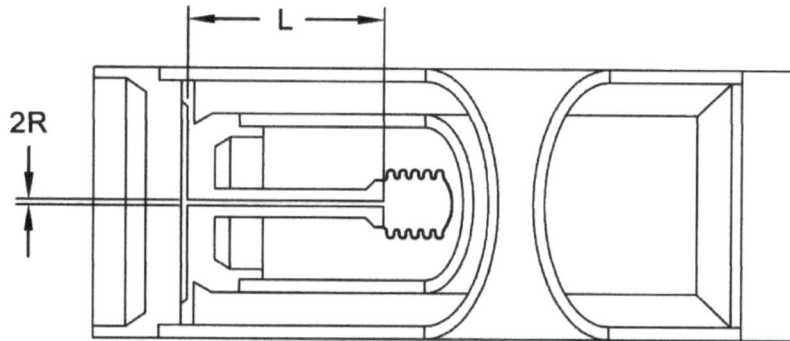

Figure 113 Dimensions Affecting Damping (D-Struts)

$$Q = \frac{\pi \, (R)^4}{8 \, \mu \, L} \, (\Delta P) \left(\frac{in^3}{sec} \right)$$

Q = V A, ΔP = F/A, F = C V

$$A = \pi \left(\frac{(2R)^2}{4} \right)$$

$$\Delta P = \frac{C \, V}{A} \left(\frac{lb}{in^3} \right)$$

$$C = \frac{8 \, \mu \, L \, A^2}{\pi R^4} \left(\frac{lb \, sec}{in} \right)$$

Non-Fluid Dampers:

Elastomeric Shear Dampers

The Voyager spacecraft used a non-liquid damper to control micro vibration. Dave Otth authored a paper "Shear Dampers for Deflections of Micro-Inch Magnitudes" in the proceedings of the institute of environmental sciences (approx date 1975). This paper describes the elastomeric shear damper washers used on Voyager to control very low amplitude boom motion. The damping material was a urethane sheet called "Dyad".

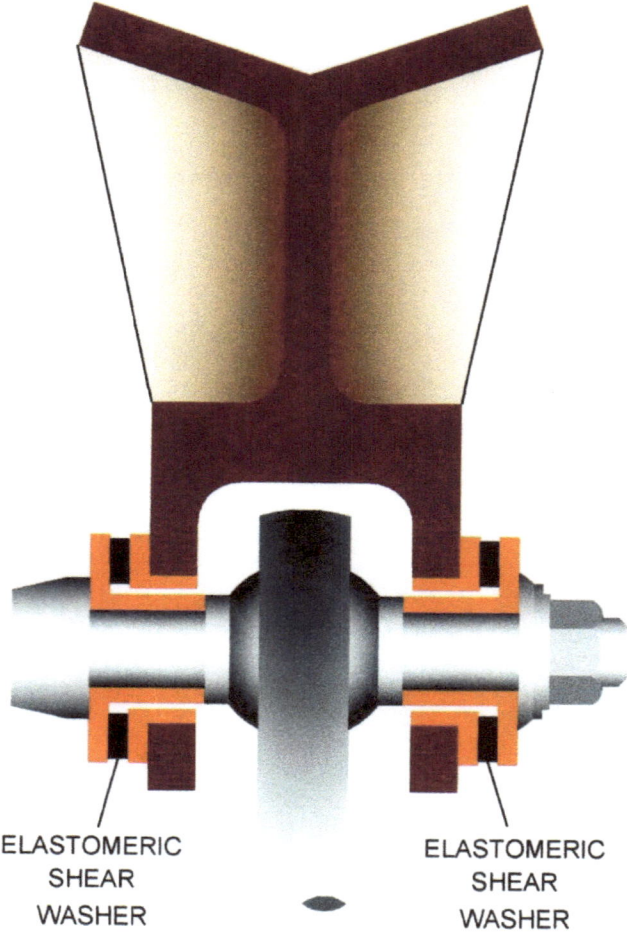

ELASTOMERIC SHEAR WASHER   ELASTOMERIC SHEAR WASHER

Figure 114 Elastomer Shear Dampers

Coulomb Friction Damping

The second non-liquid damping application occurred in the Galileo spacecraft. The probe relay antenna actuator required coupling-to-ground to assure stable pointing. This Coulomb friction device produced a constant drag force as the antenna rotated. The drag was sufficient to prevent vibration coupling at any input frequency.

PRES	TEMP (°F)	COEF OF FRICTION							
		STATIC				SLIDING			
		NORMAL FORCE (LBS)				NORMAL FORCE (LBS)			
		1.02	2.12	4.22	6.21	1.02	2.12	4.22	6.21
AMB	-30	.306	.230	.221	.216	.247	.217	.198	.181
	73	.191	.179	.188	.177	.170	.157	.157	.150
VAC	73	.196	.195	.182	.173	.170	.166	.151	.151
	160	.164	.115	.125	.138	.127	.096	.089	.098
	-30	.374	.361	.328	.319	.369	.302	.271	.235

**Figure 115 Coef of Friction at Temperature
(Delrin AT against Alum)**

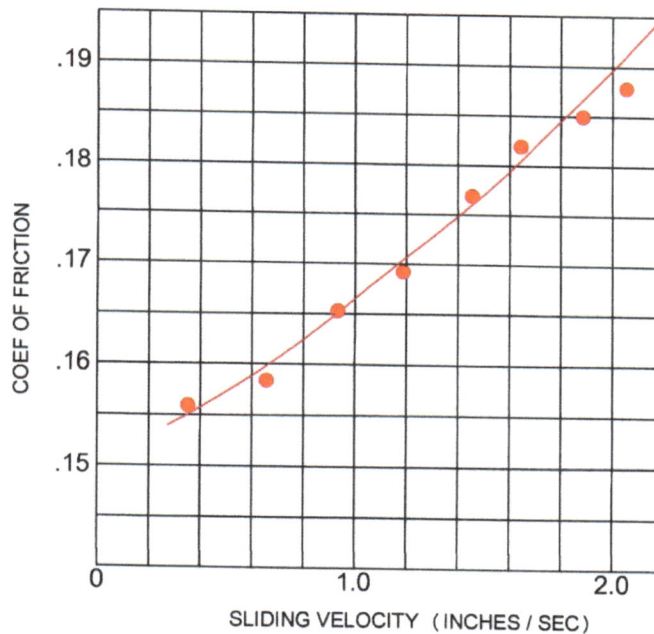

**Figure 116 Coef of Friction vs Sliding Speed
(Delrin AF against Alum)**

Eddy Current Rotary Damper

Figure 117 The Eddy Current Damper

This damper is commercially available. I have not used the unit, and data supplied by the vendor is not sufficient to prove to me that the unit will perform as described. The lack of a specific load / life specification only increases my concern.

This high-torque-capacity damper (up to 700 in-lb) was designed and qualified to serve as a rate-limiting device for the deployment of a large solar array.

A copper allow disk rotating between pairs of samarium-cobalt magnets creates a generated voltage in the disk. This voltage produces circulating currents within the disk which result in a restraining torque proportional to input velocity. The restraining torque is multiplied through a 1600:1 four-stage planetary gear train. A simple external adjustment allows user to select damping rates ranging from 10,000 to 20,000 in-lb-sec/rad.

EDDY CURRENT ROTARY DAMPER	
DAMPING RATES (IN-LB-SEC PER RAD)	10,000 TO 20,000
DAMPING TORQUE CAPABILITY (IN-LB)	700 (MAX)
ROTATIONAL RANGE	CONTINUOUS
TOTAL WEIGHT (LBS)	1.55
QUALIFICATION TEMPERATURE RANGE (°F)	-60° TO + 220°

Figure 118 Performance Specification

So You Want To Land Your Mini Cooper On Mars:

This is the challenge that JPL was faced with for the MSL Rover. The conventional damping techniques are simply not capable of absorbing this amount of energy in the time required. Your Cooper would land into Mars not on Mars. However, an electrical generator and resistor bank can do that trick. It is even possible to segment the generator so that multiple independent generators exist to provide redundancy for the damper function. The MSL Team found that this was the practical way to do the job. Contact Ensign Bickford for details.

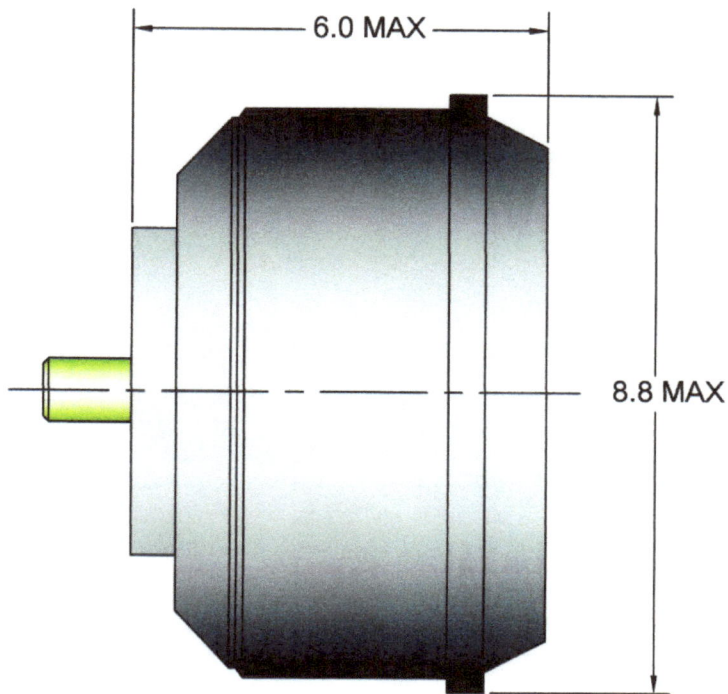

Figure 119 Electrical Generator as a Damper

COMPONENTS	TI MASS (Kg)	Be MASS (Kg)
GENERATOR	>2.0	>2.0
RESISTORS	>4.0	>4.0
GEAR BOX & HOUSING	>8.0	>6.0
TOTAL MASS	>14.0	>12.0

Figure 120 Mass Estimate

CHARACTERISTIC	
DAMPING RATE (N-m-SEC /RAD)	APPROX 10.5
FRICTION (N-m)	APPROX 2.0
REFLECTED INERTIA (Kg-m^2)	APPROX 10.0

Figure 121 Performance Estimate

Chapter 12   Rotary Seals

Introduction:

There are four types of truly hermetic rotary seals that have been used in aerospace applications. These include:

(1) Magnetic Coupling

(2) Nutating Bellows Seal

(3) Harmonic Drive Seal

(4) Ferrofluid Seal

Each seal type is capable of providing millions of revolutions of seal life with no measurable leakage. O-ring seals (rotary seals) are sometimes used for shaft sealing but they are not long-life seals. The typical o-ring seal will begin to "burp down" after only a few revolutions and total failure (gross leakage) usually occurs after a few thousand revolutions.

Sealing was of primary importance prior to the advent of brushless motor and optical encoder technology. These technologies matured in the mid 1970s and there has been little Aerospace use of "rotary seals" since that time. However, the semi-conductor industry makes extensive use of this technology.

Magnetic Couplings:

The magnetic coupling is used to transmit rotary or linear motion through a solid wall. There are three general types of magnetic couplings: (1) Synchronous, (2) Eddy Current and (3) Hysteresis. There are many companies which produce commercial magnetic couplings. The couplings are produced as rotary and linear motion transfer devices.

Synchronous Couplings

The synchronous coupling provides a 1:1 motion relationship between the driving shaft and the driven shaft. These couplings use the attraction / repulsion characteristics of permanent magnet pairs (N-S-N-S) to produce coupled motion. An array of alternating pole magnets on the driver couples with similar alternating pole magnets located on the driven shaft across an "air gap". The sealing wall material is located in that "air gap". There is a peak coupling torque which is a function of the magnetic circuit design. If a torque greater than the peak value is applied, decoupling will occur. This condition is similar to a "torque drop-out". The driver and driven shafts will re-couple as soon as the torque is reduced. There is a "compliance" in the magnetic coupling (think of it as a torsion spring). The driving shaft will wind-up slightly as the transmitted torque increases.

Eddy Current Couplings

This coupling is an "asynchronous" device which requires a speed mismatch between the driver and driven shafts. an array of alternating pole magnets is located on either the driver or driven shaft. An electrically conductive material is placed on the shaft which has no magnets. Any time that the driver moves in relation to the driven shaft, eddy currents flow in the conductive material and a magnetic field is produced. The magnetic field opposes the permanent magnets and couples the driven shaft to the driver. The strength of the coupling force is directly related to the magnetic material properties and the speed differential between the driver and driven shafts. If the coupling force is exceeded, a ratcheting effect (non-smooth motion) will occur and serious heating can result.

Hysteresis Couplings

This class of coupling combines the characteristics of both synchronous and eddy current couplings. An array of magnet pairs is placed on either the driver or driven shaft. The shaft which has no magnet pairs has an easily magnetized material (Hysterloy) placed on it. The permanent magnet array is designed to achieve a synchronous coupling to the driver at low torque values and will produce what appears to be a "synchronous coupling" until torque increases to a value where de-coupling occurs. However, when the shafts de-couple, the characteristics of the Hysterloy material allow the pole states in the Hysterloy to switch. Effect allows the Hysteresis coupling to run smoothly and with greatly reduced heating.

Nutating Bellows Seals:

The next figure shows a sealed, 10-turn potentiometer that was produced for the aerospace industry. The rotary seal is an all-mechanical device that transfers motion to the potentiometer wiper through a system of eccentric shafts/disks. A nutating metal bellows provides the motion seal.

A problem has been encountered during seal development. Initially, an "electroless" nickel bellows was used. This is a metallic bellows produced by a chemical-plating process. It was found that small (microscopic) nodules formed during the plating process and then broke off during use causing the bellows to leak. The bellows fabrication process was revised to an electroplate process and these bellows were free of nodules.

The nutating seal is only applicable to low-speed, low-torque applications.

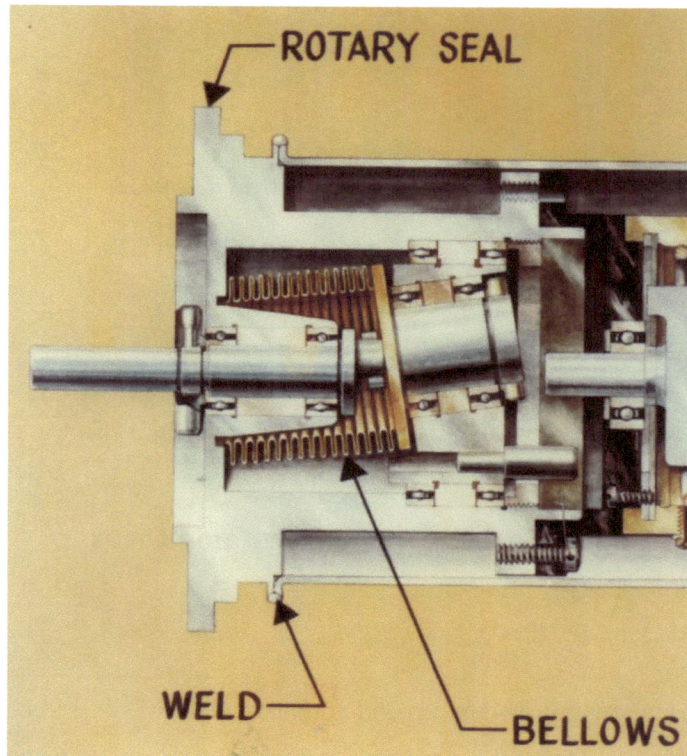

Figure 122 The Nutating Bellows Seal

Harmonic Drive Seals

A few aerospace applications of this seal type have been developed. One notable application was the wheel drive for the lunar rover. Most of these applications occurred in the 1960s when space actuator technology was very new.

The harmonic drive principle allows the transmission of rotary motion through a solid steel wall. The harmonic drive principle involves three basic components: the wave generator, the flexspline, and the circular spline. In a normal configuration, as shown here, the wave generator is the input element that imparts an ellipse-like shape to the fixed flexspline. The flexspline is hermetically sealed to the barrier so that it becomes, in effect, an integral part of the barrier. The ellipse-like shape of the flexspline, but not the flexspline itself, rotates at the same speed as the wave generator. As this shape rotates, it causes progressive engagement of the external teeth of the flexspline and the internal teeth of the circular spline, thereby causing the circular spline to rotate in the same direction as the wave generator.

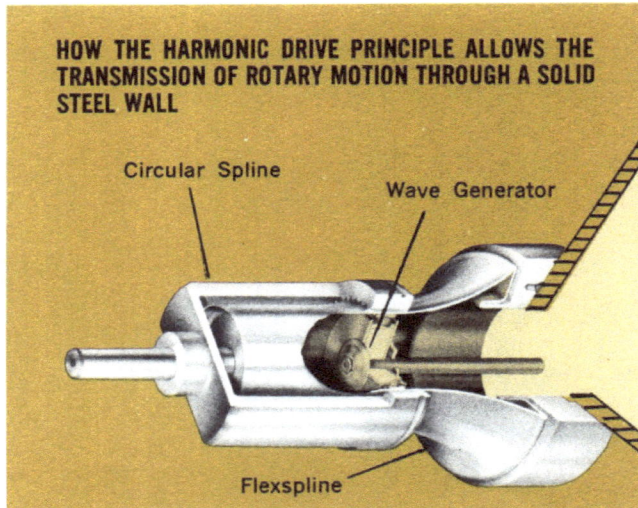

Figure 123 Sealed Harmonic Drive

Ferrofluid Seal

The first two figures below show a sealed motor and potentiometer. An actual cross-section of the motor seal is shown in the third figure. Many actuator vacuum test chambers contain commercial ferro-seals which transfer rotary motion out of the vacuum chambers. I believe that some of these seals have been in use at JPL for nearly thirty years.

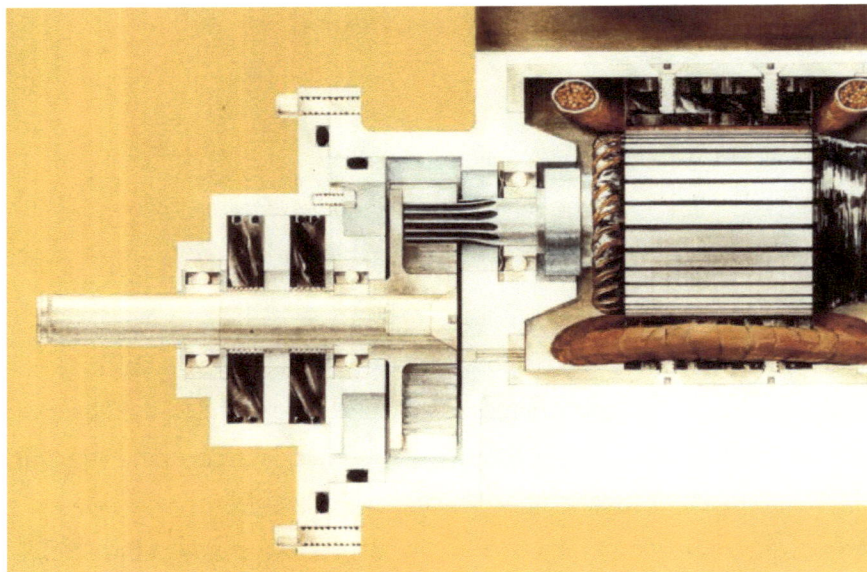

Figure 124 Brush Motor Sealed with Ferrofluid Seal

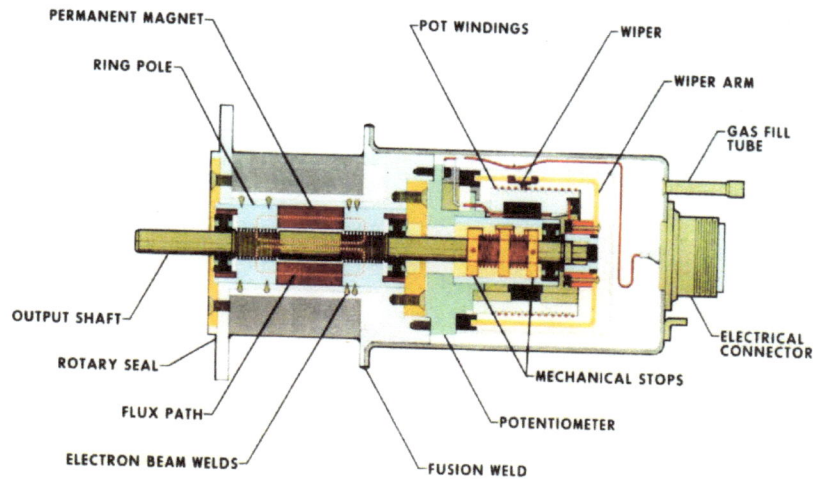

Figure 125 Wire Wound Pot Sealed with Ferrofluid Seal

The rotary seal is achieved by a magnetic fluid which is held in place by a strong magnetic field. Sharp pole tips on the rotating shaft create a series of liquid o-rings. The o-rings create a highly redundant and very reliable seal. The magnetic fluid is a mixture of very fine iron oxide particles permanently suspended in a base fluid. Very extensive development work was done to find base fluids which would not react with the sealed atmosphere.

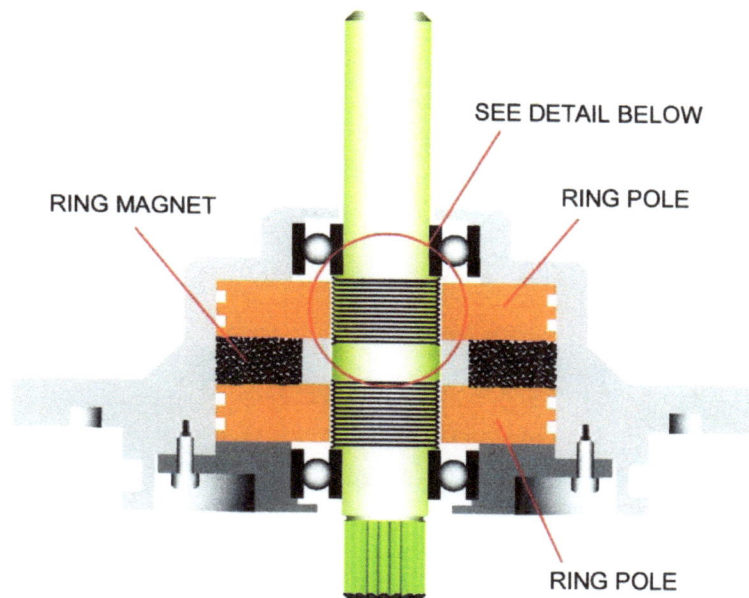

Figure 126 Ferrofluidic Rotary Seal

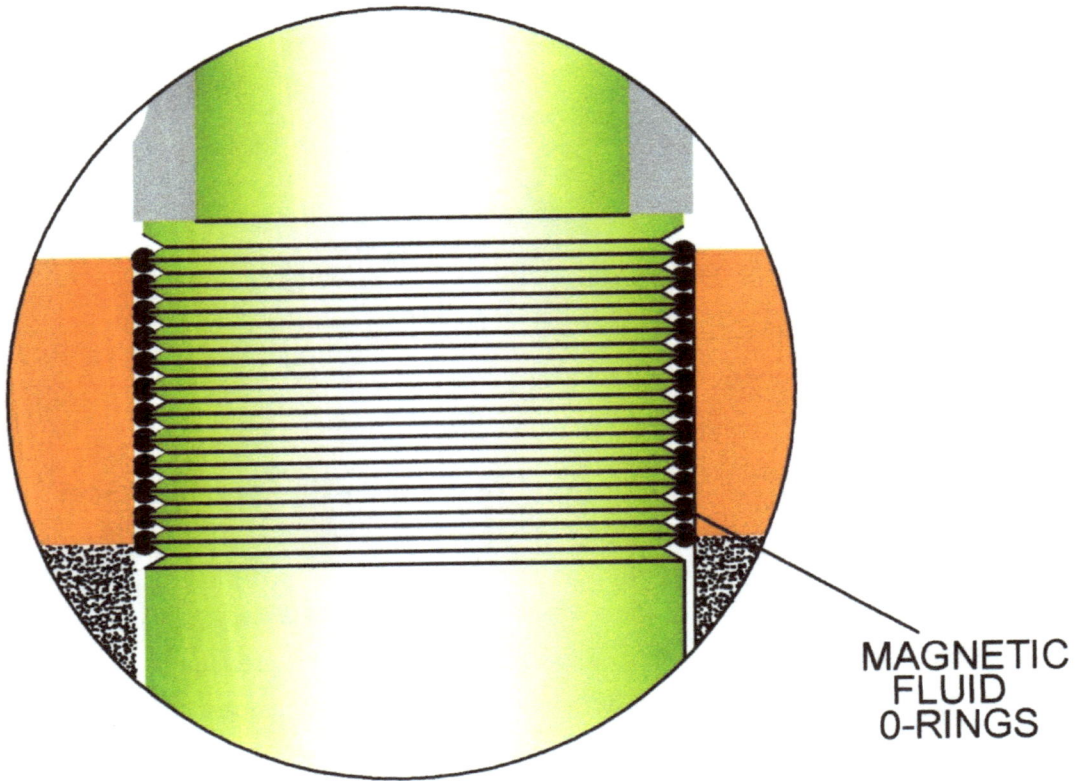

Figure 127 Detail of Fluid O-Rings

Chapter 13 Signal/Power Transfer Across a Rotating Joint

Flat Conductor Cable Wraps:

Source Information

NASA Tech Memorandum, NASA TM X-53960, NASA

Flat Conductor Cable for Limited Rotary or Linear Motion, Marshall Space Flight Center (Oct 1970)

The Twist Capsule

The flat conductor cable wraps discussed in the previous section form the basis for most twist capsule designs. However, the complete twist capsule must include several additional features. None of these additions were discussed:

(1) A special very reliable cable management system is required both on the input to the cable wrap and exiting from the cable wrap.

(2) A ball bearing pair is required if long operating life is a goal. And, some form of debris shield should protect the ball bearings.

(3) A mounting interface must be provided.

(4) A mechanical stop must be provided to protect the cable wrap from excessive wind-up. The design must allow for installation of the stop at the earliest possible stage of assemble in order to prevent human error from damaging the cable wrap.

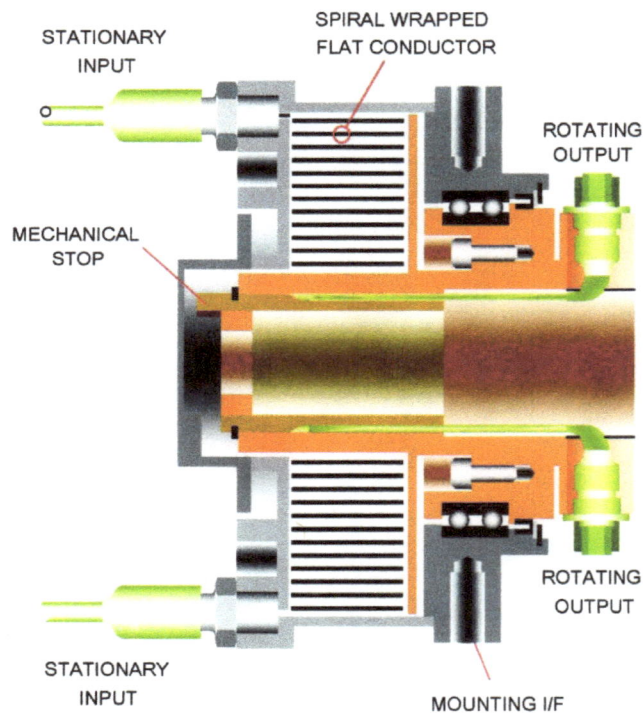

Figure 128 Mars Pathfinder Cable Wrap

Slip Rings

The slip ring assembly is capable of continuous rotation. But, the capability is achieved by using brush contacts which are susceptible to wear and noise causing debris generation.

A good general rule is "There is no shelf." This device is an excellent example ! This unit has extensive flight history; however, because it involves sliding contact, problems occur and reoccur with every new production lot. And, as we know from sad experience (Seasat) a slightly different application can result in failure.

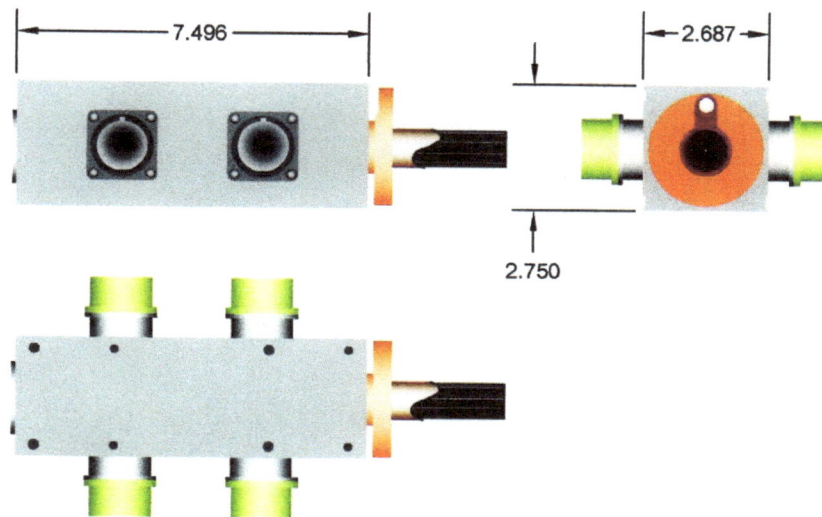

Figure 129 Slip Ring Assembly

Roll Rings

A device which is proprietary to: (Honeywell Space Systems) & (Diamond Roltran Inc)

In life-testing roll rings completed 35 million revolutions by early 1994 and were still performing to original specifications. For example, this far exceeds the 10 million spins required of any device transmitting power across a rotating axis on a trip to Jupiter.

Roll ring performance is based on a rolling technology similar to spin bearings. The "roll rings" do not have gross sliding as in slip ring applications.

Flexures in roll rings resembling thin wedding bands fit between the grooves of inner and outer concentric cylinders, creating a precise, stable electrical coupling. So stable, in fact, the rings cannot escape the grooves even under high-G loading and misalignments in operation.

The technology enables tailoring of the size of a power or data transfer assembly exactly as needed. Because roll rings are built into stand alone modules they can be configured for many different applications.

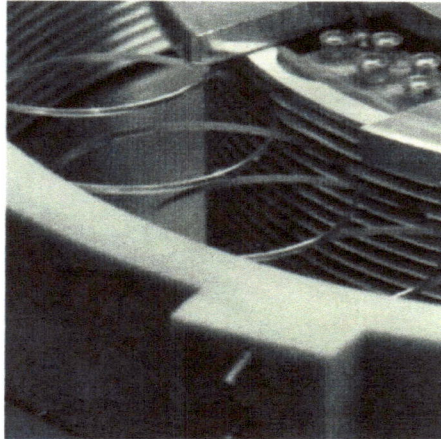

Figure 130 Roll Ring System

Rotary Transformers

The book "Space Vehicle Mechanisms", by Peter Conley, John Wiley 1998, contains a discussion of rotary transformers written by William T. McLyman (Chapter 15, Part II, Space Vehicle Mechanisims). He developed the rotary transformers for the Galileo spacecraft spin-bearing assembly. His article plus the listed reference material constitute a good starting point for understanding the very simple device. He has also published a comprehensive handbook for transformer and inductor design which is now in its third edition (see below).

"Transformer and Inductor Design Handbook"

Mc Lyman, Colonel Wm. T.

ISBN: 0824751159Publisher: Marcel Dekker Inc,

Pub Date: Jan 2004From Publisher:

Flexible Wave Guide

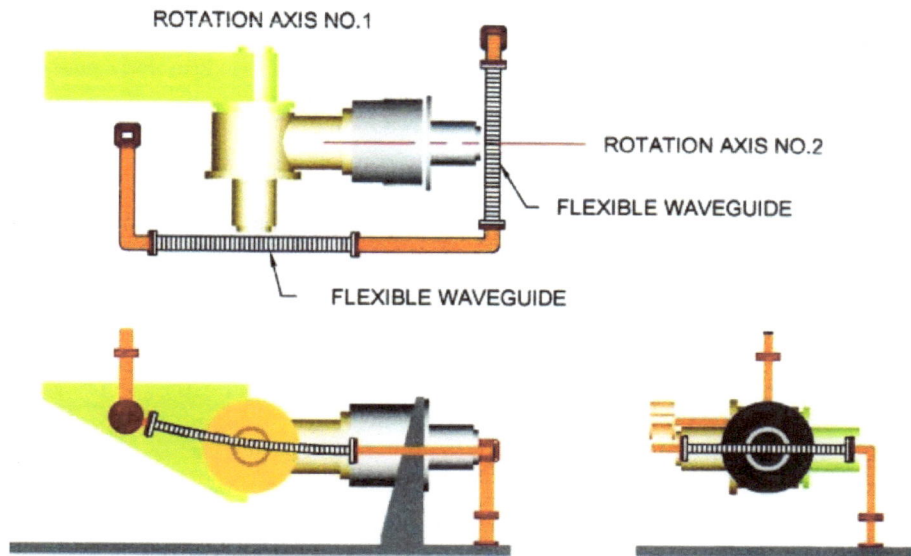

Figure 131 Limited Rotation Using Flex Wave Guide

Paired Rigid Wave Guides

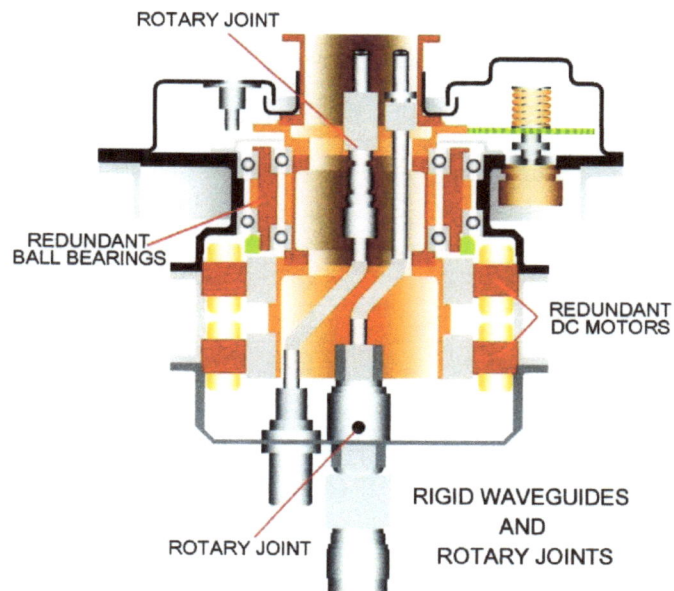

Figure 132 Limited Rotation with Wave Guide Pairs

160

Twist Flex

The "Twist Flex" cable wrap was developed in 1973 at Lockheed Missiles and Space Co.

Tests have shown that the Twist-Flex unit has a definite cycle life. It was shown that shield damage is sustained on both power and the RF (Twinax) cables after extensive life testing. However, The same tests also showed that the design could provide adequate life margin for missions lasting several years.

The Twinax RF cables require care be taken to select a wire with no loose strands in the shield that might result in reduced cycle life. In the case of the AWG 16 twisted-pair shielded power cables, cycle life of approximately three times the required life was demonstrated before failure.

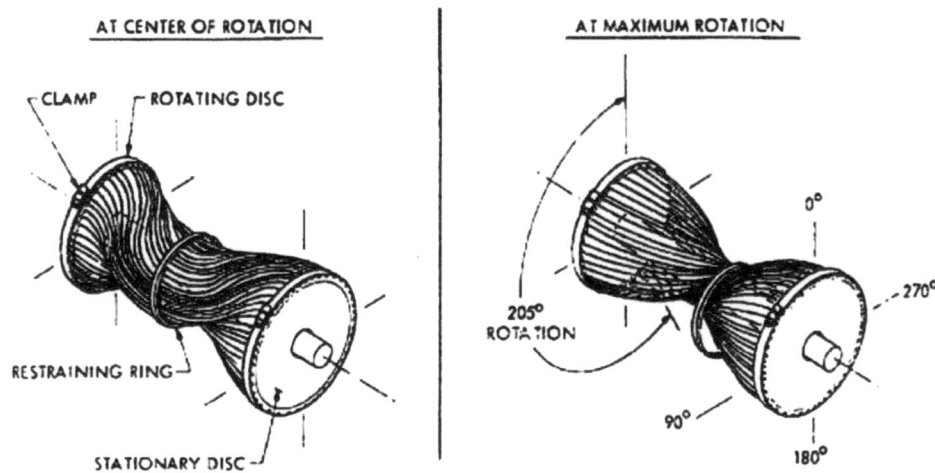

Figure 133 The Twist Flex Concept

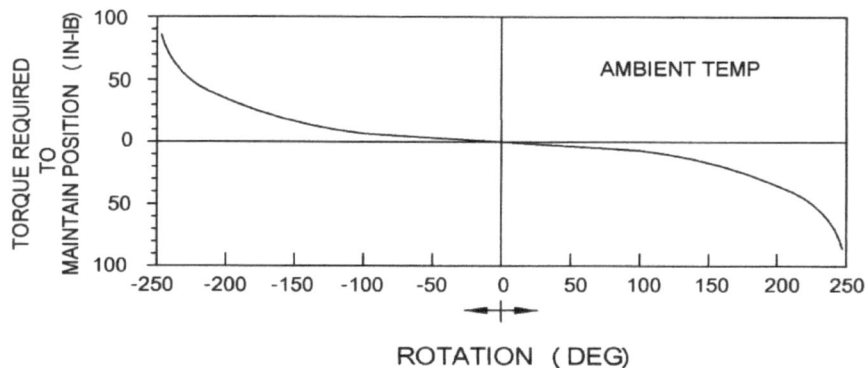

Figure 134 Twist Flex Rotational Travel

REQUIREMENTS	MODEL NO. 1	MODEL NO. 2
CONDUCTOR QUANTITY		
SIGNAL	60 PAIRS	29 PAIRS
POWER	41 PAIRS	17 PAIRS
RF	8 PAIRS	8 PAIRS
ROTATION ANGLE	+/- 205°	+/- 40°
TORQUE	60 InLb @ 200°	24 InLb @ 40°
LIFE	10000 CYC @ +/- 205° 140000 CYC @ +/- 180° 350000 CYC @ +/- 10°	150000 CYC @ +/-35° 350000 CYC @ +/- 10°
SIZE	10 DIAMETER BY 18 INCHES LONG	10 DIAMETER BY 12 INCHES LONG

Figure 135 Twist Flex Wire Count

Chapter 14   Brushless DC Motors

Advantages of the Brushless DC Motor:

I am a complete advocate of Direct Current Motors for use in space. I was working in the field when we struggled with DC brush motors and I was one of the first aerospace mechanisms engineers to use electronically commutated DC motors as a replacement for brush motors. I worked with Aeroflex labs in 1982 to develop a brushless motor for use on several applications on the JPL built Galileo Spacecraft and with that successful development, I stopped having motor problems. The electrical connection of that motor was identical to a brush motor (two wire interface) and its performance duplicated brush motor performance. You can read more about it in the January 1983 issue of Design News. I have waited thirty years to see a general interest in this technology develop within the aerospace community. I understand that it is happening but very, very slowly.

A Case Against Stepper Motors

In the late 1960s, stepper motors began to be used extensively in aerospace actuators. They were touted as a solution to brush wear in DC motors; however, the stepper motor has numerous characteristics that can make it very troublesome. The primary problem results from the fact that the load motion and the electrical pulses are not synchronous; motor steps are completely open-loop! All brush and brushless DC motors have some form of commutation signal that tells the electronics when to send out the next power pulse and which winding to energize. This feedback is totally missing in stepper motor systems. Each stepper motor power pulse is sent out in a timed sequence and the motor rotor may or may not be at the right position to produce usable torque (it's a gamble).

The position of the load and the rotor shaft is only a function of the spring-mass and friction in a system. And the system friction is significantly affected by operating temperature.

Reducing the size of each motor step helps to synchronize the electrical pulse and mechanical motion. Small angle stepper motors (1.2° - 1.8°) and micro-steppers (multiple phase excitation) were introduced to help solve synchronization problems; however, both methods are far less efficient than commutated DC motors, and the micro-stepper has no position holding torque when power is off. Also, the maximum operating speed of all steppers is much slower than commutated DC motors. Most of the input power creates heat not output power.

The Great Unknown

Later in this chapter, I will shown how the performance of a DC motor can be evaluated with only a little measured data. This same approach is not possible with stepper motors. The stepper motor does not have a speed-torque curve; however, a plot of drop-out torque verses step-rate can be measured and plotted. Suppliers who advertise "off-the-shelf" stepper motors should be able to supply this information, but they rarely can define the effects of temperature on this data and they obviously have no knowledge of the external load.

The design of the electronics can also have a major impact on motor performance. The lack of Zener diodes at critical locations within the stepper circuit can reduce achievable step rate (the motor windings are inductors which must be discharged quickly after each step). Many times I have seen cases where the electronic engineers blame the mechanical system and the mechanical engineers blame the electronics. Usually both parts of the system have defects.

My point is that with stepper systems, you have to commit to all elements of a design long before you have a clue whether it will work! Then, you begin a long, expensive process of "fail-fix-fail" until enough Band-Aids are applied. Also, once you do invest all that time and effort necessary to characterize and de-bug stepper systems, you will most likely lock yourself into the use of that stepper system on all future applications whether it makes sense or not.

Bells and Whistles

Some mechanical features can be added to stepper motor actuators to make them "behave." The main aperture door on the space telescope is a massive, 13-foot diameter structure. Management dictated that a stepper motor be used to open and close the door. The "management" selected actuator could not directly torque such a large inertial load without causing loss of synchronization between the rotor and electronics (drop-out). The problem was solved by placing a soft torsion rod between the large inertial mass and the actuator, effectively decoupling the load from the actuator. This solved one problem but introduced a new one. The door hinge was now so torsionally soft that the whole door could oscillate violently as it rotated. The solution was yet another mechanism: A drag brake was added to keep the oscillations in check. These "add-ons" created significant, extra cost and weight. Use of a DC motor would have avoided these problems altogether.

One More Advantage for BDC

I realized, in 1983, that the brushless DC (BDC) motors that I developed for Galileo could be used in a unique way to simplify any overall control system. An electronic sensing device (a magnetic switch) is used to commutate each phase of the brushless motor. Think of these devices as an "electronic brush". Together, the sensors tell you exactly where the motor rotor is located. The sensors are an incremental encoder. The same information (from the sensors) can be sent directly to the spacecraft central processor (main computer) to provide position information and the computer can easily sum the incremental signals and derive an absolute position. I co-authored a paper at the 18th Aerospace Symposium in 1984. The paper was titled "Smart Motors". The really great idea languished for many years. But, in 1996, JPL got a chance to do it that way. The Mars Pathfinder (MPF) mission needed a "super" small control electronics for the pointing control of the High Gain Antenna which was attached to the MPF lander. You may remember all those color pictures which were "phoned home". Well, we got so many pictures because the pointing control of the MPF antenna was good enough to allow data rates greater than expected.

Now Let's Talk About BDC Motors

Basic Speed/Torque/Current Data

The following section shows how supplier data can be used to analyze motor performance at various temperatures. Current limit checks will be discussed and alternative current limit techniques will be recommended.

The DC motor speed/torque/current data shown next is typical of all permanent magnet DC motors including brush and brushless units.

The current/torque curve is constant regardless of temperature. The maximum output torque of a hot motor will always be less and the maximum output torque of a cold motor will always be more. This is because winding resistance varies with temperature. However, the current curve does not change. The slope of the current curve is defined as (K_T) or the motor torque constant.

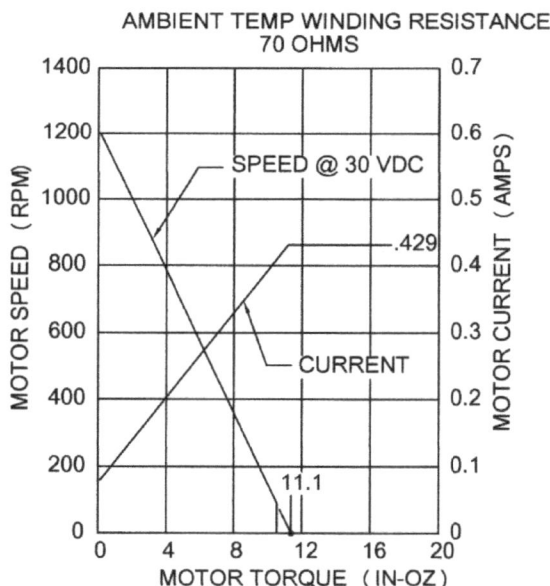

**Figure 136 Supplier Advertised
Performance**

Calculating Winding Resistance At Temperature

Winding resistance at temperature can be calculated as follows:

$$\mathbf{R_{Temp} = R_{Ambient}\left[1 + 0.00393(T_{Temp} - 20°C)\right]}$$

For our example:

$R_{Ambient} = 70 \text{ Ohms}$

T = -85°C (cold environment)

$$\mathbf{R_{Temp} = 70[1 + 0.00393(-85°C - 20°C)] = 41.11\Omega}$$

when 30 V is applied to the motor the current flow will be:

$$\mathbf{I = \left(\frac{V}{R}\right)}$$

The maximum (stall) current that can flow at ambient and cold limit will be:

R = 70 Ω	I = 0.429 A (@30 VDC)
R = 41.1 Ω	I = 0.730 A (@30 VDC)

The output (stall) torque is then calculated as follows:

Where: current at zero speed = 0.075 A and K_T = slope of speed /torq curve

$$\mathbf{K_T = \frac{Torque}{(I - I_o)}}$$

K_T = 11.1 in-oz / .429 amps - .075amps = 31.35 in-oz/amp (from curve)

Stall Torque @ -85°C = (.73 amps - .075 amps) (31.35 in-oz/amp) = 20.5 in-oz

Different Voltages and Temperatures

Unlike the current / torque curve, the speed / torque curve is very much altered by changing motor temperature and operating voltages.

The effect of voltage change is easy to determine. The operating speed of the motor is directly proportional to the applied voltage. If (as in our case), the speed / torque curve at 30 VDC is known, then the 24-VDC curve will be parallel to the 30V curve and have a velocity equal to 24/30 of that curve. Likewise, a 36-VDC curve will be 36/30 of the 30V curve.

The effects of temperature are equally significant and only a little more difficult to understand. If you refer to the first speed -torque curve the current plot can be extended to intersect the horizontal axis. That extension represents the torque loss internal to the motor. Next, a vertical line is extended up from the horizontal axis. The 30VDC speed/torque curve is then extended left until it contacts the new vertical axis. That intersect is the point of generation for all 30-V speed/torque curves regardless of temperature. The other end of the speed torque curve is the intersection of that W/T line with the horizontal axis. It is stall torque! And, as was discussed earlier:

Stall torque = $K_T(I - I_o)$

At ambient temp: $I_{24V} = \dfrac{24V}{70\Omega} = .343$ amps

At -85 °C: $I_{24V} = \dfrac{24V}{41.1\Omega} = .584$ amps

At ambient temp: $T_{stall} = 31.35 (0.343 - 0.075) = 8.4$ in-oz

At -85 °C $T_{stall} = 31.35 (0.584 - 0.075) = 16.0$ in-oz

The intercept speed at 24 V is calculated to be 24/30 x 1463) = 1170 rpm

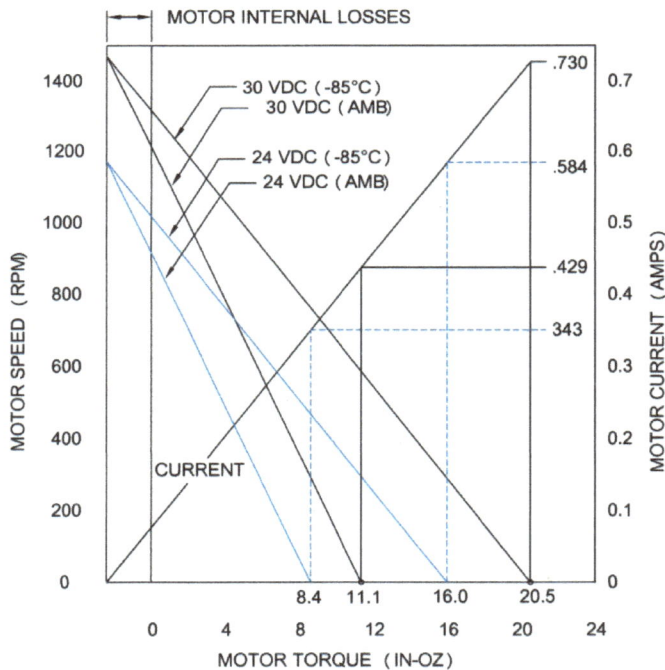

Figure 137 Speed / Torque at Temperature

The same analysis process would be followed to calculate the motor performance at high temperature. There is now enough data to plot the "new"(-85°C and 24 V) speed/torque curves. The resulting plots show that the ambient temperature curves are parallel and that the -85°C curves are parallel. This confirms that we've done the job correctly.

This modified speed/torque data will next be used to determine a motor speed-torque curve at -85 °C. The first step is to determine the actual motor internal loss at cold temperature.

We will create a speed / torque curve specifically for the -85°C environment. The motor will have an actual no-load speed at -85°C that is much slower than the ambient temperature no-load speed. This is easy to measure by running the motor (without external load) at -85°C. **This test is a "must" for development of the final -85°C speed / torque curve.**

The measured -85°C, no-load speed of the motor was 1000 rpm at 30 VDC. A horizontal line is drawn at 1000 rpm to the intercept of the 30-V speed/torque curve. A vertical line is then extended downward to the torque axis. The value of torque is 4.9 in-oz. This is the additional amount of parasitic drag that occurs within the motor at -85°C.

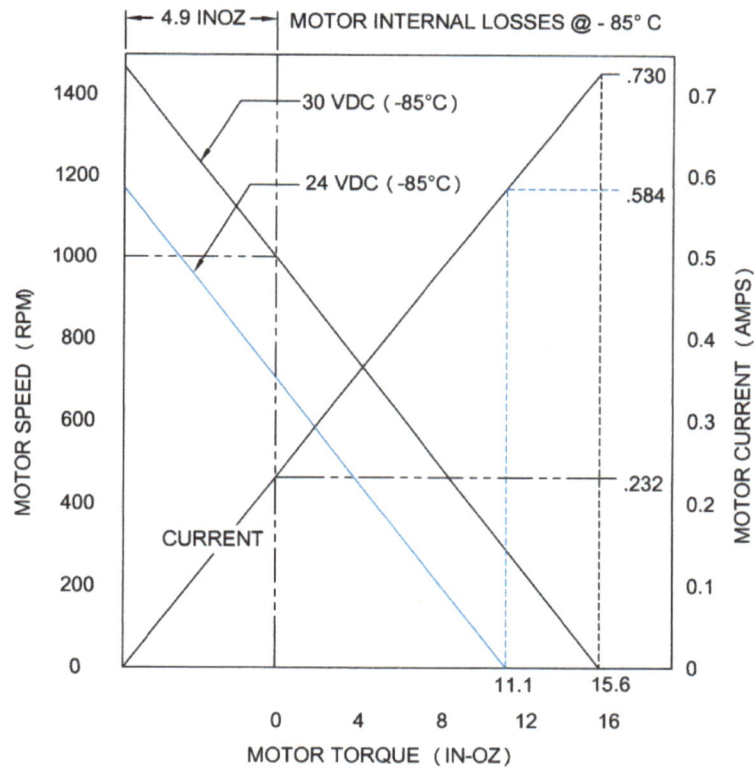

Figure 138 Speed / Torque at -85°F

The previous figure shows the scale of the torque axis shifted to re-zero torque about the old value of 4.9 in-oz. And finally, the -85°C speed / torque/current plot is created as shown next.

The "new" (-85°C) plot shown next allows evaluation of available output torque at that temperature. If the motor voltage can be guaranteed at 30 V, the available output torque will be 15.6 in-oz. But, a margin (torque margin) should always be applied. A margin of 2 is a good conservative value. So, the available output torque will be 7.8 in-oz. The operating speed of the motor and its load (7.8 in-oz) will be 508 rpm at 30 V or 215 rpm at 24 V. And an operating current of 0.48 A must be allowed (i.e., the current limit provided by the control electronics must be above 0.478 A). This current level may very well create an over-torque condition for ambient temperature operations. In order to evaluate the potential for over-torque we must understand the speed-torque characteristics of the driven load (usually a multi-stage gearbox).

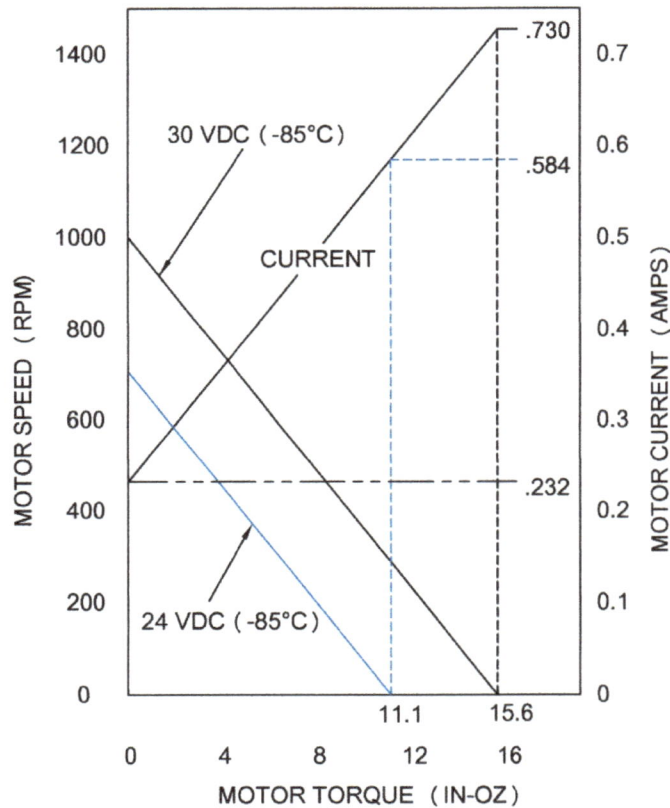

Figure 139 Speed / Torque at -85°F

169

Output Load Characteristics

Analysis of a motor driven gear system requires that knowledge of the speed/torque characteristics of the driven load (gearbox) be available. Data is needed at ambient temperature and at the temperature extremes. The next figure shows this data for a family of pancake harmonic drive sizes. The data has been accumulated over the last thirty years by testing of the various sizes.

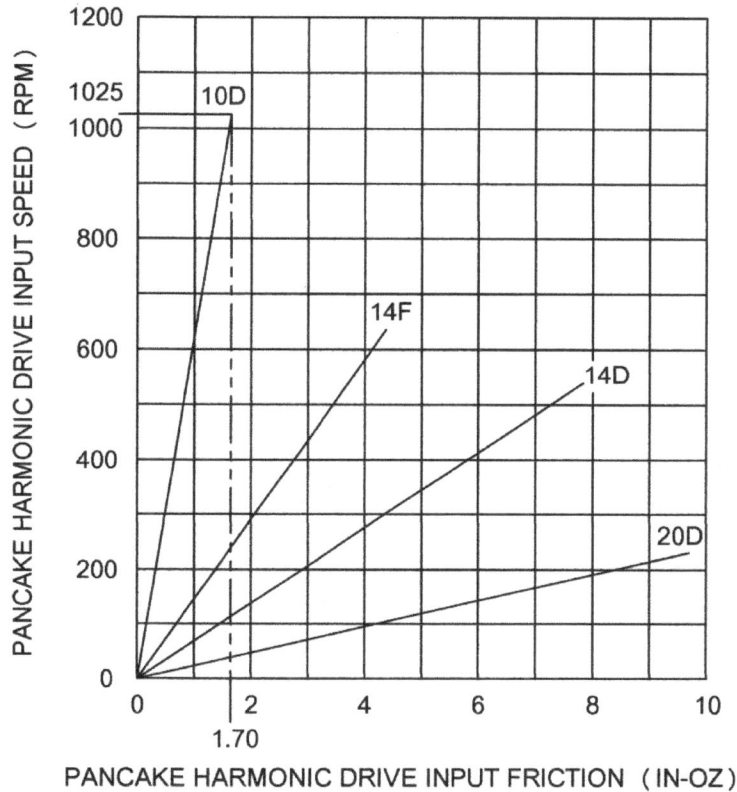

Figure 140 Measured Friction Characteristics

Parasitic Drag

The previous figure shows that the gearbox speed / torque characteristic is a linear function (nearly linear). This means that two points will describe the curve with reasonable accuracy.

The first point is zero/zero (the origin) and the second point is a drag value at a specific speed. A very easy point to measure is no load speed/drag. When you run a motor/gear box combination with no output load, the no-load speed for the combination will be somewhat slower than for the motor alone. Plotting the intercept of the new slower speed with the motor speed / torque curve yields the magnitude of gearbox parasitic drag associated with a speed equal to the motor no-load speed of the combination.

This simple measurement can be made at any temperature. A motor speed/torque for that same temperature can then be created using the methods outlined previously. Finally, combining the data yields parasitic drag. A plot can then be created for any desired temperature.

An alternate method for evaluating parasitic drag is to drive the gear box input shaft with an external motor while placing an in-line torque transducer between the motor and gear box. This is a more elegant and costly approach but it will measure changes due to run time as well. It is money well spent.

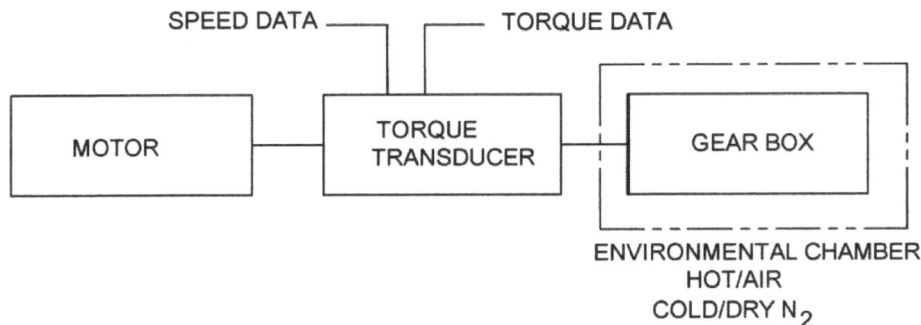

Figure 141 Optimized Test Equipment

Torque Efficiency

In order to calculate output torque for a motor/gear box combination, it is necessary to define an input/output torque efficiency factor. The factor can then be applied to the stall torque value derived from a motor speed/torque curve:

Combined output stall torque = motor stall torque x gear ratio x efficiency

The parasitic drag should not be deducted from the motor stall torque value because it is a function of velocity while stall torque is a stationary measurement.

The procedure for obtaining input/output torque data is a simple torque-in-torque-out measurement using appropriate sized torque watch/wrench.

When the efficiency data is obtained it can then be used as described in the next section to develop "actuator" speed / torque plots.

Precautions

The standard lubricant Bray 6XX grease allows operation at low temperatures down to -40°C with parasitic drag characteristics remaining nearly uniform. However, at lower temperatures, the liquid lubricants begin to significantly affect parasitic drag. The plot of parasitic drag/speed will likely become highly non-linear.

However, these non-linearity's may be caused by design errors within the actuator. Non-metallic ball bearing separators may clamp metallic balls, thermal gradients may increase ball preloads or the thermal expansion characteristics of materials may cause binding. **DO NOT ASSUME THAT ALL PARASITIC DRAG IS LUBRICANT RELEATED!** Recheck the parasitic drag without lube. If parasitic drag increase is still major, you have a faulty mechanical design.

Sample Performance Calculation

Next, we will create an ambient temperature speed/torque curve for the combined motor and gearbox as follows:

Motor performance is per the figure titled "Supplier Advertised Performance"

Size 10D pancake harmonic drive gear ratio (R) = 244:1

Parasitic drag = 1.7 in-oz at 1025 rpm (see Pancake H/D data))

$$\%EFF = \frac{300}{300 + R} = .55$$

(USM equation from antiquity) (for high ratios)

R = Gear ratio

Max allowable output torque at gearbox = 30 in-lb (stall)

Max operating voltage = 30 V

The term "actuator" will now be used to indicate the motor and gear box combination. The next figure combines the above data. It shows that the actuator motor will have a no-load speed of 1025 rpm. The no-load speed of the actuator will then be:

$$\textbf{Actuator noload speed} = \frac{1025}{244} = 4.2 \textbf{RPM}$$

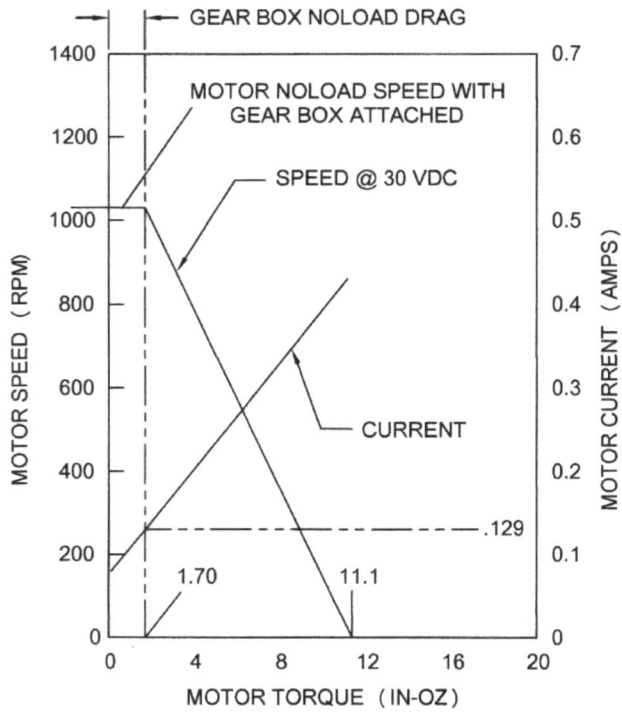

Figure 142 Testing with a Gear Box

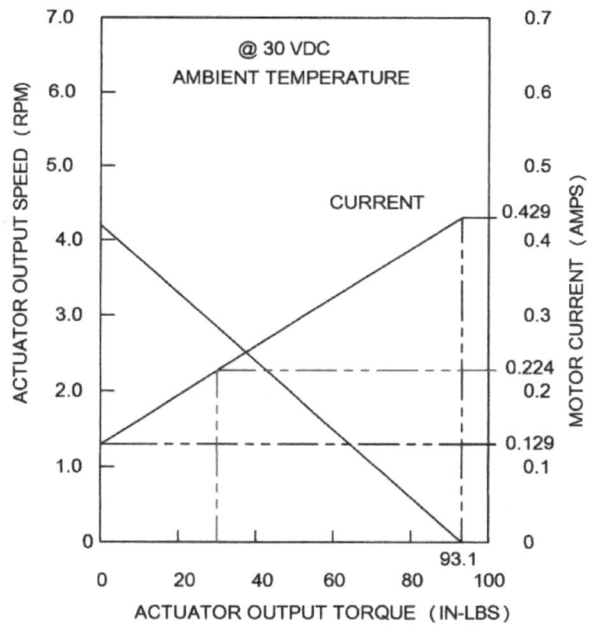

Figure 143 Gear Box / Motor Performance

173

Over-torque Protection

Our example actuator has a specified maximum torque capability of 30 in-lb. But, our motor can produce 93 in-lb of torque. "We have a problem!"

The same figure indicates that a current limit of less than 0.224 A is required to limit output torque to less than 30 in-lb.

If we assume that the parasitic drag of the gear box increases by a factor of 2 at -85°C (real test data is mandatory), then we will have 1.7 x 2 or 3.4 in-oz of parasitic drag and the torque required to produce 30 in-lb of actuator output torque will be :

$$T_{Motor} = \frac{30 \times 16}{244 \times 0.55} = 3.58 \ inoz$$

The total load for a 30 in-lb output torque is then:

3.58 + 3.4 ≈ 7 in-oz

But from our (-85°C) motor plot , 7 in-oz of torque will require in excess of 0.45 A. This far exceeds our 0.224 A ambient temperature limit. In fact, the motor will draw more than 0.224 A under cold no-load operation.

The solution is to provide a moving current limit where motor temperature is used as a feedback to the current limit circuit. The "cold motor" is allowed to draw more current than the warm motor.

In order to understand that a real problem existed, it was necessary to plod through these calculations and also necessary to have a minimum number of test data points to support the analysis. With these, a full understanding of the "system" becomes possible.

Developing A Motor Specification

The starting point for small BDC motor performance specification is the output power requirement. The output load defines output power.

> OUTPUT SPEED X OUTPUT TORQUE
> EQUALS
> OUTPUT POWER

Figure 144 Output Power Requirement

1. A good conservative initial estimate is that the input power (electrical watts) will equal approximately two to three times the output power.

2. The peak actuator power efficiency occurs at approximately 50% of no-load speed (i.e., efficiency at both ends of the speed/torque curve is zero because no output work is occurring).

3. The maximum motor speed should probably be limited to 10,000 rpm. If you need more input speed than that, you're in the world of "spin systems" (see Chapter 4).

4. When operating a maximum output load, the motor should be operating near the peak-power point.

With this data, we can proceed to "spec" a motor.

Sample Motor Spec Calculation

Given: Output torque to be 200 in-lb at 10.0 rpm

$$T = \frac{200}{12\frac{in}{ft}} = 16.67 \text{ ftlb}$$

$$\textbf{Speed} = \textbf{10}\frac{\textbf{Rev}}{\textbf{Min}}\left(\frac{\textbf{2}\pi\,\textbf{Rad}}{\textbf{Rev}}\right)\left(\frac{\textbf{Min}}{\textbf{60 Sec}}\right) = \textbf{1.05}\frac{\textbf{Rad}}{\textbf{Sec}}$$

$$\textbf{Output Power} = \textbf{16.67 X 1.05} = \textbf{17.5}\frac{\textbf{FtLb}}{\textbf{Sec}} = \textbf{23.7 watts}$$

We will assume a motor speed of 3000 rpm at peak-power point. No-load speed will be twice this or 6000 rpm.

The required input/output gear ratio will be 300:1 (3000 rpm/10 rpm).

Typically a harmonic drive could provide the required ratio in one stage, but it is not the right choice. The input speed is far too high and parasitic drag would be out-of-sight. Also, the harmonic drive ratio can't be lower than 50:1. This would allow a 6:1 input gear but the resulting 1000 rpm input is still too high.

In our example, a multi-pass spur gear is appropriate. It can be planetary or spur. We have used many 4.33:1 planetary gear systems so the number of stages will be four and the efficiency per stage will be approximately 0.90. Overall efficiency will then: $0.9^4 = 0.65$.

The peak power point dictates a stall torque equal to twice the required output torque. Next, if we assume that electrical and mechanical efficiency is equal, then overall efficiency will be:

Eff $_{total}$ = 0.65 x 0.65 = 0.42

The input power required at the peak power point will be: 23.7 W / .42 = 56.5 W

Current at Peak Power will be: 56.5W/30V = 1.88 Amps

Now, it is possible to create an output speed/torque/current curve as shown on the next page. Note that the slope of the current / torque curve is not defined yet!

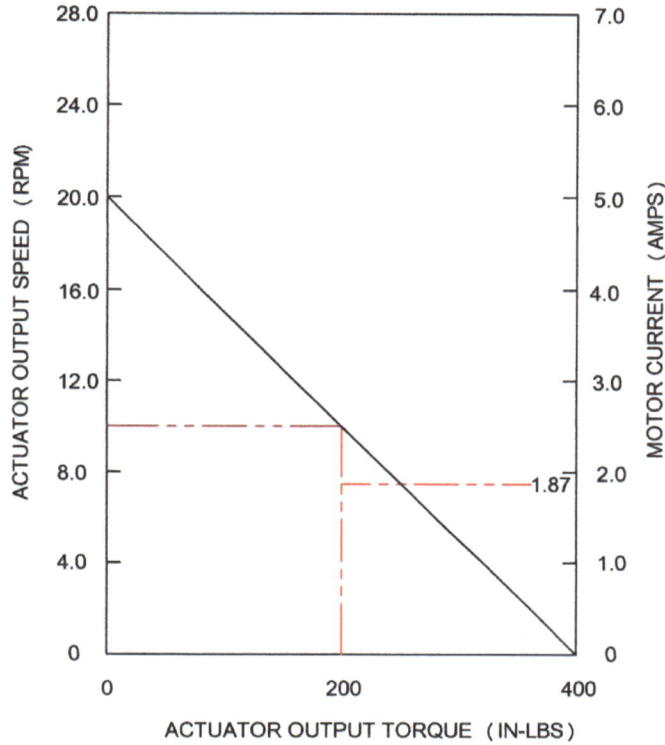

Figure 145 Output Performance

The motor torque equivalent to 400 in-lb output needs to be calculated next.

$$T_{in} = \frac{T_{out} \, X \, 16}{RATIO \, X \, EFF} = \frac{400 \, X \, 16}{300 \, x \, 0.65} = 32.8 \, in-oz$$

Then, we must determine the magnitude of parasitic drag (gearbox drag) either by guessing or from prior test data. My estimate is 2 in-oz

We can develop the speed/torque curve (motor) knowing that motor speed should be 3000 rpm at a torque value of:

176

$$\text{Torque}_{\text{Operating Point}} = \frac{32.8}{2} + 2 = 18.4 \text{ inoz}$$

and 6000 rpm at 2.0 in-oz.

The current curve can be developed in a similar manner (1.87 A at 18.4 in-oz) and an internal loss approximately 0.1 A.

This data is then plotted to form the motor speed/torque/current curve shown in the final figure. This is the single most important element of a motor specification.

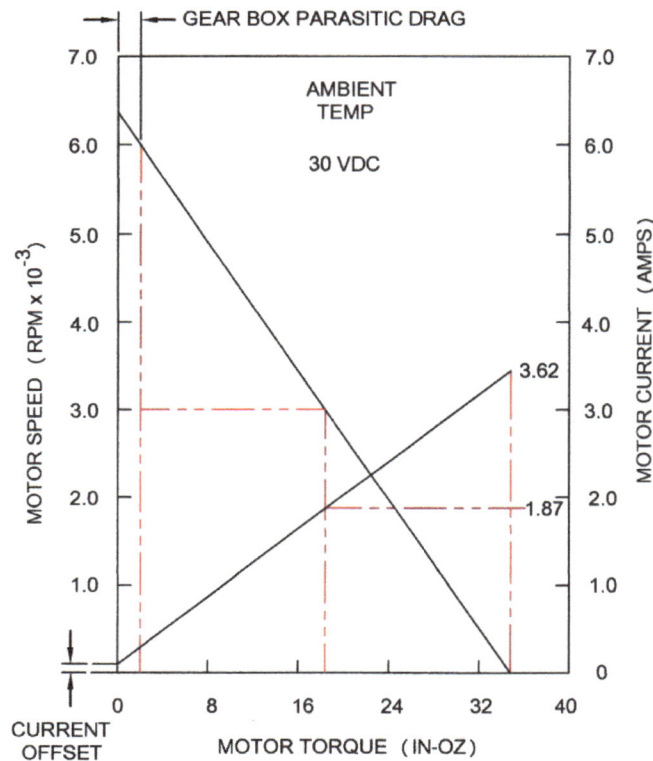

Figure 146 Speed / Torque Data for Specification

However, this is only a first cut. Minor adjustments may be required to the slopes of both the speed/torque plot and the current/torque plot. These adjustments are the response from a motor manufacturer as a real (producible) motor is created. It is important to identify the hard requirements (i.e., characteristics at the peak power point) and then allow adjustments about these points (during initial motor design. The motor manufacturer will need to have the latitude to rotate the speed / torque requirements about a specified point on the curve). And, you will need to indicate which direction of rotation is best for you. Is a lower speed / higher torque better or is a higher speed / lower torque better.

Chapter 15   Momentum Compensation

What is Momentum Exchange:

The acceleration of a mass or inertia attached to a spacecraft creates a condition of momentum exchange between the base body and the accelerating body. The exchanged momentum can be linear, rotational, or a combination of both.

The actuator reacts torque back into the spacecraft as its output shaft applies torque to accelerate an inertial mass.

If the applied torque creates an acceleration of mass/inertia, an equal but opposite force/torque will occur at the actuator housing. It will be transmitted to the base body as long as the acceleration continues. It is this impulse that must be reacted in order to maintain a fixed position base body.

However, the existence of actuator torque does not automatically mean that a momentum match is disturbed. If the output is rotating at a fixed rate, there is no momentum disturbance! Nevertheless, torque must be continuously applied to overcome friction. If this "drag make-up" is stopped, the moving body will experience a deceleration and that will create an inertial torque which will accelerate the base body until both bodies match speed and no friction is produced.

A reverse situation can exist where the entire spacecraft is spinning in order to maintain attitude, but a portion is de-spun in order to point antennas or instruments. The Galileo spacecraft was this type of "dual spin spacecraft."

Most often the spacecraft attitude control system can be sized to handle small, infrequent impulses. But there are special cases where very large impulses may be required at frequent intervals. These special cases are candidates for momentum-compensated drives.

Many, many years ago, a few propeller driven aircraft were fitted with a single engine having counter rotating propeller blade sets. The idea is not a new one.

Linear Momentum Compensation:

This example includes both linear and rotary momentum. The drive motor is part of I_2. A band-drive system imparts counter rotation to $I1$ at a ratio of 2:1. $I1$ then imparts opposing linear motions to M1 and M2. The system is capable of very rapid motion reversal without generating vibration of the base body. Also, the system can be operated in 1 "g" gravity horizontally or vertically without affecting performance.

During launch only base body (spacecraft) torque will couple with the linear elements. And, since torsional acceleration of the spacecraft is a smaller effect than linear accelerations, it is possible to launch without restraining the moving elements if a small restoring force is present in the structural support at the outboard ends of the moving masses (flexure supported optics). Momentum matching can provide benefits greater than elimination of base body reactions.

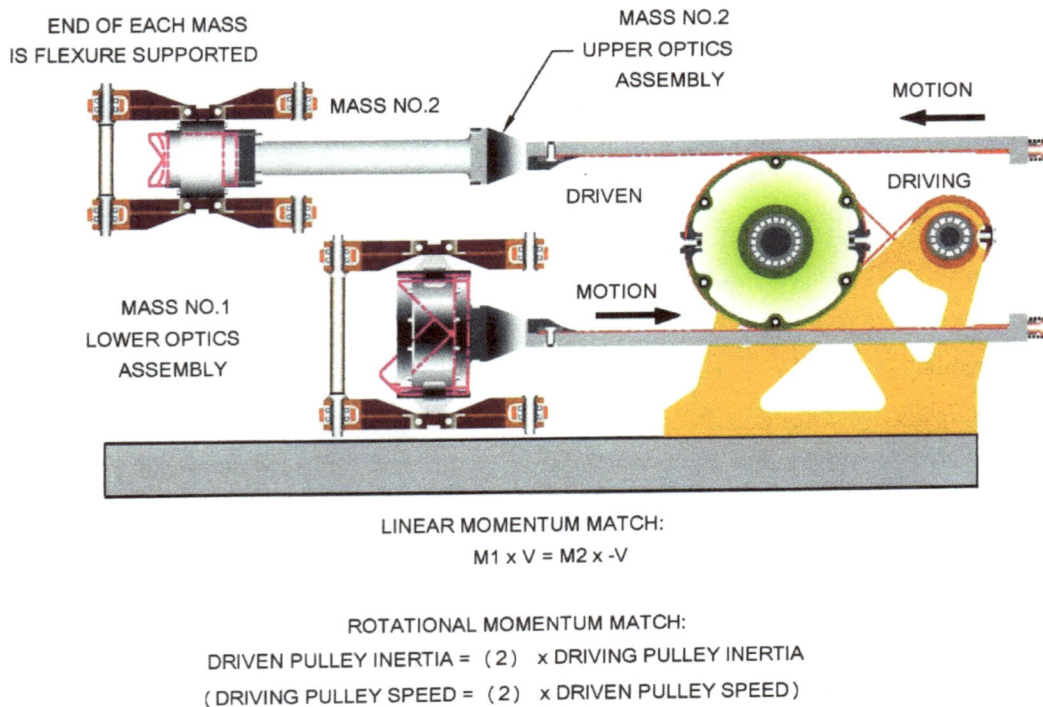

LINEAR MOMENTUM MATCH:
M1 x V = M2 x -V

ROTATIONAL MOMENTUM MATCH:
DRIVEN PULLEY INERTIA = (2) x DRIVING PULLEY INERTIA
(DRIVING PULLEY SPEED = (2) x DRIVEN PULLEY SPEED)

Figure 147 Linear Momentum Compensation

Rotational Momentum Compensation:

In example No. 1, a small "gear ratio" was provided between the momentum matched rotational elements (I_1 and I_2). This allowed the driver pulley to be a smaller, lighter element. Consider now, a system where the output is massive and must be very agile.

There is a solution that can allow the output to be rotated without causing a gross displacement of the base body. This is achieved by using a counter-rotating flywheel.

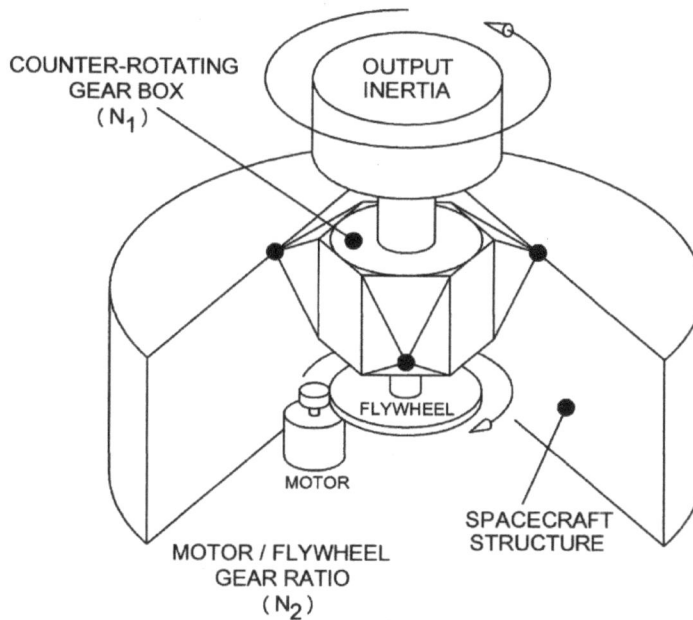

Figure 148 Rotational Momentum Compensation

Problems:

Continuous Rotation in one direction

It is never possible to achieve a perfect momentum match. Very slight errors that can't be detected for small angles of rotation will integrate if rotation is continuous in one direction. The base body will eventually move. Conversely, if the rotation is restricted to a finite angular travel, the slight errors will be self-canceling as motion is reversed.

Required Efficiency

N_1 can be a low-efficiency ratio. That is true because very little power is transferred through N_1 (most of the system kinetic energy is in the rotating flywheel not the output). But N_2 must be a very high-efficiency ratio because all of the motor power passes through N_2.

Acceleration occurs in 1 sec. Beyond that the system is operating at a constant rotational speed of 6°/sec and the motor is providing drag makeup only until deceleration is required. The average speed during the 1-sec acceleration is 3°/sec and an angle of only 3° is traversed. During most of a rotation the primary load is friction. Having a large ratio (N_2) reduces the magnitude of the friction reflected to the motor.

$$\textbf{Motor Friction Load (Ext Friction)} = \frac{\textbf{Flywheel Friction}}{\textbf{N}_2}$$

The need for high efficiency power transfer and low friction transfer dictate a very high efficiency for N_2.

Cross Products of Inertia

The output needs to be dynamically balanced (zero cross-products of inertia) if near perfect momentum compensation is to be achieved. The existence of a cross-product will result in a pitching moment as the output is rotated. This effect can be minimized by assuring that output mass is distributed in a manner which will create minimum cross-product.

Effects of Gearing Errors

The discussion of gear errors in the chapter on gearing, shows that the ratio of a gear system is quite non-linear for small motion increments. In a momentum-compensated system, this means that a measurable vibration occurs as the output is rotated. Therefore, gear drives are not recommended if smooth, continuous rotation is required.

It is possible under special circumstances to use gearing. This requires that three conditions exist. First, for optimum performance the base body attitude control system should be inhibited during rotation so that it does not fight the torque ripple. Secondly, any spacecraft appendages must have a high natural frequency and/or be highly damped. The torque ripple during rotation will excite the appendage (see Section x). If rapid settling time is desired, then high frequency/high damping are mandatory. And third, if any high-precision sensors, requiring stability, are present, they could not operate effectively during rotation.

Example Calculations

I will begin this example by defining a set of functional characteristics for a rotary system which is to be momentum compensated. I will use a very large output mass for starters. Let's try two tons (4000 lbs). The inertia of such a massive object can be derived as follows. We can assume that the outside diameter of the spacecraft is similar to Galileo or Cassini in their stowed configurations. A diameter of 5 feet will be used. The output inertia will then be calculated:

$$\mathbf{I_{out}} = \tfrac{1}{2} \left(\tfrac{4000}{32.2} \right) (2.5)^2 = \textbf{388 slug feet}^2$$

We began by describing the system as agile. Now, let's put some numbers on the agility:

Output speed: 1 rpm

Output acceleration: reach speed in 1 sec

Output velocity = 6°/sec

Output Acceleration = 6°/sec^2

The motor will be large and powerful so a maximum speed of 5000 rpm is reasonable. Motor life also dictates that maximum speed be limited.

If we check the energy distribution in the system, we discover that

$E_{F/W}$ = E_{OUT} x (gear ratio)

We are really accelerating a flywheel with the output (massive output) taking a ride.

An assumption will be made that the motor armature inertia is very much smaller than the flywheel inertia.

 This is not a good assumption if a very close match is required (such as 0.1%).

A large gear ratio at N1 will result in a low-mass flywheel rotating at a high speed. This will be a maximum-energy solution (most electrical power required).

At the other extreme, a smaller gear ratio at N_1 will result in a higher-mass flywheel rotating at a lower speed. This will be a minimum-energy solution.

First Try (N_1 = 100)

$$T_{f/w} \; = \; 600 \; \frac{deg}{sec^2} \left(\frac{2\pi}{360}\right) \left(\frac{388}{100}\right) \; = 40.63 \; ft-lb$$

$$PWR_{f/w} = 40.63 \left(\frac{600°}{sec}\right) \left(\frac{2\pi}{360}\right) = 426 \; \frac{ft-lb}{sec} = 578 \; watts$$

The properly designed control system will have a motor power level approximately equal to the output power level.

The total peak power in the 100:1 system will be:578 W x 2 = 1156 W   (Without friction effects, which will add.)

Typically, 20 V would be reasonable operating voltage. This would yield an operating current of 58 A. It would be difficult to handle this current level, and power dissipation would create significant thermal problems. Remember, we said this would be an agile system, dynamic braking is required to stop. You must reabsorb energy or dump it as heat!

Second Try ($N_1 = 50$)

$$T_{f/w} = 300 \frac{\text{deg}}{\text{sec}^2} \left(\frac{2\pi}{360}\right) \left(\frac{388}{50}\right) = 40.63 \text{ ft} - \text{lb}$$

$$PWR_{f/w} = 40.63 \left(\frac{300^{\circ}}{\text{sec}}\right) \left(\frac{2\pi}{360}\right) = 213 \frac{\text{ft} - \text{lb}}{\text{sec}} = 298 \text{ watts}$$

The total peak power in the 50:1 system will be: 298 W x 2 = 578 W

This will yield an operating current of (V = 20 V) 29 A. This is still a large current but within reason. There will also be a significant additional power required to overcome friction (See paragraph: Power required to overcome friction.)

Flywheel Mass

The electrical power requirements dictate a lower ratio for N1 but this will require a more massive flywheel:

N = 100   IF/W = 3.88 SF2

N = 50 $I_{F/W}$ = 7.76 SF^2

For the flywheel we can assume that the mass is concentrated at the outside diameter of the wheel and that the wheel must fit within the spacecraft diameter. A 4-ft diameter would be reasonable:

N=100

$$M = \frac{3.88}{4} = 0.97 \text{ slugs} = 31.2 \text{ lbs}$$

N= 50

$$M = \frac{7.76}{4} = 1.94 \text{ slugs} = 62.5 \text{ lbs}$$

This calculation indicates that the lower gear ratio, which will make the electronics design easier, will also not add too much mass to the spacecraft. If we assume that the total spacecraft weight is twice as much as the movable output, we are looking at an 8000 lb system which will only gain 31.2 lbs.

A 31.2-lb flywheel mass increase for an 8000 lb spacecraft is reasonable. In fact, that much mass might be saved in reduced power system requirements.

Confirmation of Design

There now is sufficient information to calculate the actual motor inertia. Again, the motor load is assumed to equal the total output load inertia reflected to the motor:

Output Inertia = 388 slug ft^2

Flywheel Inertia = 388/50 = 7.76 slug ft^2

$$\textbf{Motor Inertia} = \frac{388}{(N_1)^2\,(N_2)^2} + \frac{7.76}{(N_2)^2} = \mathbf{79.15\,(10)^{-5}\ slug\ ft^2}$$

(This is a power calculation) We use N^2 !

Assume: motor armature diameter = 2.5 in. = 0.2083 ft

$$\textbf{Motor Mass} = \frac{2I}{R^2} = \frac{2(79.15)(10^{-5})}{(0.104)^2} = \mathbf{.146\ slug = 4.71\ lb}$$

$$\textbf{Armature Volume} = \frac{4.71\ lb}{.3\left(\frac{lb}{in^3}\right)} = \mathbf{15.71\ in^3}$$

$$A = \frac{\pi}{4}\ (2.5)^2\ = 4.91\ in^2$$

$$L = \frac{15.71}{4.91} = 3.2\ in$$

We are now closing in on a motor spec:

I_{REFL} + I_M = (79.15 x 10^{-5} + 79.15 x 10^{-5}) SF^2

I_{TOTAL} = 158.3 x 10^{-5} SF^2 (This is a load inertia.)

Assume that we will limit the motor speed to 5000 RPM maximum.

It's a large motor so this is a reasonable first assumption.

Peak armature acceleration will be:

$$\textbf{Motor Acceleration} = \mathbf{5000\ (6)\ \frac{deg}{sec^2} = 523\ \frac{rad}{sec^2}}$$

$$\textbf{Peak Torque} = \mathbf{(158.3)(10^{-5})sf^2 x\ (523)\left(\frac{rad}{sec^2}\right) = .829\ ftlb}$$

$$\textbf{Peak Power} = \mathbf{(.829)ftlb\ x\ (523)\frac{rad}{sec^2} = 433\frac{ftlb}{sec} = 588\ watts}$$

This power value is 10 W more than initially estimated because we have included the output load as well. Next, the effect of systems friction must be added.

Power Required to Overcome Friction

Motor friction and flywheel friction must be estimated at this point.

$$\textbf{Flywheel Speed} = (6)\frac{\textbf{deg}}{\textbf{sec}} \textbf{x}(50) = 300\frac{\textbf{deg}}{\textbf{sec}} = 5.24\frac{\textbf{rad}}{\textbf{sec}}$$

$$\textbf{Motor Speed} = 5000\frac{\textbf{rev}}{\textbf{min}}\left(\frac{\textbf{2}\boldsymbol{\pi}\textbf{ rad}}{\textbf{rev}}\right)\left(\frac{\textbf{min}}{\textbf{60 sec}}\right) = 524\left(\frac{\textbf{rad}}{\textbf{sec}}\right)$$

Assume: Flywheel friction = 10X motor friction (because the F/W bearings are much larger).

Motor friction (at 5000 rpm) is 1.0 in-lb

Gear Ratio between armature and flywheel (N_2)= 100 / 1

Power required to overcome flywheel friction will be equal to the power required to overcome motor friction.

$$\textbf{Power loss @ Motor due to friction} = \left(\frac{\textbf{1.0inlb}}{\textbf{12}}\right)(\textbf{524})\left(\frac{\textbf{rad}}{\textbf{sec}}\right) = 43.6\left(\frac{\textbf{ftlb}}{\textbf{sec}}\right)$$

Power loss @ Motor due to friction = 59 watts

$$\textbf{Power loss @ FW due to friction} = \left(\frac{\textbf{10 inlb}}{\textbf{12}}\right)(\textbf{5.24})\left(\frac{\textbf{rad}}{\textbf{sec}}\right) = 4.3\left(\frac{\textbf{ftlb}}{\textbf{sec}}\right)$$

Power loss @ Motor due to friction = 5.9 watts

Total power (All Friction) = 59 x 5.9 = 65 watts

Total motor power is 65 watts + 588 watts = 653 watts

The motor is a big, powerful unit! A D.C. permanent magnet motor won't be the best choice. Consult motor manufacturers.

Quality of the Momentum Match

$$(\textbf{I}\boldsymbol{\Omega})_{\textbf{Out}} = (\textbf{I}\boldsymbol{\Omega})_{\textbf{Flywheel}} + (\textbf{I}\boldsymbol{\Omega})_{\textbf{Motor}}$$

(assuming flywheel and motor rotate in same direction)

The (I) values are the actual inertias not the reflected inertias!

Motor Momentum = $79.15(10)^{-5}$ sf^2 x $524\left(\frac{\text{rad}}{\text{sec}}\right)$ = .415 (ftlbsec)

Output Momentum = 388 sf^2 x $0.105\left(\frac{\text{rad}}{\text{sec}}\right)$ = 40.7 (ftlbsec)

If the motor inertia is not included, the match error will be:

$$\textbf{Match Error} = \left(\frac{.415}{40.7}\right) = .0102 = 1.02\% \textbf{ (not a very precise match)}$$

If a better match is required then slightly reduce flywheel inertia (by 79.15 x 10^{-5} SF^2 x 100).

An experienced Controls Engineer would simply develop a transfer function for the system . But all this information is required for that also.

Chapter 16   Special Devices and Materials

Special Actuators:

Magnetostrictive Actuators

      Etrema Products Inc. / Edge Tech Inc., Ames, IA 50010

Piezoelectric Actuators:

      Burleigh Instruments Inc. , Fishers, NY 14453

Rolling Bellows Actuators:

      Bellowfram Corp., Newell, WV 26050

Dimple Motor Actuators:

      Hercules Inc., Wilmington, DE 19808

      Network Electronics, Chatsworth, CA 91311

Ball Lock Actuators:

      Quantic Industries Inc., San Carlos, CA 94070

Thermoelectric Heating / Cooling:

      Marlow Industries, Dallas, TX 75238

      Thermoelectric Cooling America Corp (TECA) Chicago, IL 60639

Special Rolling Element Devices

Sprag Clutch Assemblies

      Form Sprag Corporation, Warren, MI 42090

      Zurn Industries Inc., La Grange, IL 60525

      Borg-Warner Automotive, Bellwood, IL 60104

      Morse Ind/Emerson Power, Ithaca, NY 14850

Cam Followers

      McGill Precision Bearings, Valparaiso, IN 46383

      Radial/Thrust Bearing   (Needle Bearings)

      Nadella (Subsidiary of Torrington)

      U.S. Contact SKF Needle Division, Breman, IN

Rotary/Linear Ball Bushing

      Linear/Rotary Bearings Inc., Westbury, NY 11590

      Rotolin

      Landis & Gyr Inc., New York, NY 10036

Control Cables (Flexible Ball Bearing Cables)

    Controlex, Croton Falls, NY 1051Couplings

Couplings

Shaft Locks and Couplings:

    Ringfeder Shaft Locking AssemblyRingfeder, Westwood, NJ 07075

Tran Torque Coupling

    Fenner-Manheim, Manheim, PA 17545

Helical Shaft Couplings

    Helical Products Company, Santa Maria, CA 93456

Locking Shaft Coupling

    Innovatex Corporation/Acrotech, Lake Zurich, IL 60047

Infinite Shaft Indexer

    Harmonic Drive Technologies, Peabody, MA 01960

Special Gears:

Evoloid (2 & 3 tooth pinion gears)

    Quaker City Gear Works, Huntingdon Valley, PA 19006

High-Performance Bevel Gears

    Arrow Gear Co., Downers Grove, IL 60615

Hi-Prec Gears of all types

    INSCO Corporation, Groton, MA 01450

Helicon/Spiroid Gears

    Spiroid Div of Illinois Tool Works In,..Chicago, IL 60639

Special Springs

Bi-metallic Belleville Washers

    Chicago Wilcox Manufacturing, South Holland, IL 60473

Zero-Twist Helical Springs, Rectangular Wire

    Kinemotive Corp, Farmington, NY 11735

    Helical Products Company, Santa Maria, CA 93456

Load Cells:

Load Sensing Bolts, Clevis Pins and Load Cells

Strainsert Co.,Conshohocken, PA 19428

Special Materials:

Porous Plastic

Porex TechnologiesFairburn, GA 30213

Porous Glass

Corning Glass, Corning, NY 14830

Porous Metal

Mott Metallurgical Corporation, Farmington, CT 06032

Microwell Sponge

Monarch Marking, Dayton, OH 45401

Free Machining Material:

Macor Glass Ceramic, Corning Glass, Corning, NY 14830

Mallory 1000 Sintered Tungsten (.6 lb/in3)

Mallory Metallurgical Co, Indianapolis, IN 46206

Material with Unique Performance

Low-Melting-Point Lead:

Cerro Base

Cerro Metal Products, Bellefonte, PA 16823

High-Expansion Wax:

Epolene Wax

Eastman Chemical Products, Kingsport, TN 37662

Impact-Resistant Putty:

Silly Putty (Dilatant Compound 3179)

Dow Corning, Midland, MI 48686

Actuation Materials:

Magnetostrictive Materials, Terfenol D

       Etrema Products Inc.(Edge Tech Inc), Ames ,IA 50010

Piezoelectric Ceramics

       Burleigh Instruments, Fishers, NY 14453

Nitinol (Memory Metal)

       Tini Aerospace Inc.   San Leandro, CA 94577

Magnetic Fluids:

Ferrofluids

       Ferrofluidics Corp.,   Nashua, NH 03061

High Friction Material:

Adiprene L-100 (see Chapter 5)

       DuPont Corporation, Elastomer Chemical Department,   Wilmington, DE 19898

Mechanism Components

Pic Design

Boston Gear

Grainger

Mc Master / Carr

Sterling Instrument

Winfred Berg

Chapter 17   Protection

Introduction:

Great effort is expended to assure that a new mechanism will function as planned. But, often little or no effort is spent to assure that the new mechanism is protected from un-planned damage caused by un-foreseen events. It is very important that every functional mechanism be "bullet proof" with regard to technician errors, handling damage and un-planned environmental events.

Examples:

The following case histories really happened!

It is always prudent to provide over-torque protection at the output of a high-ratio gear system because this type of actuator can't be easily back-driven.

Manually Applied Output Torques

(If it can happen, it will happen!)

A visitor to a test area lifted the tip of a large flat folded antenna. The antenna panel was several feet long and a fold actuator was attached to the base of the panel. Operating requirements for the system dictated a high, non-back-drivable gear ratio in the actuator. Wisely, the actuator had been fitted with a roller clutch (see the discussion in this chapter regarding roller clutches for over-torque protection). Yes, the visitor caused the clutch to ratchet, but the gearbox was not harmed and the culprit was caught because the panels remained apart.

Test Equipment/Testing Anomalies

A similar non-back-drivable actuator was used to deploy a very large, rigid-panel array. In the stowed position the pair of large panels fit closely together. And, as the initial unfolding began, the clutch would ratchet many times. The cause of the problem was traced to the fact that first motion of the panels during ambient atmospheric testing produced a slight vacuum (lower pressure) between the panels. This "sucked" the panels together and "stalled the drive, causing the clutch to ratchet. This overlooked problem could have caused the actuator to destroy itself. Or, worse, the actuator might have been degraded without anyone's knowledge

Protection from Inertial Torques

A large flywheel is attached to a non-back-drivable worm drive. The flywheel is slowly accelerated to 50 rpm. The system is evaluated at speed, and when the tests are complete, power is cut. Someone should have shouted, "DON'T STOP THE TEST!" The angular momentum stored in the flywheel snapped the gearbox output shaft, and the flywheel then gracefully exited the area.

Faulty Test Equipment

In large organizations, it is not unusual for the mechanism engineer to delegate responsibility for test equipment to another group such as manufacturing or test engineers. This can lead to very serious problems. The following events actually happened!

I discovered that cold-plate testing was being used for some hardware in 1994. The technicians had built the test equipment and were completely unaware of any danger and actually thought the rapid action of the test equipment was great! I asked that temperature monitors be put on the cold plate (T_1), the actuator outer housing (T_2), and the actuator rotor (T_3). The next figure shows that we generated a 30°F gradient in less than three minutes.

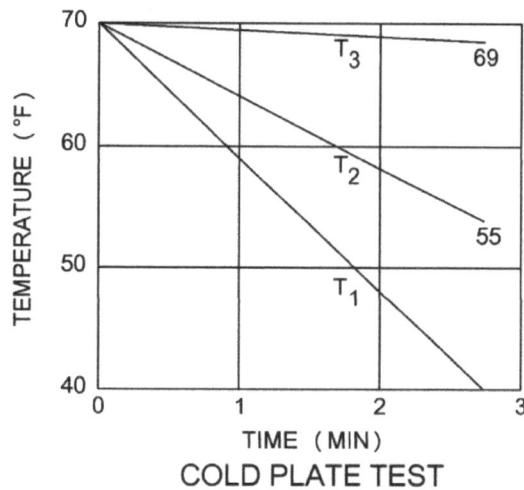

Figure 149 Generated Thermal Gradients

Conductive heat sinking is a very effective way to transfer heat quickly. A copper plate has copper tubing soldered to it. And, liquid nitrogen (-320° F) is then pumped through the tubes. This "cold plate" is capable of drawing heat out of a test specimen very rapidly.

However, great caution must be taken when testing actuators or other devices containing ball bearings. The ball bearings within the actuator causes a very high impedance to conductive heat transfer. A vacuum is not necessary. Testing at ambient pressure with heat sinks can damage internal ball bearings in seconds. The subject of thermal gradients and ball bearings is discussed in more detail in Chapter 4 (ball bearings).

The Bad Boys

There are three general categories of protection needed for mechanisms. These include:

Over-torques:

These failure modes include excessively high internal torques inside of an actuator because the motor is not torque limited. Or, by unexpected, external torques being applied at the actuator output shaft.

Over-travel:

Failure due to over-travel usually happens because the "end-of-travel" stop design is faulty (or non-existent).

Friction / Stiction:

Deployment devices are very sensitive to this failure mode. The mechanism designer must assure that a deploying object receives an initial helping "push-off" and that a reasonable deployment torque margin exists throughout the full deployment. The problem is that the deploying object will continue to accelerate if active damping is not present and an "Over-travel" problem will be created.

The present day solution is usually to provide push-off springs, a very large drive spring, and over-damp the deployment using a fluid filled damper. This approach has worked very successfully on many spacecrafts but it is very hard to achieve redundant operation. It is also possible to use electric motors which can easily be made redundant. However, now days, lead time and cost often make the approach impractical.

Over-Torque Protection

It is always necessary to assure that the maximum load occurring at an actuator output shaft does not exceed the peak design allowable value. The allowable "peak load must always be significantly greater than the normal operating load. I have used the word "load" because the loading condition may be a linear force (a linear actuator) or a rotary torque (a rotating actuator).

Three types of load limiting could be used:

(1) Motor Current Limiting

(2) Shear Pins

(3) Detents

(4) Tooth Clutches

(5) Roller Clutches

Motor Current Limiting:

This technique is a good way to protect the actuator from itself but it will not protect the actuator from externally created overloads. The current limit can actually be used to modify performance in response to changing environmental conditions. The Mars Pathfinder High Gain Antenna Actuator required a current limit system (when you limit motor current, you limit motor torque). In the early hours of the morning on Mars, the Actuator would become so cold (-150 ° F) that the greases and oils in the actuator would freeze, making it impossible to point the High Gain Antenna. Electric Strip Heaters were placed on the Actuator but were only needed at temperatures below - 40°F. If the heaters operated above - 40° F, they just waste electrical power. The solution was simple and very effective. Thermistors (temperature monitors) were mounted on the "actuator" and their output information was fed back to the current limiting electronic circuit. The actuator heaters were powered-up at - 40° F and at lower temperatures, the motor itself was given more current, generated more torque and could then power through the frozen grease even before the actuator warmed-up.

Shear Pins:

Never a good idea!! Any shear pin can be "partially sheared" and you will never know it. Also, if you fail to capture the pin and it shears, pin pieces will float around potentially doing even more damage to the host vehicle.

Detents:

Many years ago, a paper titled "Serrated Clutches and Detents", was written by L.N. Canick (Servomechanisms Inc.). The paper analyzes tooth clutches and pin detents.

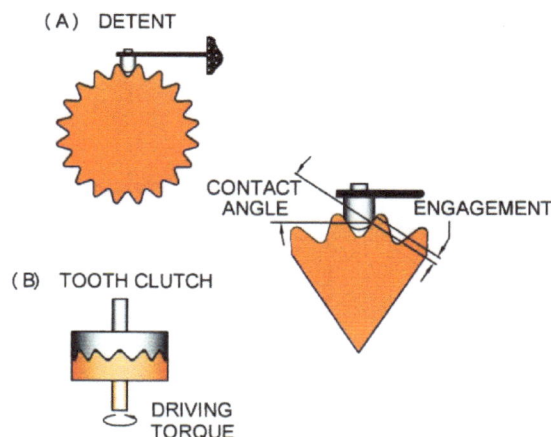

Figure 150 Detent Type Clutches

Friction is the biggest enemy of this type of device. Factors like contact angle and the length of the surface that the pin must drag on grossly affect performance and repeatability of operation. Also, non-symmetric features, like the detent shown in item (A) will operate differently in each direction.

Tooth Clutches:

The clutch (Thompson Linear Ind) shown below is typical of most tooth clutches. Mating face gears mesh to produce a very high strength coupling. This type of clutch may be the only solution if very large torque protection is required in a very small volume. The tooth profile should be altered as necessary to provide required performance. I have designed, built and tested this type of clutch and I found that it has substantial performance variation because it requires sliding surfaces (Friction) to operate. I also found that release at high torque levels generates shock and vibration. It is a useable device concept but its operation can be troublesome.

Figure 151 Tooth Clutch

Roller Clutches:

I was required to develop a smoothly operating over-torque clutch in 1982 for the SIR-B Mission. I decided to design a new type of clutch which would have a precision breakaway characteristic, smooth ratcheting and the ability to have performance easily altered. The resulting design is shown below.

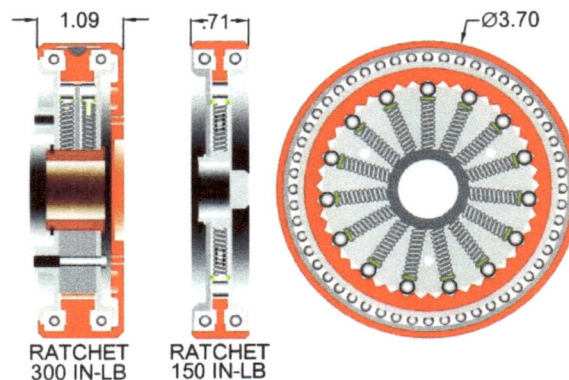

Figure 152 First Roller Clutches

The working surfaces of the clutch are fabricated from age hardened Vasco Max 300 maraging steel and the rollers were hardened 52100 steel (RC60-64). The rollers were lubricated with Bray Grease (for vacuum operation). Special care was taken to assure a smooth ratchet action (see discussion of design details).

A Challenging Roller Clutch Design

The SIR-C Program presented the most challenging roller clutch design to date. This clutch was designed to prevent an ac motor from stalling when the JPL Tri- Drive Actuator reached end of travel (stalling an AC motor will cause severe overheating). The ratchet speed was approximately two revs per second. And, the maximum ratchet torque was 67 in-lb. The clutch had to be capable of continuous ratcheting for an extended time period.

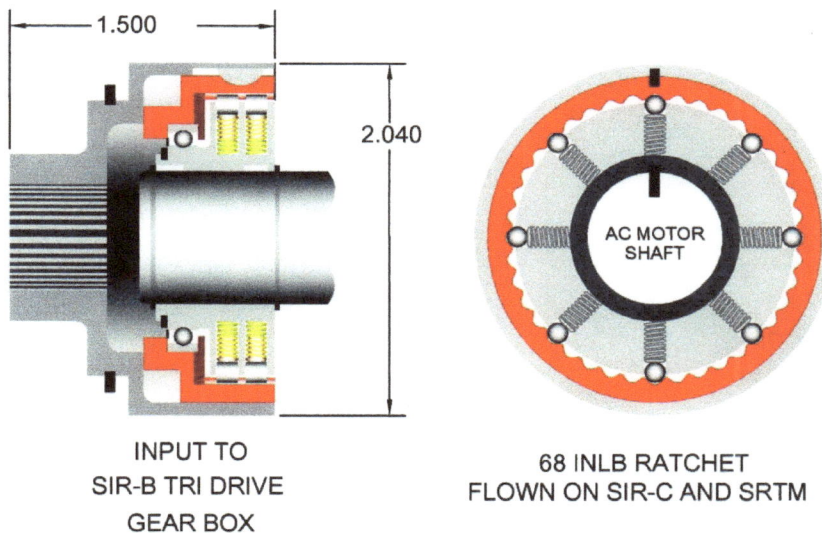

INPUT TO
SIR-B TRI DRIVE
GEAR BOX

68 INLB RATCHET
FLOWN ON SIR-C AND SRTM

**Figure 153 High Speed Roller Clutch
Flown on SIR-C and SRTM**

Test Results for SIR-C Clutch

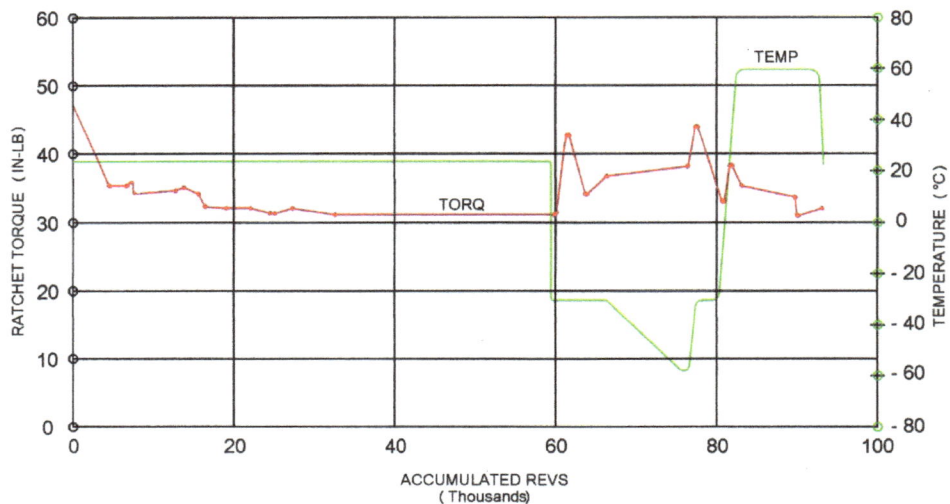

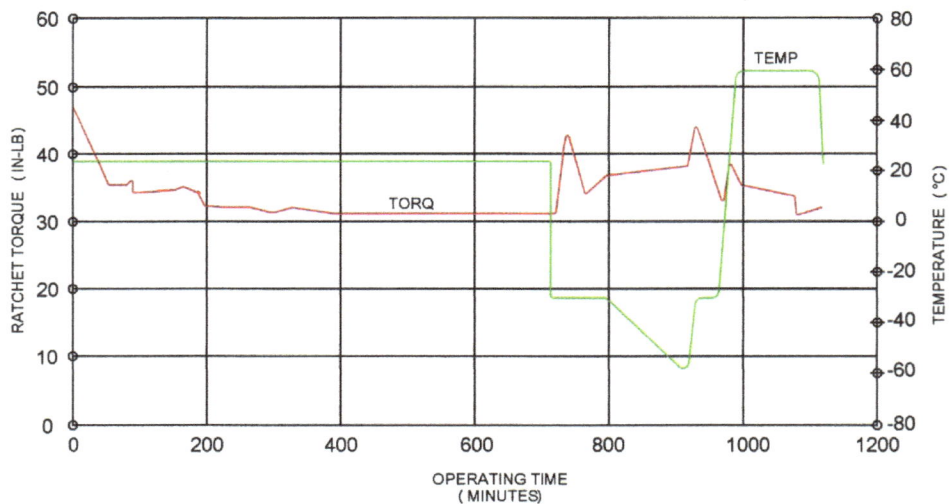

Figure 154 SIR-C Clutch Life Test (with AC Motor)

The Smallest Roller Clutch

A very small clutch was also designed . It used the same proven materials that have been used in all previous units.

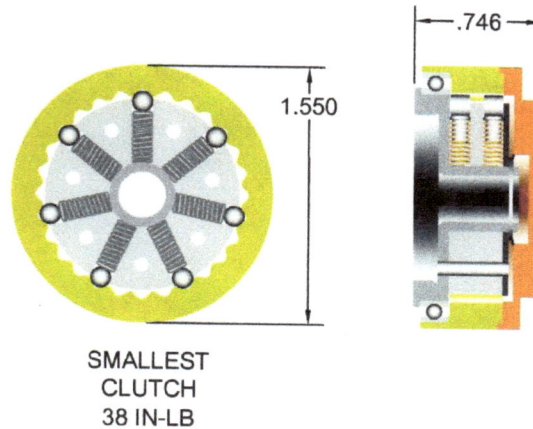

SMALLEST
CLUTCH
38 IN-LB

Figure 155 Smallest Roller Clutch (38 in-lb)

Roller Clutch Design Calculations

$$T = \frac{RF}{\dfrac{\cos \Phi}{K} + \sin \Phi}$$

$$K = \frac{1 + \mu \tan \theta}{\tan \theta - 2\mu - \mu^2 \tan \Phi}$$

T = Transmitted Torque (in. lb)

R = Effective Radius (in.)

F = Radial Sprg Force (lbs)

μ = Coef of Friction

Φ = Angle of Tangency at Contact Point $= \sin^{-1}\left(\dfrac{V}{R-V}\right)$

STEPS:

1. Select a tooth layout using data on following two pages. (This yields R_{EFF})

2. Design or pick a spring that fits within envelope. [This yields F/spring (roller)]

3. Check contact stress on roller. (See sample problem)

4. Calculate clutch performance for $\mu = 0$,
    $\mu = 0.05$, $\mu = 0.10$

If performance is acceptable within this range you have a design.

A =   Pressure Angle

N =   No. of Teeth

B =   Tooth Half Angle

P =   Tooth Pitch = 360/N

RR =   Roller Radius

RT =   Tip Radius

C =   Clearance (Ball contact point to start of RT). (Typically 0.01 inch is OK)

Equations

$$X = \frac{R_T}{\tan B}$$

$$B = A + \frac{180}{N}$$

$$K = R_r + C + X$$

$$H = K (\sin A)$$

$$Y = \frac{H}{\tan \frac{P}{2}}$$

$$R = H + Y$$

$$S = RP \left(\frac{\pi}{180} \right)$$

$$P_o = \frac{H}{\sin \frac{P}{2}}$$

$$T = P_o + Z - R_T$$

$$Z = \frac{R_T}{\sin B}$$

$$V = R_r (\sin A)$$

$$E = 2V + R_r$$

$$M = R - E$$

$$R_{EFF} = R - V$$

$$\text{Test Radius} = 2M$$

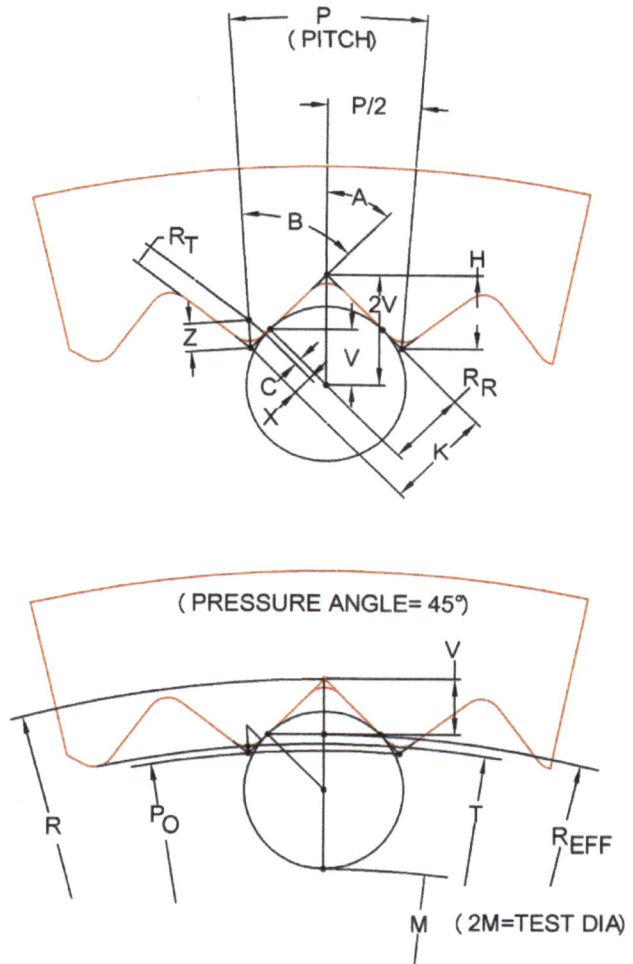

Figure 156 Roller Clutch Geometry

200

Tooth Contact Stress

Roller Dia (D_1) = 0.1250   Tooth Dia (D_2) = 0.05

Roller Width   =0.125   Load = 4.88 lb total

Max Contact Stress (τ_c) = .591$\sqrt{\dfrac{PE}{K}}$

$$K = \frac{D_1\,D_2}{D_1 + D_2} = \frac{0.125 \times 0.050}{0.125 + 0.050} = .0357$$

P = Load/Linear inch = 39.04 lb/in.= $\frac{4.88}{0.125}$ = 39.04 lbs/inch

E = 30 x 10^6

Max Contact Stress (τ_c) = .591$\sqrt{\dfrac{39.04 \times (30\,xE^6)}{.0357}}$ = 107,045 psi

☺ **Looking Good!**

Over-Travel Protection

All systems which operate over a limited linear/rotary distance must have "end-of-travel" stops. The need for stops is easy to understand. The "requirement" that the system and the stops must remain fully functional after repeated stop contacts is far less clear. No amount of redundancy of the operating elements in the system will help if "one stop" contact breaks your little beauty! This need for survival also means that the over-traveled elements must be capable of returning themselves to normal operation. You've got to be able to back-off from the stops and return to normal operation. The amount of design effort that is needed to assure system survival and continued operation is usually seriously underestimated and the resulting protection is marginal.

Typically, over-travel problems occur for one or more of the following reasons:

(1) Jamming occurs at end-of-travel

(2) The drive motor produces excessive stall torque.

(3) An operating system contains a large amount of momentum when it is operating. Hitting the stops will produce a very large impulse. Remember: Iω (momentum) = Torque x Time (impulse)

(4) The allowed stopping distance is insufficient.

Non-Jamming Stops

Most rotating screw / nut systems can be stalled at either end of travel using a non-jamming dog-stop. However, when driver torque is very large this type of stop can still sustain damage (see: "Decoupling Screw Torque").

Nut travel along the screw should be limited in order to prevent accidental screw disassembly or damage to the machine in which the screw is installed. Most machine tool manufacturers are now using timed dog-stops for this purpose (Figure 157). These stops can be used with a rotating screw and a fixed nut, or with a rotating nut and a fixed screw. To make certain that the input torque does not exceed the capacity of the stop, a torque-limiting device, such as a slip clutch, should be used between the prime mover and the screw.

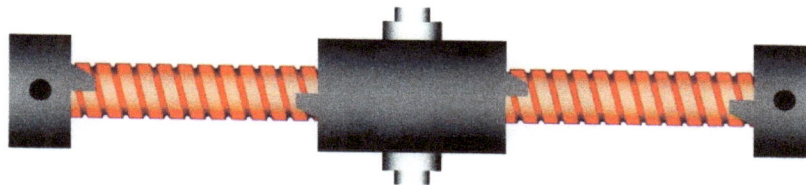

Figure 157 Dog Stops (Phased)

Timed dog-stops miss each other in the revolution just before impact and make contact entirely in torsion one revolution later. The contacting stops can't jam but they also have minimal energy absorbing ability. If you have significant kinetic energy in the moving system, Dog Stops are probably not the best solution.

The spiral groove stop is a non-jamming stop. It also can provide rotation angles much greater than 360°. Stop contact does not create radial loading because the arm pairs have opposite and equal forces. This type of stop was used on the Mars Pathfinder High Gain Gimbal Azmuth Actuator.

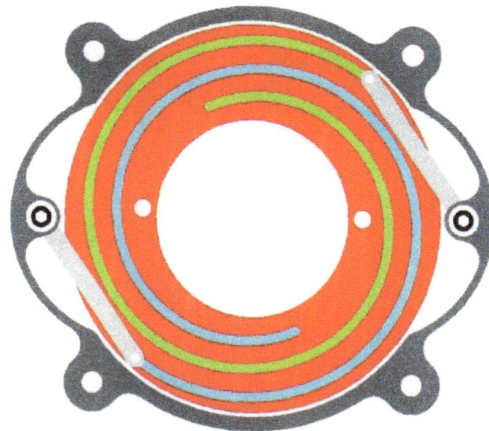

Figure 158 Spiral Groove Stops

Limiting Motor Stall Torque

Chapter 14 discusses motors and their speed / torque characteristics. If a motor must operate over a very wide environmental temperature range, some form of current limiting (torque limiting) will be necessary. Some possible "tricks" which can be performed with a carefully thought-out current limiting system were discussed previously in this section. You, the mechanical engineer/designer may have to fight to get a "proper current limit design". Just Do It!. Be a real pain in the butt until the problem receives serious attention from the electronic design group. Without proper attention, the entire mechanical design could be at jeopardy.

A system that has a very large input-stall torque must be protected in a special way. The system shown next has an enormous stall torque, which would destroy a stalled screw. "Dog-Stops" are not applicable. The screw must decouple from the torque-producing bevel gear when the slider reaches either end of travel. This is accomplished by providing a slip coupling between the screw and bevel gear. Normally the screw just rotates but when the slider reaches either end of travel and can't continue to move, the screw will continue to rotate if it is also free to translate. This screw translation can be used to cause the screw to decouple from the driving gear (screw torque is limited by axial force).

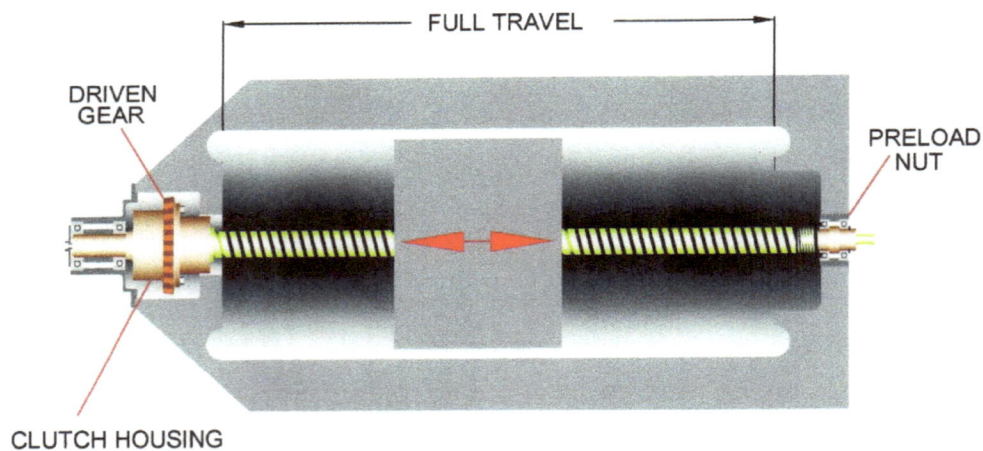

Figure 159 Force Limiting Over-Travel Protection

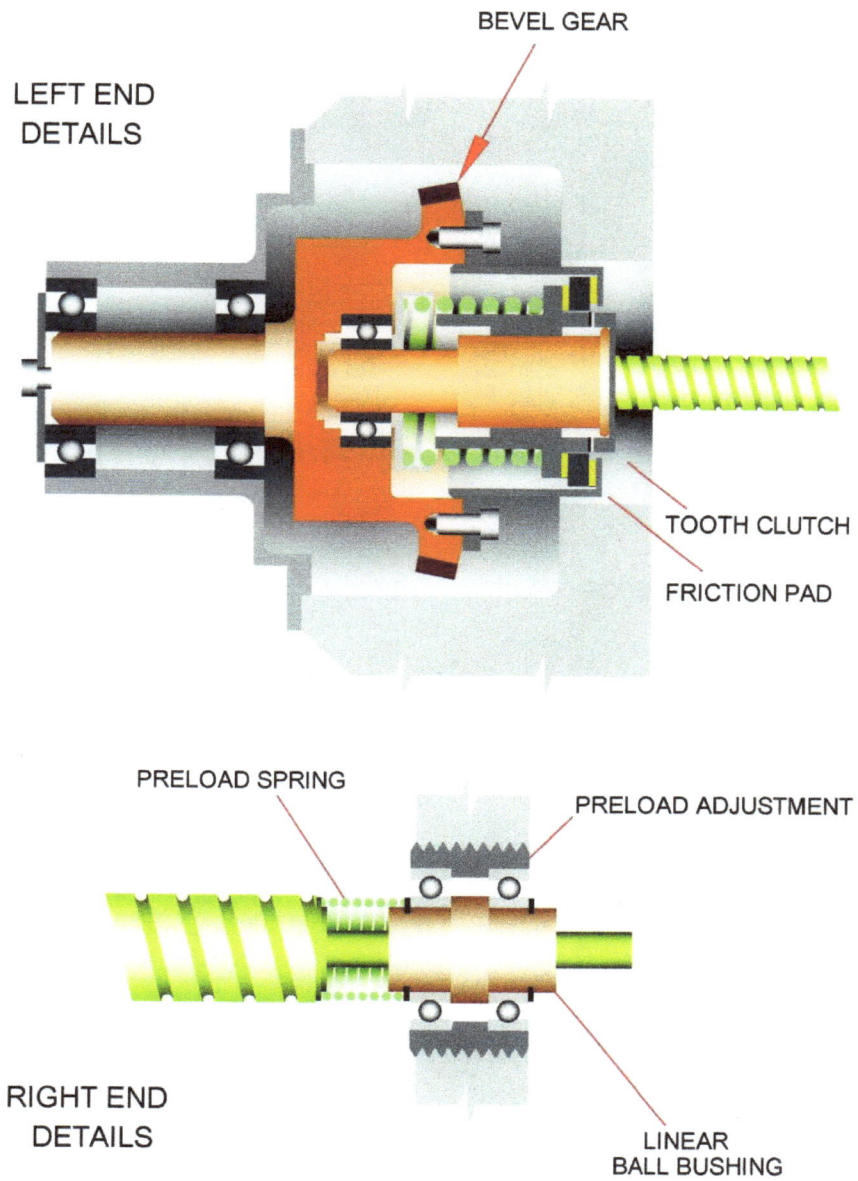

Figure 160 Details of Force Limiting System

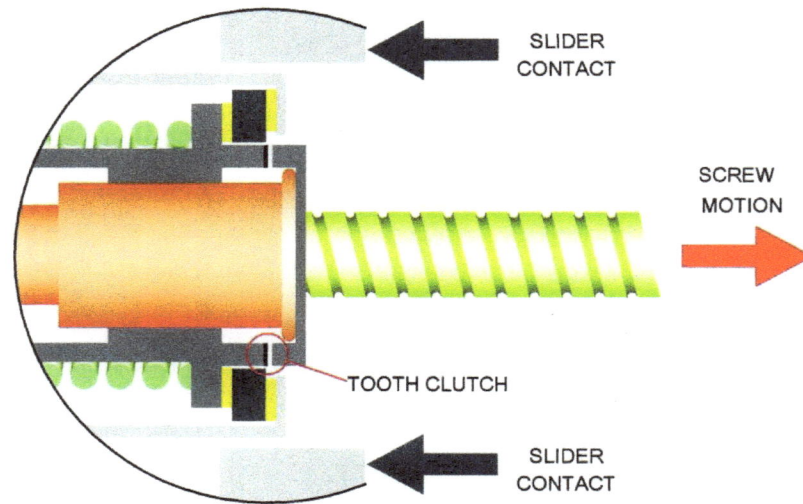

CLUTCH OPERATING DETAILS

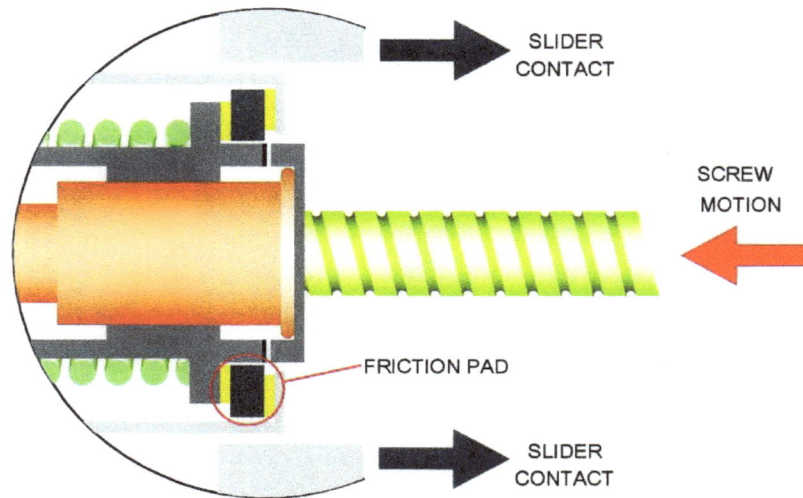

Figure 161 Details of Bi-Directional Clutch

The **Kinetic Energy Problem**

Any system that is in motion contains stored energy which must be eliminated if that system is to slow down and stop. If the system is simply "deploying" one time, then the only required elements are: (1) A prime mover, (2) A form of deployment rate control or a device to re-absorb the energy of motion at the end of travel and (3) some method to indicate that deployment is complete (a simple two position switch) and assure that the deployed object does not rebound (A capture latch).

The prime mover can be a motor/gear box or a simple spring. But the "simple spring" isn't so simple if you consider the need for deployment rate control. A drive spring and a fluid filled damper (see Chapter 11) will provide a controlled rate of deployment but the damper increases system complexity big time.

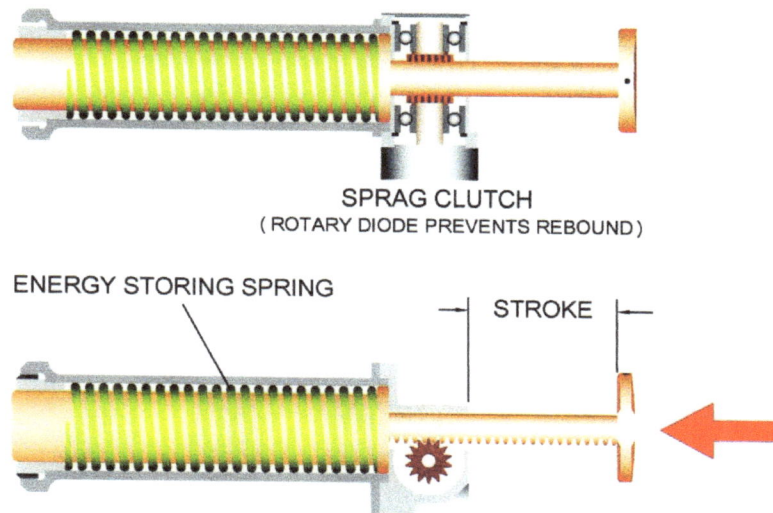

SPRAG CLUTCH
(ROTARY DIODE PREVENTS REBOUND)

ENERGY STORING SPRING

STROKE

Figure 162 Reusable Energy Storage System

If the rate of deployment is not critical then some form of energy absorbing end-of-travel bumper can be used. The bumper can be as simple as crushable honeycomb which must be replaced after each use. Or, if replacement is a problem, a reusable energy absorbing spring bumper can be used.

You may think that using a very small spring will solve the problem without all the fancy energy absorbers. Not so! You must have a significant torque margin. The energy that you put into the system to make it move must be significantly greater than "nominal" in order to assure that your mechanism will function at the extremes of the environment.

I My message:...... "Do Not Minimize Torque Margin"! A half open instrument aperture will cause the "PI" (Principle Investigator) great un-happiness..

Capture Latches and Sensors

The magnetic latch provides an excellent way to secure a deployed cover or other similar device. Latches of this type have been used in space since 1972. More recently, hall sensor packages (OPTEK P/N OHM 30208) have become available. They can be placed in the magnetic circuit of a magnetic latch to provide indication of deployment completion.

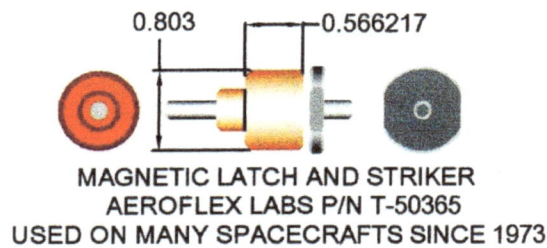

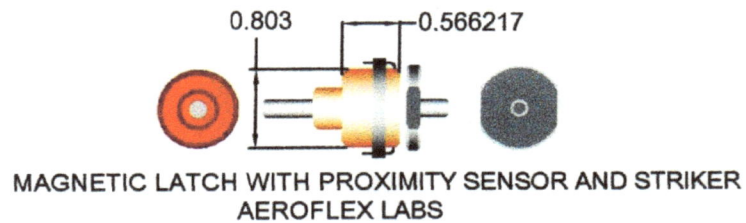

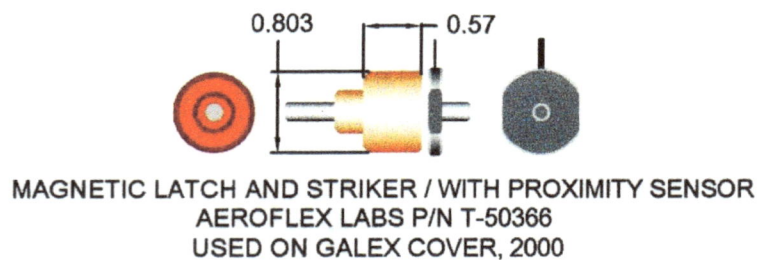

0.803   0.566217

MAGNETIC LATCH AND STRIKER
AEROFLEX LABS P/N T-50365
USED ON MANY SPACECRAFTS SINCE 1973

0.803   0.566217

MAGNETIC LATCH WITH PROXIMITY SENSOR AND STRIKER
AEROFLEX LABS

0.803   0.57

MAGNETIC LATCH AND STRIKER / WITH PROXIMITY SENSOR
AEROFLEX LABS P/N T-50366
USED ON GALEX COVER, 2000

Figure 163 Magnetic Latch Types

One additional very interesting Magnetic Latch concept has been created. If you need a "middle-of travel" latch and sensor, try this idea!

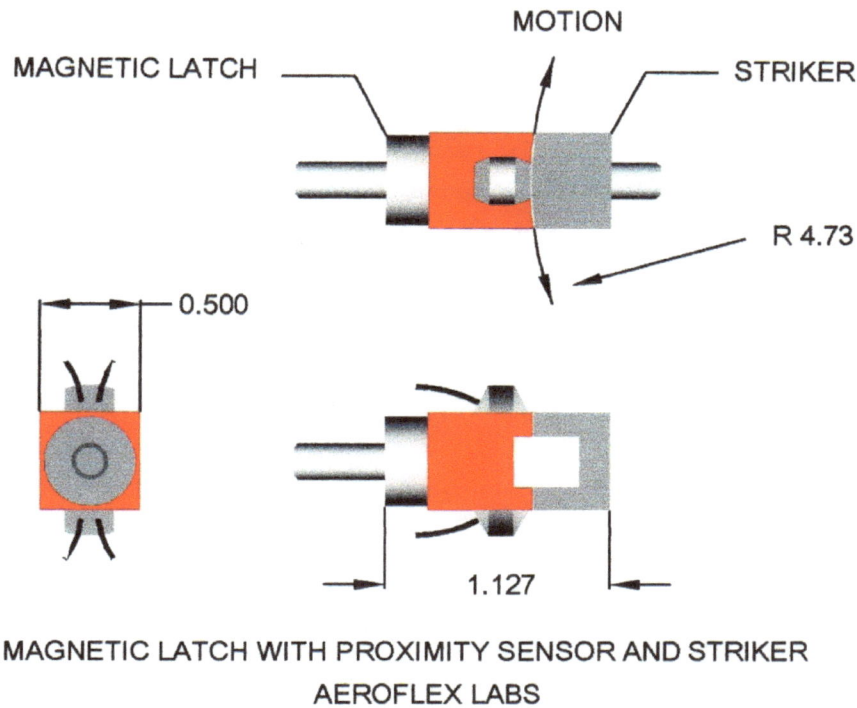

MAGNETIC LATCH WITH PROXIMITY SENSOR AND STRIKER
AEROFLEX LABS

Figure 164 Pass-By Magnetic Latch

Over-travel Protection for High Speed Positioning Systems

Any positioning system (tracking or "point to point" positioning) presents a special kind of problem with regard to over-travel protection. Examples of failure modes include:

(1) A failure in the control system causes the drive motor to have an uncontrolled run-away and the output reaches end of travel while the motor is still "pushing". This condition will break your "little beauty" for sure unless you are protected. If the controls engineers (electronics designer) recognizes this possibility, They can include some electronic protection within the control system. Sensing an "over-speed" and shutting off the drive motor helps the situation. But, every element which is added to the control system adds

additional failure modes. The best system design will share the pain between the electronics and the mechanical systems. Where have I heard that before?

(2) An equally likely over-travel failure is "coasting in to the stops". This can occur because of a control system failure or a command error. I call this "coasting, but in reality, the speed at stop contact can be near the maximum command speed.

So, what can be done? well you can provide a BIG bumper spring and let the output rebound back across the operating zone. That's always interesting to watch! Or, a bumper spring and dash-pot fluid damper can be used. But that introduces potential fluid leaks. One of these solutions is usually used for systems where the motor drives the output directly without any gear ratio (direct drives).

Motor sizes can become very large for really big, direct drive positioning systems. It may make more sense to use a gear ratio between the motor and the output load. This presents a new set of over-travel problems. Controls engineers like to have the motor rotor inertia and the reflected output inertia to be about equal. They want the load to be:

$$\textbf{(Output Inertia)}_{\textbf{reflected}} = \frac{\textbf{Actual Output Inertia}}{\textbf{N}^2}$$

where: N = gear ratio

The reason for this relationship comes from the kinetic energy solution:

$$\frac{1}{2}\textbf{I}_{\textbf{motor}}(\omega_{\textbf{motor}})^2 = \frac{1}{2}\textbf{I}_{\textbf{output}}\left(\omega_{\textbf{output}}\right)^2$$

where: $\omega_{\textbf{motor}} = \textbf{N}\,\omega_{\textbf{output}}$

The motor rotor and output have equal amounts of stored energy while operating.

If the motor inertia is larger than the reflected output inertia, more kinetic energy will exist in the rotor. Remember that stopping in over-travel requires that all energy be absorbed. You will be transferring all the motor kinetic energy through the gear box to the bumpers located on the output.

There is a practical upper bound on how large the motor rotor will be. This condition occurs when the rotor is purposely made massive enough so that:

I rotor = I output / N

If the rotor and the output counter-rotate the condition is called "Momentum Compensation"

$$(\mathbf{I}\boldsymbol{\omega})_{\mathbf{rotor}} = -(\mathbf{I}\boldsymbol{\omega})_{\mathbf{output}}$$

Accelerating torques exactly balance each other and the fixed mounting platform does not feel the accelerations.

The significance with regard to over-travel protection is that the momentum compensated system will have a high speed rotor which contains (N) times more kinetic energy than the output and all of that energy needs to pass through the gear box on its way to the output stops. This presents a really tough problem.

The problem of stopping any geared system that stores large amounts of kinetic energy in the rotor can be solved by recognizing the relationship of momentum change and impulse:

The change of angular momentum (Iω) = The impulse (Stopping Torque x Time)

In our worst case model: $(\mathbf{I}\boldsymbol{\omega})_{\mathbf{rotor}} = -(\mathbf{I}\boldsymbol{\omega})_{\mathbf{output}}$

If we can apply a braking action between the rotor and the output, the gear box will be totally protected. No braking torques/forces will be transmitted through the gearing.

Soft Stops

Systems which contain substantial kinetic energy need a special over-travel protection which will absorb energy. The soft stop is a friction brake. The friction element is a polyurethane tire mounted on a sprag clutch (one clutch for each direction of travel).

The sprag clutch is a rotary diode which will slide into over-travel but roll out of over-travel. This makes escape from over-travel possible and allows normal operations to continue using a redundant motor and control electronics.

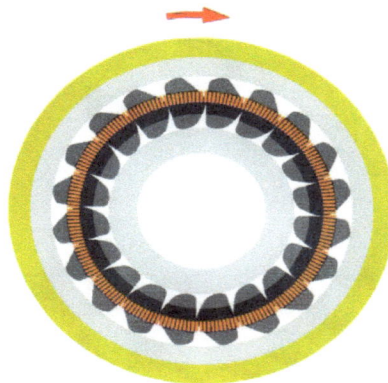

**Figure 165 Sprag Clutch
(A Rotary Diode)**

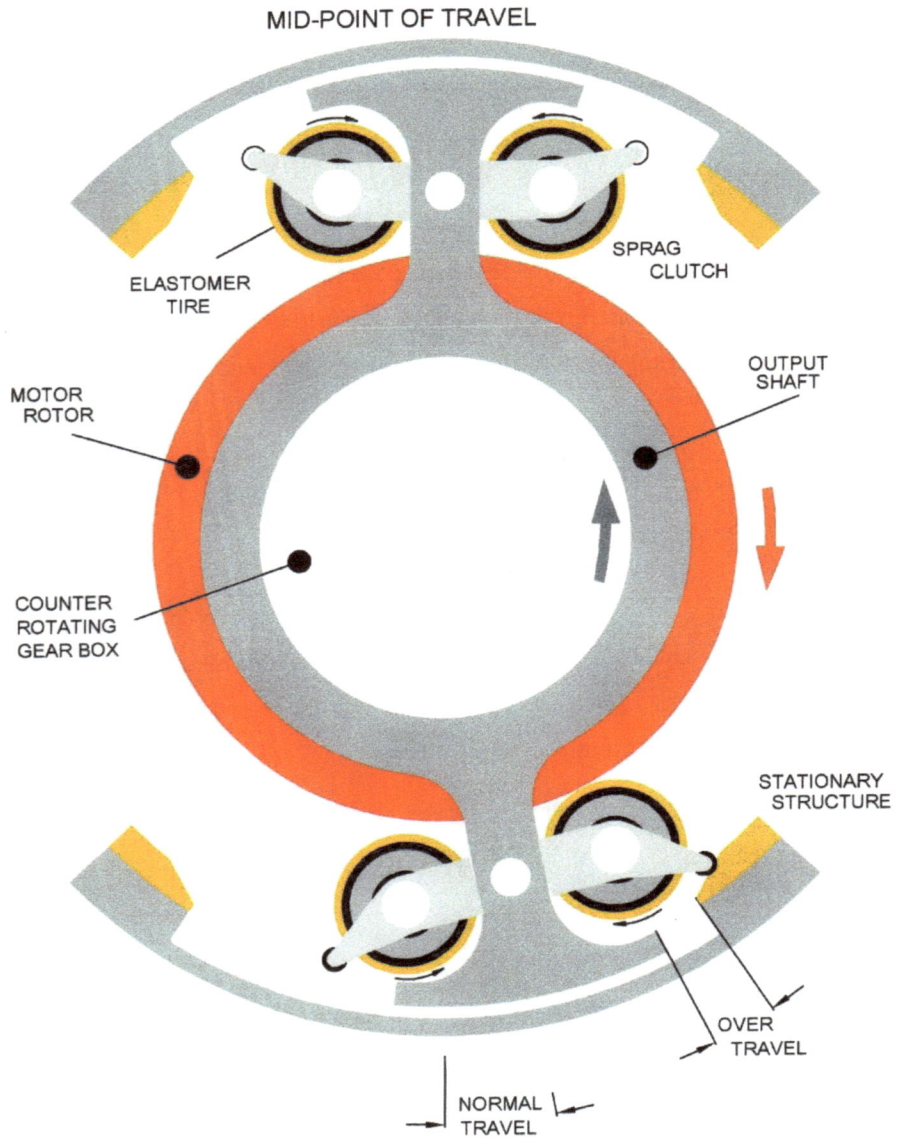

Figure 166 Soft Stop System

Miscellaneous Protection Devices

Heavy Duty Spring Bumper

A conventional spring with a heavy initial preload will also store more energy for a given displacement than a non-preloaded spring. However, the s-glass rods of this design act like constant force springs and provide very high strain capability.

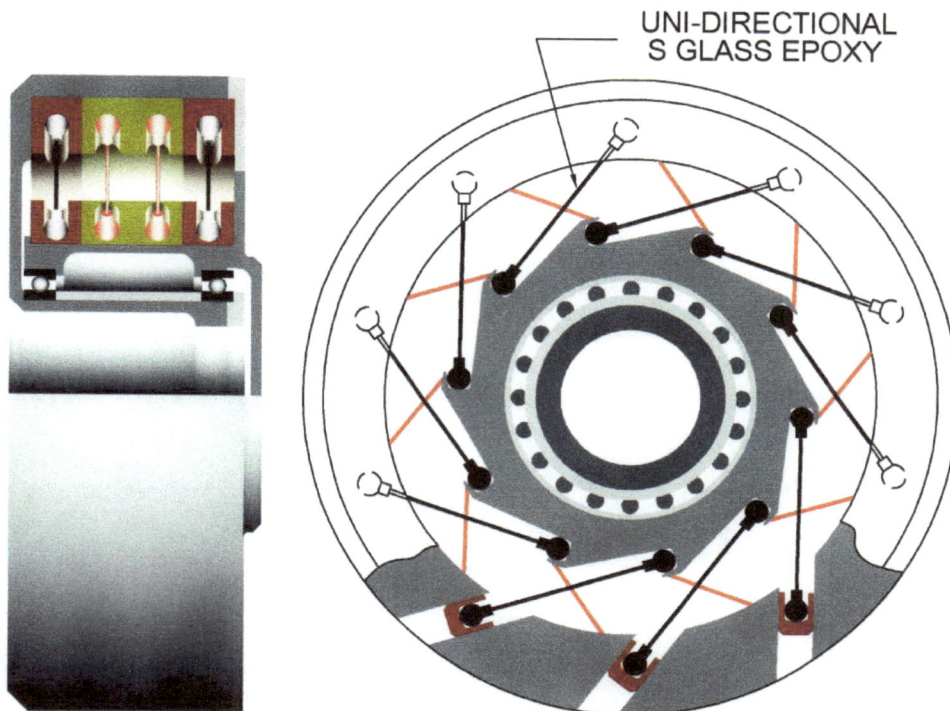

UNI-DIRECTIONAL
S GLASS EPOXY

MEGA BUMPER
MAXIMIZES STORED ENERGY

Figure 167 High Capacity Rotational Bumper

(1) The line of action should be offset in order to induce buckling in a predetermined direction.

(2) Very low friction pivots/flexures should be used to provide very precise end fixity. (But don't give up zero backlash if you really need it.)

Emergency Release of Belts

The figure below shows a belt-driven system that requires release of the primary belt drive in order to operate the secondary drive system. The same figure shows an emergency release system capable of freeing the primary motor from the system. A secondary bearing pair is located within the timing belt pulley. Those bearings are non-operating until the pulley is cut free by an explosive charge firing radially inward. An outer notched tube is cut (see picture) freeing the pulley to rotate on the inner shaft. Then the pulley and belt can continue to rotate with the driven system.

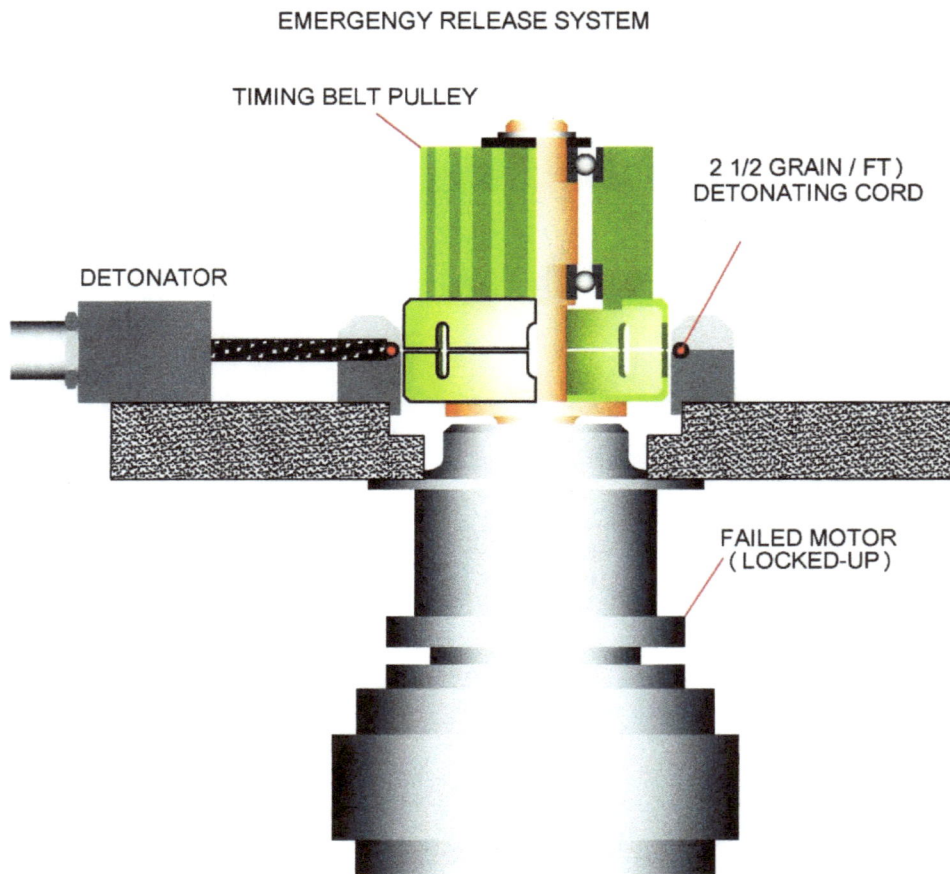

EMERGENGY RELEASE SYSTEM

TIMING BELT PULLEY

2 1/2 GRAIN / FT)
DETONATING CORD

DETONATOR

FAILED MOTOR
(LOCKED-UP)

Figure 168 Emergency Disconnect for a Locked Motor

Crushable Honeycomb

This material provides a one-shot method for energy removal. But like a fuse, it must be replaced after each use, and some degree of paranoia always exists as to possible damage that might decrease its capability. Many crushable honeycomb stops have been used.

Contents

Figure 169 Design Data for Crushable Honeycomb

Chapter 18   Reliability & Redundancy

Introduction:

Electromechanical actuators have been produced in a variety of configurations including direct drive actuators and gear drives.

It is relatively simple to achieve total redundancy using direct drive actuators. However, the direct drive configurations always result in much larger and heavier construction for a given output torque and the motor current levels are usually much higher.

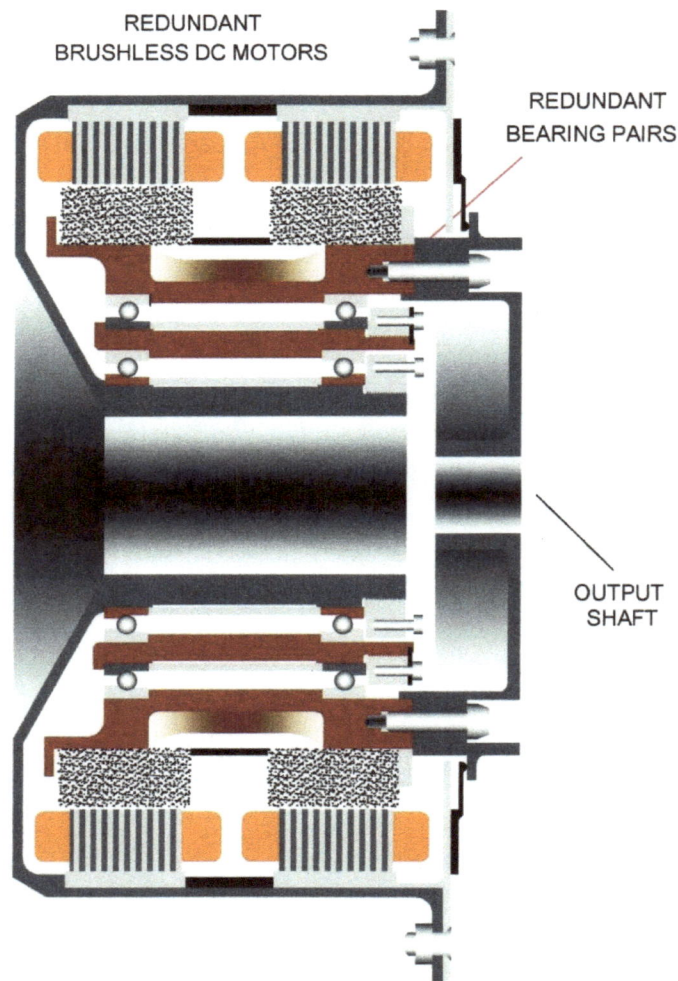

REDUNDANT
BRUSHLESS DC MOTORS

REDUNDANT
BEARING PAIRS

OUTPUT
SHAFT

Figure 170 Fully Redundant Actuator

Gear drives are light and produce very large output torques. However, gear drive configurations normally compromise reliability to some degree. Usually, partial redundancy is achieved through the use of complex differential gearing which introduces numerous single point failures. The actuator shown below is typical of the earliest applications from the 1960 to 1970. It was originally designed for aircraft applications and then later updated for space usage.

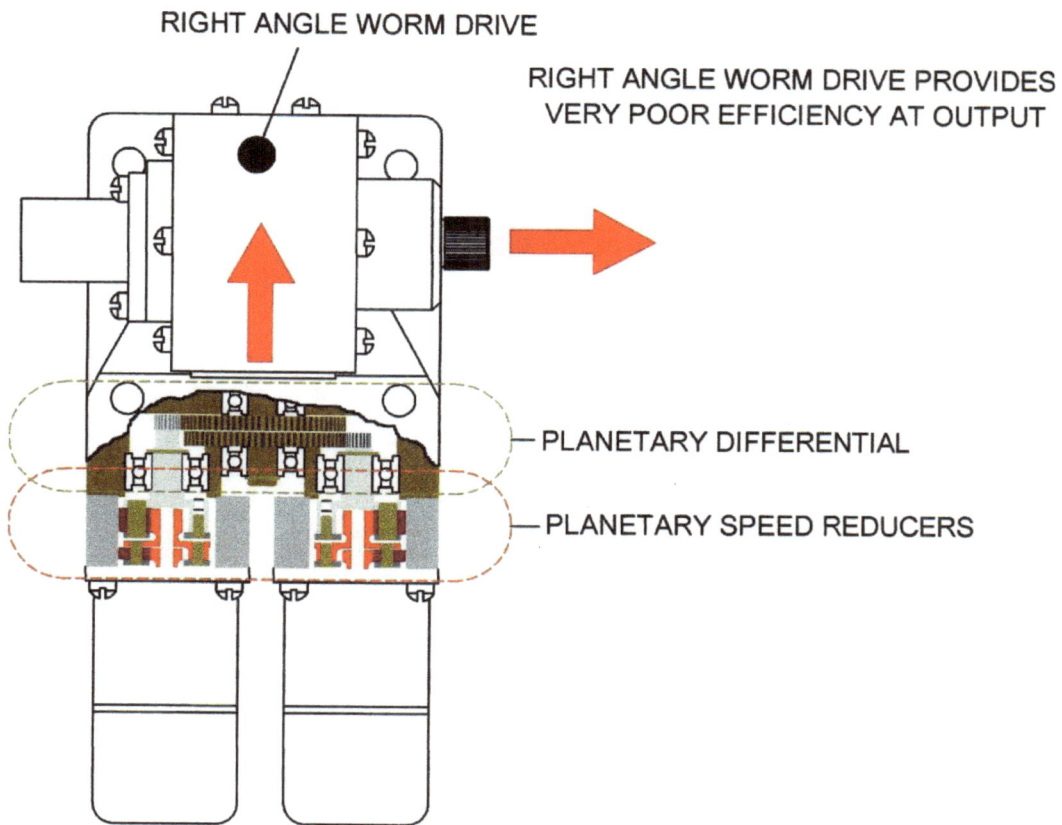

Figure 171 Partially Redundant Actuator

The next figure shows a close-up view of the numerous planetary gear stages in the actuator. The rotating elements of the differential have many credible common failure modes which could be single point failures and prevent either drive motor from operating!

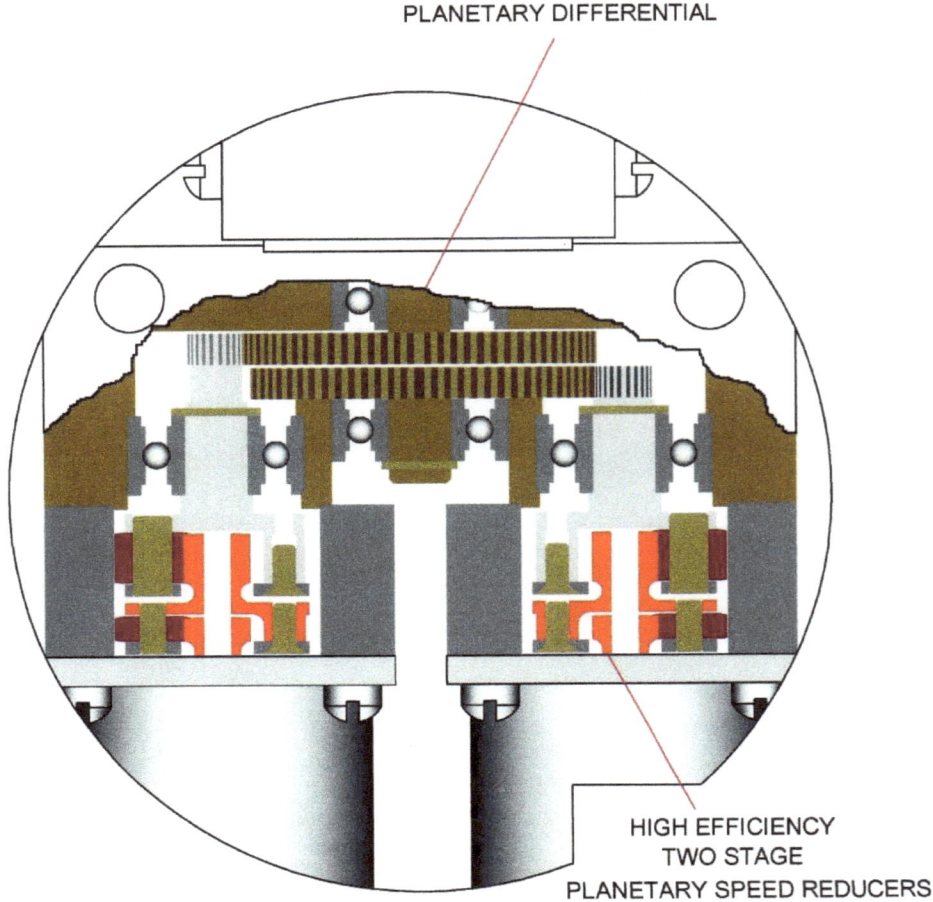

PLANETARY DIFFERENTIAL

HIGH EFFICIENCY
TWO STAGE
PLANETARY SPEED REDUCERS

WHAT'S WRONG WITH THIS PICTURE:

(1) DUBIOUS BENEFIT FROM REDUNDANCY
      SUSCEPTIBLE TO GENERIC FLAWS.

(2) EXTREME COMPLEXITY

(3) HIGH EFFICIENCY GEARING NEAR INPUT
      REQUIRES BRAKES ON MOTORS BECAUSE
      THE NON-0PERATING MOTOR WOULD
      BACK-DRIVE.

Figure 172 Details of Complex Planetary Differential

The first truly redundant geared actuator capable of continuous output rotation in either direction was developed at JPL in 1980. That unit was called the "Dual Drive". Tandem gear sets with hollow center shafts combine to form a truly redundant drive.

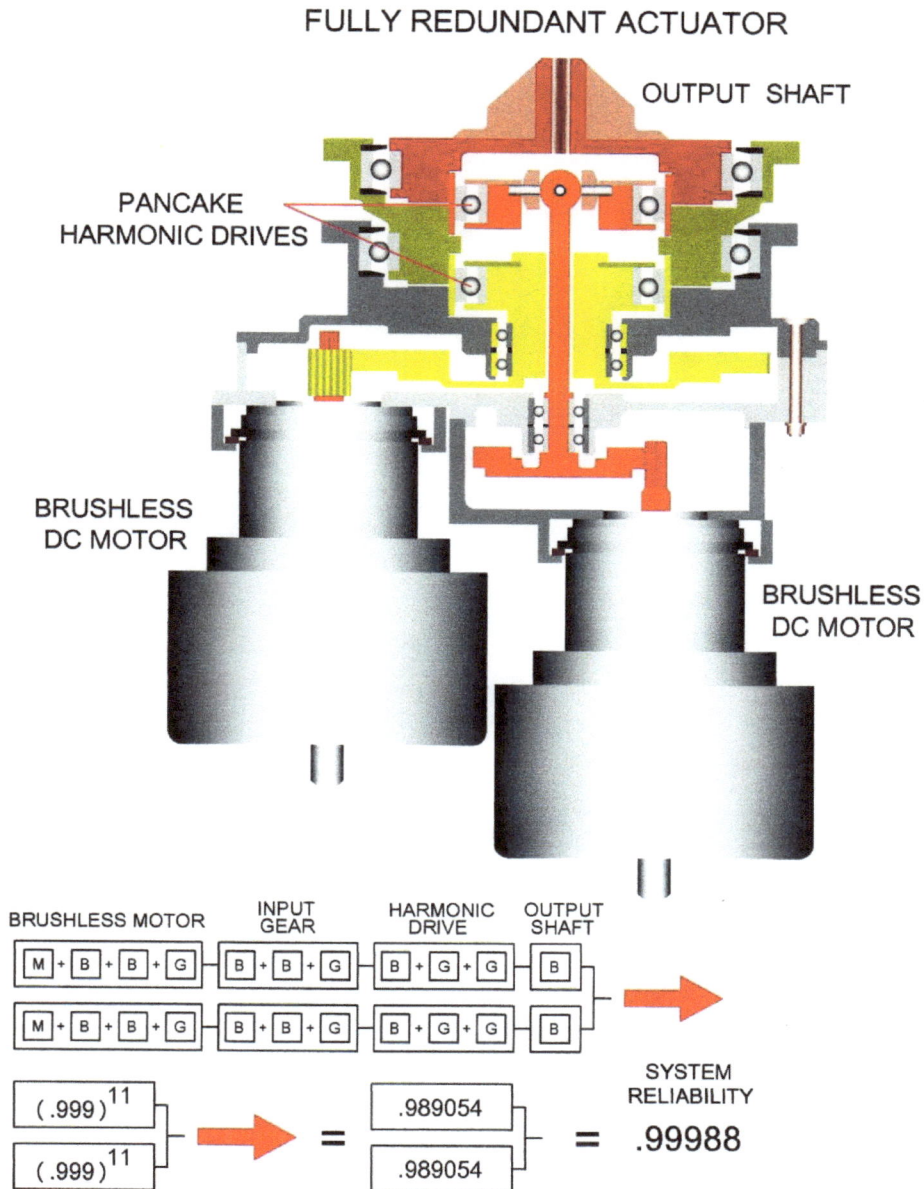

Figure 173 Fully Redundant Dual Drive Actuator

Let's go on an Excellent Adventure

I want to take you back to 1965. A group of engineers at United Shoe Machinery Inc in Beverly Massachusetts develop a very special "Inside-out" Pancake Harmonic Drive.

The design was destined to play a major part in changing our world.

Figure 174 Inside-Out Pancake Harmonic Drive

Now let's "fast forward" to 1974, USM develops a custom "pancake" gearbox shown next. USM realized that a commercial product was possible. The HDUF pancake harmonic drive became a standard product.

A year later in 1975, USM proposes a redundant version of its pancake actuator. Their unit had two significant drawbacks: (1) it was not truly redundant -- the output bearings were common, and (2) it required that the redundant motor be located on the rotating output. We were getting closer to a truly redundant actuator but we weren't quite there yet.

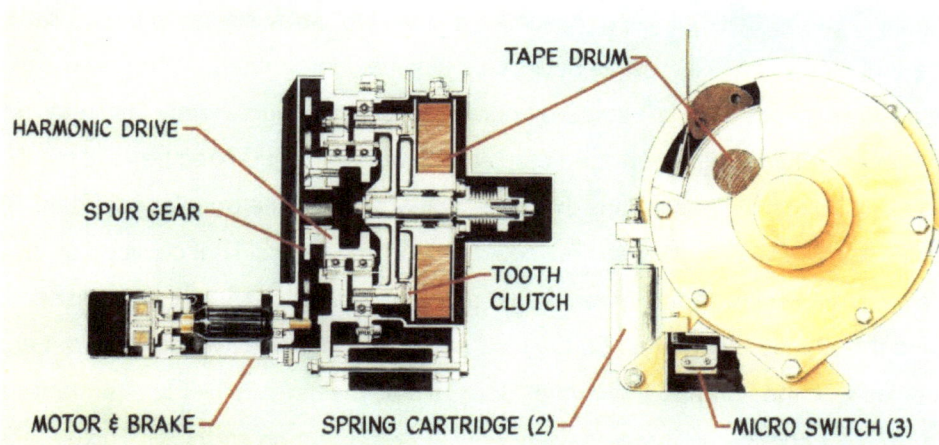

Figure 175 First Pancake Harmonic Drive

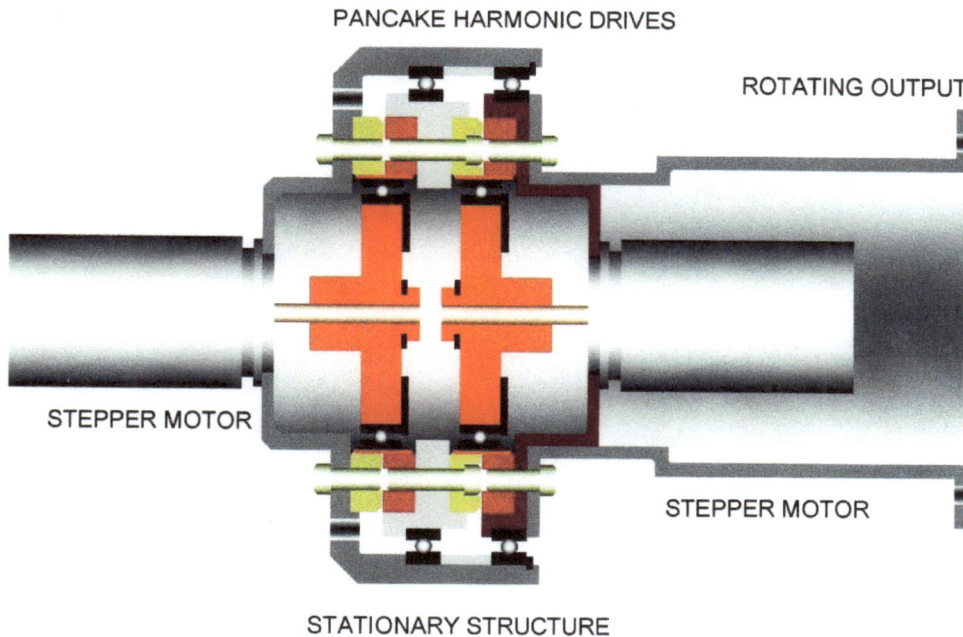

Figure 176 Dual Tandem Pancake Harmonic Drive (1975)

Now let's fast forward to1980. The need develops for a very high-reliability actuator to be used to lock-out the Galileo Spacecraft nutation damper during orbit insertion at Jupiter. JPL was willing to try something new. The resulting design became known as the "Dual Drive" (see Figure 173).

 Next, we move on to 1990.The SIR-C (Shuttle Imaging Radar- Version C) program is in really serious trouble! Cost projections indicate a massive over-run which will kill the program. The problem results from too many mechanisms. The SIR-C concept called for a "Fold-Up" array similar to the earlier SIR-B instrument. The problem with SIR-C results because a new very large flat panel array was to be used. The array was so large that unfolding it triggered numerous Shuttle Flight Safety Issues! When it was fully open, it nearly filled the entire Shuttle payload bay. Any object which extended beyond the Shuttle Doors had to be "Two Fault Tolerant". This means that each actuator had to be double redundant. The JPL engineers decided that the large antenna array could be built fully open. That decision eliminated nearly two dozen mechanisms. However, there was a much smaller x-band panel which still needed to be extended beyond the Shuttle Bay Doors. So they still had a need for one two fault tolerant actuator. The problem was solved with the "Dreaded Tri-Drive" Sorry, it's an insider joke! A triple tandem pancake harmonic drive actuator configuration was developed (A Dual Drive on steroids). This satisfied the two fault tolerance requirement. Two successful SIR-C missions were flown in the 1990's. Sir-C 's third flight into space occurred late in 1999. The SIR-C array was fitted with an additional 200 ft long deployable boom and outrigger antenna which provided stereoscopic imaging for topographical mapping. That flight was designated SRTM. The Assistant Lab Director, Larry Dumas witnessed a full deployment of the 200 foot long boom on July 8, 1999. He sent the following e-mail when he returned to JPL:

Date: Fri, 24 Jul 1998 16:40:52 -0700 (PDT)

x-sender: 1dumas@pop.jpl.nasn.gov

To: Douglas Packard <Douglas.t.Packard@jpl.nasa.gov>

Subject: Visit to AEC Able

Doug, I've been meaning to drop you a note ever since Ed Stone and I visited AEC Able July 8 to witness a demonstration of the deployment of the 60 meter boom for the SRTM mission. It was a very impressive demonstration, which Able was very proud of, of course. Able gave every indication of being a hustling, competent, and successful company. The thing that caught my attention, though, was that they gave credit to JPL for giving them their first real chance to prove themselves with space hardware with the Galileo magnetometer boom. You were specifically credited with giving them very valuable advice and coaching in their formative stages of corporate learning on how to design, develop, and test space quality hardware. It's a real success story and you clearly had a hand in making it happen. Thought you might like to know that you were the subject of an unsolicited testimonial.

Regards,

Larry

Amazingly, the American taxpayers obtained two science missions and a critical mapping mission for a very low cost. I am extremely proud to have been part of it from womb to tomb.

PS: You can pay a supplier with money and with knowledge!

Doug Packard

Reliability Analysis:

In order to begin a discussion of actuator reliability, it is necessary to understand the potential failure modes within a properly designed unit. Ted Harris, in his book, "Rolling Bearing Analysis," sums this up in a uniquely clear way when he states:

"If a rolling bearing in service is properly lubricated, properly aligned, kept free of abrasives, moisture, and corrosive reagents, and properly loaded, then all causes of damage are eliminated save one, which is material fatigue."

Conventional reliability analysis of bearings and gears assumes, as a starting point, that material fatigue characteristics govern the achievable reliability of these functional components.

The reliability of an electromechanical actuator is determined by proper summing of the reliabilities of the individual gears and bearings within that actuator. It is usual that bearings and gears form the bulk of the functional elements within any specific actuator.

Two equations govern bearing reliability as follows:

Life/reliability is shown by: $\dfrac{L}{L_o} = \left[\dfrac{\ln\frac{1}{R}}{\ln\frac{1}{R_o}}\right]^{\frac{1}{1.125}}$

(Design News, Oct 9, 1972)

Life/load is shown by: $L = L_{10}\left[\dfrac{C}{P}\right]^3$

The standard bearing life rating assumes:

$L_{10} = L_o = 10^6$ revs $\quad R_o = 90\%$ or 0.90

C= Load that produces 90% reliability at 10^6 revs $\quad$ P = New Load

R = New reliability

Also, the race hardness is assumed to be RC 58. The book, "Rolling Bearing Analysis," provides a detailed procedure for calculating the "Basic static and dynamic capacity" for other race hardness values. Slight reduction of hardness seriously reduce capacity!

A Reliability Comparison

Series elements are combined as: $\quad R_{SYSTEM} = R_1 \times R_2 \times \ldots$

Parallel elements are combined as: $\quad R_{SYSTEM} = R_1 + R_2 - (R_1 R_2)$

George Michalec "Precision Gearing Theory and Practice"

John Wiley 1966, p. 373

I will now compare the overall reliability of three actuators. The first unit is typical of actuators designed for aircraft and later upgraded for use in space. It was advertised as a redundant unit. I call this first unit "The Gilded Lilly" for reasons which will become apparent during the analysis.

The second unit is a very clean, non-redundant unit. Units like this came in to service in the mid 1970's.

The third unit is the JPL "Dual Drive" which is completely redundant and met the Space Shuttle requirement for single fault tolerance.

It is possible to compare the reliability of actuators using the value of (0.999) for each individual gear and bearing in a system (you can assign any value you prefer, the analysis technique is the same). I will use the following notations:

|BK| = MOTOR BRAKE

|M| = MOTOR WINDING

|B| = BALL BEARING

|G| = GEAR CONTACT

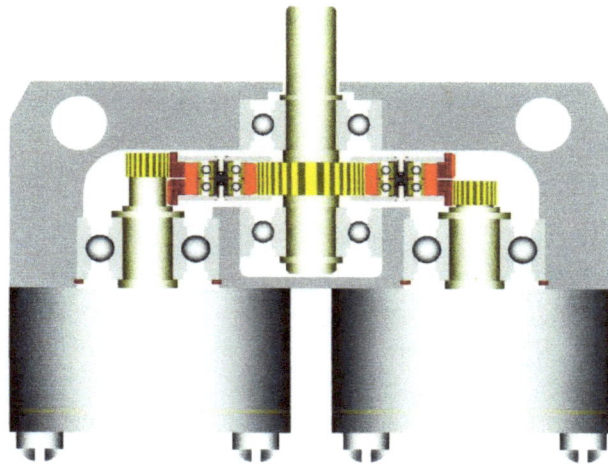

THE GILDED LILLY

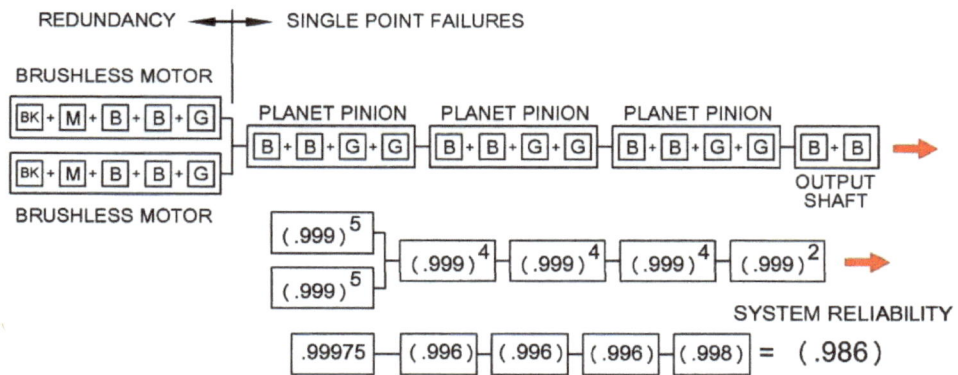

Figure 177 Reliability Analysis (Partial Redundancy)

OUTPUT

CUP
TYPE
HARMONIC

MOTOR
WITH
REDUNDANT
WINDINGS

MOTOR ROTOR

SIMPLE NON-REDUNDANT ACTUATOR

MOTOR WINDING
NO. 1

CIRCULAR SPLINE
FLEXSPLINE
GEARING

OUTPUT
SHAFT
BEARING

INPUT
BEARINGS

| M |

| B | + | B | | G | + | G | | B | | B | + | B |

| M |

MOTOR WINDING
NO. 2

WAVE
GENERATOR
BEARING

| .999 |

| $(.999)^2$ | | $(.999)^2$ | | .999 | | $(.999)^2$ |

| .999 |

SYSTEM
RELIABILITY

| .999999 | | .998 | | .998 | | .999 | | .998 | = .993

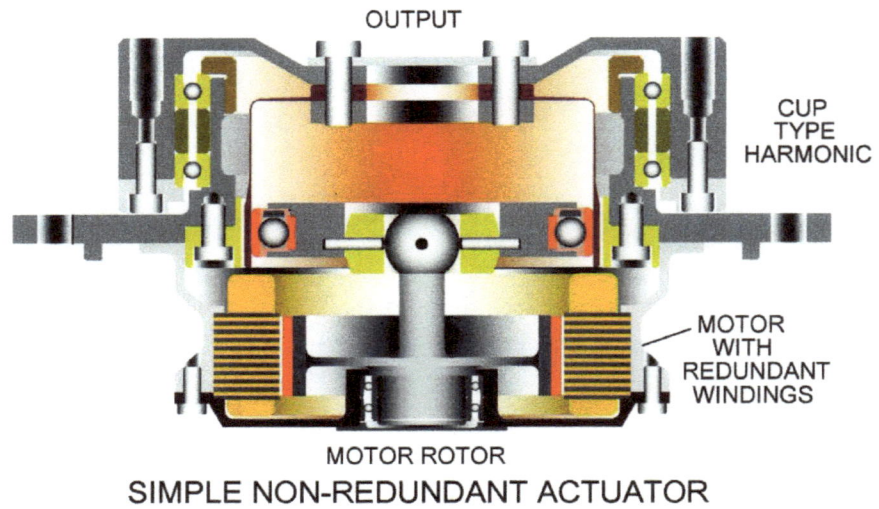

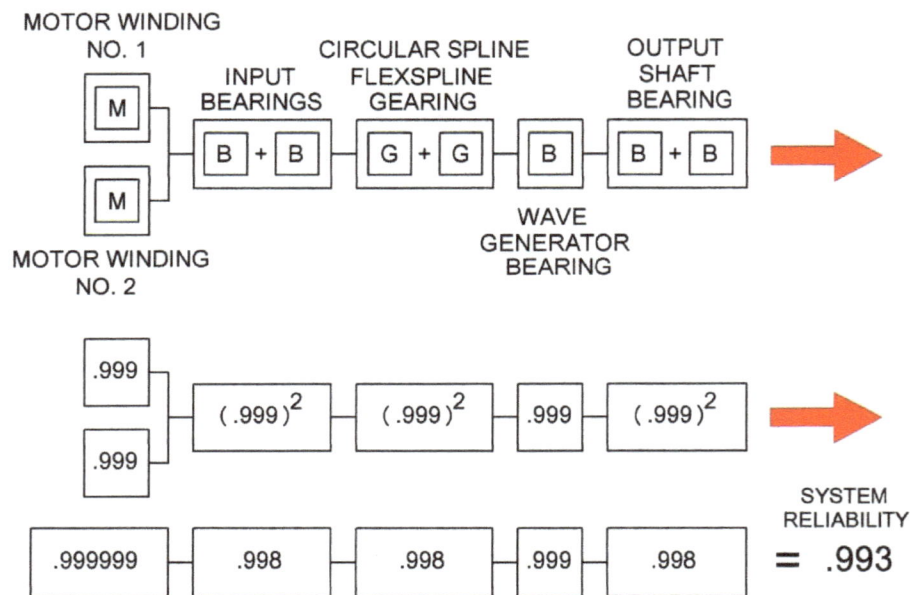

Figure 178 Reliability Analysis (Simple Non-Redundancy)

225

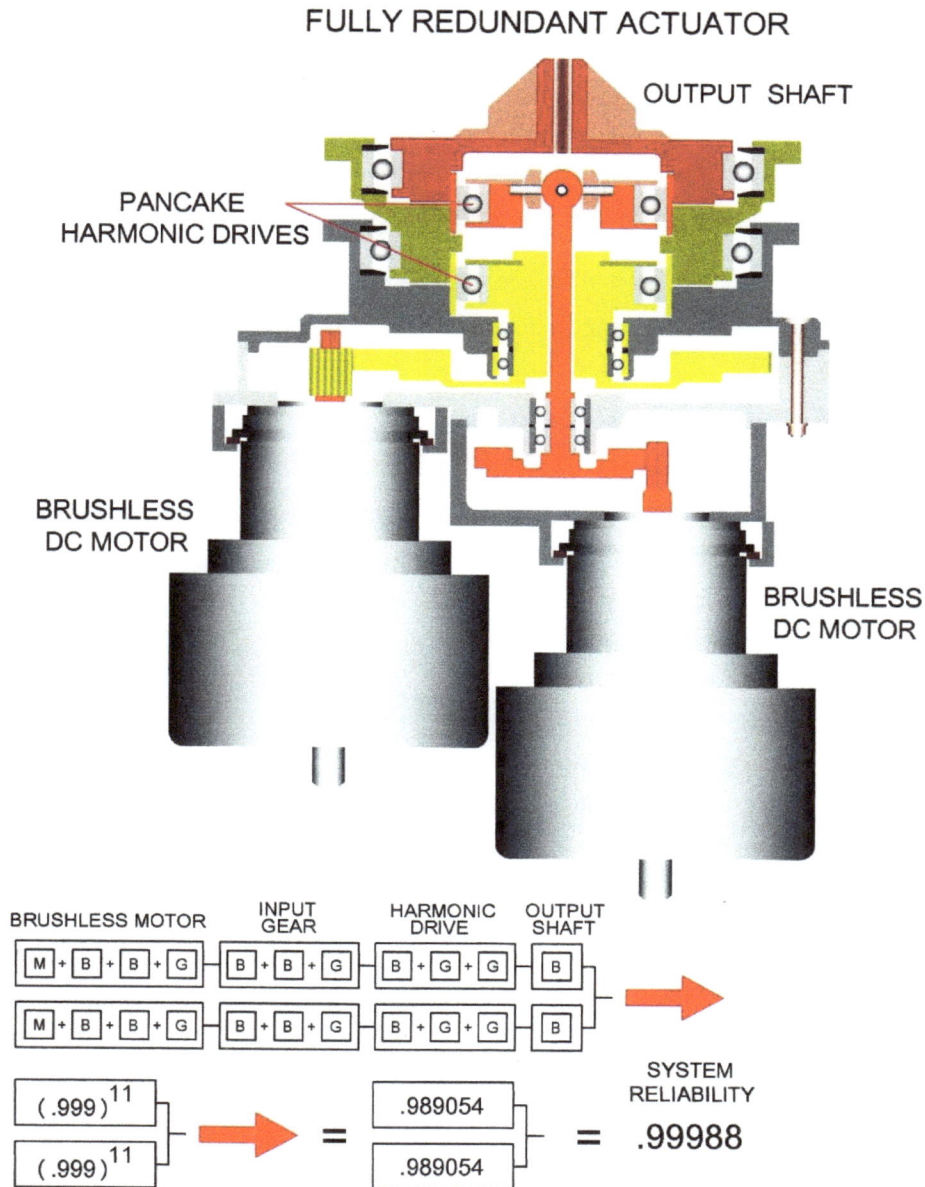

Figure 179 Reliability Analysis (Full Reduncancy)

NOTE: There is a problem with is kind of "numbers game". If the unit is properly designed, the actual reliability number for each component can approach the reliability of structural elements (1.0-) in which case the reliability comparison becomes meaningless. The Mars Exploration Rover (MER) Wheel Drive Gear Boxes are non-redundant and they also represent multiple series reliability elements but they have worked flawlessly on Mars for years. **YOU ONLY NEED ONE IF IT WORKS EVERY TIME!**

The MER gear boxes were designed by someone who had years of experience designing planetary gear systems. He got it right the first time. Sadly, the follow-on Mars program, MSL didn't fair as well.

The catch here is that years of experience and a ton of money are required to verify that a system of components is really reliable. The shorter the developmental lead time and the more cost constrained a program is, the more important true redundancy becomes.

I wrote in the introduction that "you can't tell a book by its cover". The previous reliability analysis would not have been possible without knowledge of the inner workings of each of the three actuators which were analyzed. Sometimes you have to pry this detailed information out of the actuator supplier. Tasking the supplier with the job of preparing the reliability analysis is a very good way to get in to deep do-do. First, the vendor supplied analysis will not be available until late in to the program. That's way too late to correct deficiencies without delaying delivery and causing cost increases. Second, without extensive knowledge of the unit detail design, you can't ask the right questions during design reviews.

 How many of you readers accepted my claim about redundant motor windings being parallel reliability elements? Maybe! Maybe not! It turns out that there are at least two failure modes where failure of one winding will affect the other winding. If a winding shorts to structure ground, it will act as a generator and "load down" the "good winding". You must consider this possibility and design in adequate torque margin to complete the mission task with a shorted winding.

The second failure mode would be a shorted winding which is designed in such close proximity to the other "redundant" winding so that shorting can damage the good winding and render it useless as well. You must know these things early enough during a subcontract to correct that type of design deficiency. I truly believe that the real value of this type of reliability analysis occurs because it forces the user to "open the book and read it" instead of just looking at the cover.

Several Case Histories

Next, I will present several examples of problems which have actually occurred in the Aerospace business over the last 50 years.

A Problem That Won't Go Away

Failures occurred in the early 1960's in several Agena spacecraft at booster separation. Pyrotechnic Shock was suspected of causing the failures. I do not believe that the real cause of failure was ever identified.

 I became very involved with mechanisms work starting in 1966. One particular problem seems to never go away and is with us even today. Over the years, a tiny mechanical micro-switch has caused failures on many, many spacecraft programs. I personally experienced failure of two mechanisms which used the subject micro-switch. We believed (wrongly) that a switch was being damaged when large batteries (150 lbs each) were installed near the switch location. Shortly after that failure experience, I was tasked with designing a deployment actuator (see Figure 175 titled "First Pancake Harmonic Drive"). I made sure that I buried the switch in a protected cavity so that no one could damage it. But you know what happened? The little sucker still failed! It was then obvious that the switch was defective for our operating environments.

The actual description of the failure was recorded in a failure analysis report which I authored in 1974. These are the actual comments:

Development testing of the mechanism has uncovered a serious piece part problem. Switches are employed to cause drive assembly shutoff when a predetermined tape tension is achieved. However, the unit also contains a tooth clutch which will ratchet if tape tension exceeds the predetermined value, thereby preventing tape breakage. The occurrence of clutch ratcheting imparts a substantial shock load into the mounting base where the switches are located.

Clutch ratchet tests were conducted on the mechanism in order to evaluate clutch performance and shock levels. As many as 50 separate ratchet operations were performed without problems. However, on three separate and isolated tests, the control switch failed open and the mechanism could not be operated after it had ratcheted.

Initially, it was thought that the failure might be due to incorrect switch adjustment or shifting of the switch about its mounting holes. This failure mode had been identified as the cause of numerous switch failures in many earlier applications. I personally had experienced switch failures on two occasions where the switches had been employed as separation monitors for vehicle pyrotechnic separation.

The switches and their associated actuator arms had been mounted in an exposed location where they were subject to handling damage. Thus, the conclusion of "incorrect adjustment" seemed correct. However, in this new application, the switches were purposely buried in the mounting base in order to absolutely preclude handling damage. But, when failures occurred, it became apparent that the switch itself should be investigated.

The "failed" switches were removed and tested. They all worked perfectly! After the Electron Microscope photos were obtained, I contacted the Responsible Parts Engineer for the subject switch in order to discuss the problem directly with him. He indicated that the switch manufacturer was aware of a design problem with the switch and, in fact, they had a redesigned switch available. However, the Parts Engineer indicated that none of the switches had as yet been purchased by LMSC, because no program had requested use of the improved switch. Apparently, the various using programs felt that the "old" design was acceptable and that a design change was not warranted. The Parts Engineer had to rely upon the judgment of the various program reliability representatives for a decision to change switch designs because he was not cognizant of the various switch applications.

The Parts Engineer indicated that a failure mode had been identified by another aerospace company, they also used the switch. The failure mode was identified as a movement of the two piece contact carrier. The other company had also completed a very substantial amount of testing on the new switch configuration. Thus, a thoroughly tested, improved switch design was available then (1974) if the using programs require it. But, the word never got out!

Let's discuss the early Agena spacecraft failures a little more. The failed spacecraft had a "D timer" (guidance event timer) which had been relocated near the booster separation joint (which used 10 grain explosive cord to cut the Agena free from the booster.

The "D timer" was a motor-driven mechanical timing device that used cams and, you guessed it, micro-switches.

Between 1974 and 1978, I heard of two other switch problems and in 1982. I visited Johns Hopkins University and noticed that JPL had furnished "problem" switches for use on a Galileo spacecraft instrument. I warned them not to use those switches.

I got a phone call from a Johns Hopkins reliability engineer after I returned to JPL and as I explained the problem over the phone, he had an opened switch in hand. he moved the two piece linkage and sure enough the switch failed as we talked. That story had a happy ending. JPL gave them the correct switch and problem solved.

The good switch and bad switch both look identical on the outside. You can only tell good from bad by the part number. The failure mode is insidious! A few clicks and the little buggier works fine again. I can't overstress the seriousness of using the wrong version of this device.

Problem Description

The following figure shows a cross-section of the "bad" switch. The switch is tiny. The dimensions of the case are 0.80 inches by 0.45 inches. Pushing the actuation arm should cause the red movable link to transfer the electrical path from the left hand pin to the center pin. Failure occurs when the red link fails to make contact with the center pin.

The left end of the red link attaches to a green link. The problem occurs at that attachment. The red link simply slides in a slot in the green link. There is no positive control of the relative positions of red and green. The slot in the green link is long enough so that the left end of the red link can walk up and down the slot. If the red link moves up the green slot, the electrical contact on the right end of the red link will not transfer to the center pin. So soon old and so late smart!!

The significance of this will probably be lost on the young engineer! But, after a life time of close encounters with doom, it will all become clear.

ORIGINAL SWITCH DESIGN
YOU CAN'T TELL A BOOK BY ITS COVER

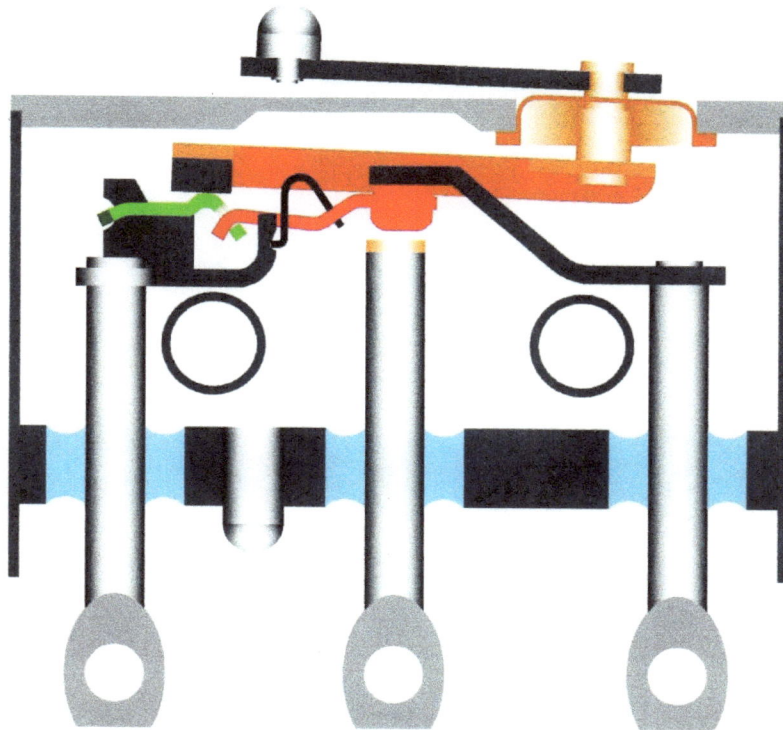

Figure 180 The Problem Microswitch

The Solution

The switch problem was solved before 1974 with the redesigned configuration shown below. A one piece "red" arm replaced the double "red / green" linkage. The new switch was successfully qualification tested and was available by 1975. But, problems didn't go away because switch users failed to understand the design details of the item which they specified for their critical spacecraft system and no one put a proper warning on the switch documentation.

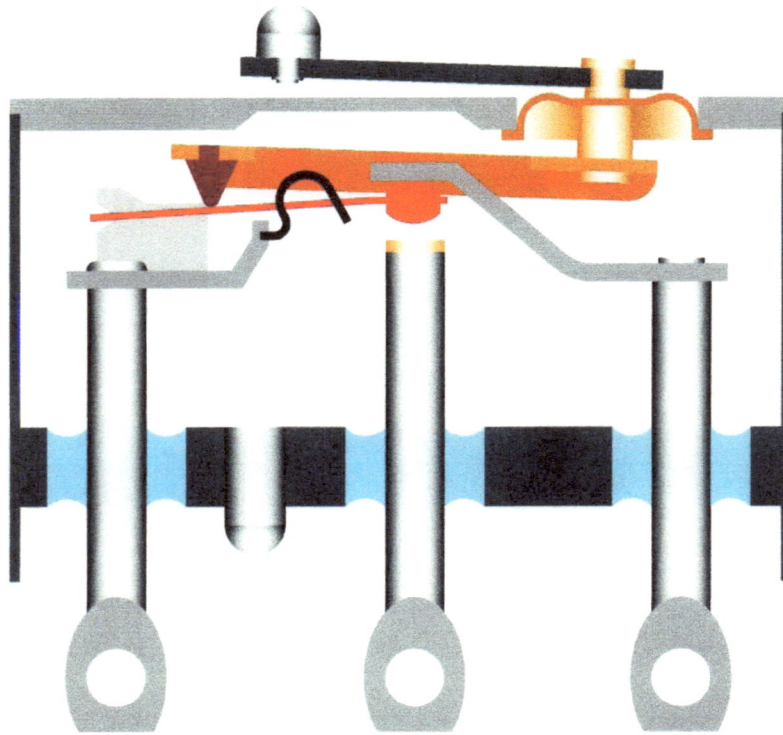

Figure 181 Redesigned Microswitch

William Shakespeare wrote words in a play in the year 1591. Those words created a saying used even today: "For want of a nail, the shoe was lost........". The words are just as accurate now as then! You must demand design details. You can't tell a book by its cover! And, that pretty catalog picture of the outside of the switch doesn't help either.

Keep an Open Mind

My thoughts regarding the need for redundancy of ball bearings have changed since I wrote the JPL Mechanisms Handbook in 2000. Then, I did not believe that redundant ball bearings were of any real value. I stated earlier in this chapter that properly designed ball bearings (bearing systems) will fail due to material fatigue. Material fatigue is a condition which occurs over time when highly loaded balls roll on hardened metallic races. Small sub-surface cracks begin to form within the metallic races and then small bits of the races begin to break-away. Eventually the debris will accumulate and destroy the ball separator causing the bearing to fall apart. This failure would also prevent redundant operation. Operating at low loads will assure that material fatigue never occurs.

The book "Space Vehicle Mechanisms" has an excellent discussion of ball bearing technology. One of the topics concerns retainer related torque losses. There is a condition that may occur where the friction of the ball bearing can temporarily increase by as much as 6X. The problem results from poor control of manufacturing tolerances, improper design with regard to ball/race conformity, and use of thin section bearings which are inherently more difficult to manufacture with great precision. The condition is called blocking, cage wind-up and groan. It happens when balls within the bearing want to roll at different speeds. The balls push against the ball separator (retainer) and may even cause the separator to shift position enough to begin dragging against one of the races (the control land). The condition is temporary because the tight/loose areas within the bearing are continually changing due to speed differences between all moving elements (balls, races, separator, etc).

I have encountered "cage wind-up" problems many times. I can assure you that the phenomenon is real. I say this because recently (2008) several actuator engineers at a major aerospace company did not believe that cage wind-up happens. These folks design actuators which are stepper motor driven and have high ratio gearing. With that combination you can have a 6X friction increase at the ball bearings and you will never recognize it.

Anyone who designs continuously rotating devices which are driven directly by a motor knows about cage wind-up. I now believe that there is a reasonable case for using redundant bearings to negate the effects of temporary friction increases in direct drive actuators. Typical candidate systems would be active aperture doors and direct drive gimbals.

So What Does a Redundant Ball Bearing System Look Like

You can design your own redundant bearing by purchasing precision duplexed ball bearing pairs (machine tool spindle bearings) and machining matching spacers. The length of the spacer pair is not critical. However the lengths of both inner and outer race spacers must match exactly. If you surface grind both spacers together in one set-up that's as exact as it gets.

A custom redundant bearing can be purchased if you have lots of money and lots of time.

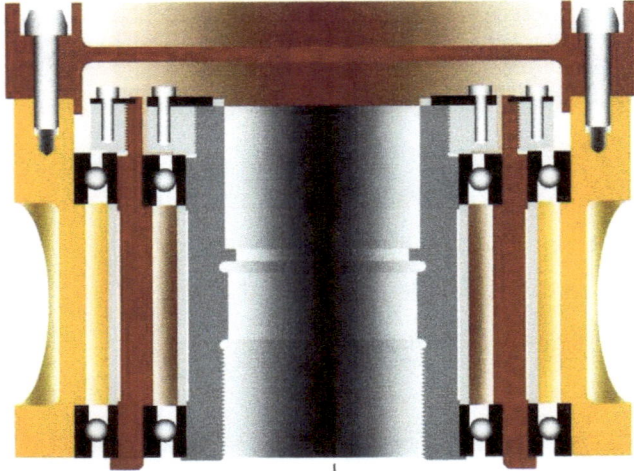

REDUNDANT BEARING ASSY
USES PURCHASED CATALOG BEARING PAIRS

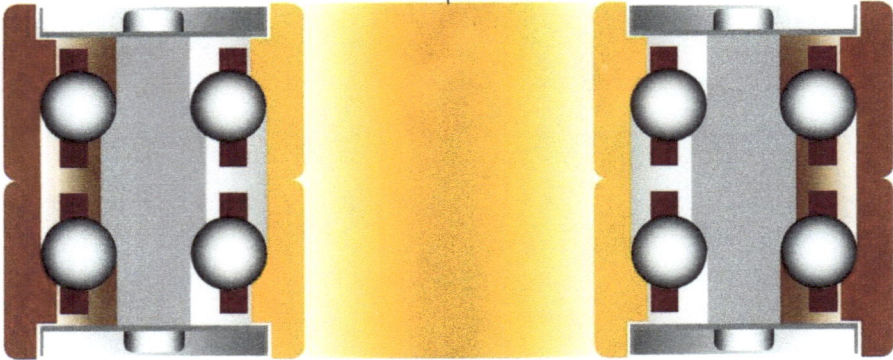

REDUNDANT BEARING ASSY
USES SPECIAL CUSTOM MADE SINGLE ASSY

Figure 182 Examples- Redundant Bearings

General Discussion

The following topics are of general interest and I feel that the information is worth sharing.

Excessive Testing

New requirements for the design, fabrication and testing of electronic components were developed. This was necessary because early use of "smart" weapons had uncovered serious reliability problems. The "Hi Rel" components and circuit design margin requirements greatly improved the performance of later weapon systems. But, along the way some genius decided to require mechanical devices to meet similar criteria. One of the most troubling requirements was: "300 hour burn-in ". Defects in mechanical systems become apparent at assembly or with a minimal run-in. Actuators or devices run for 300 hours will be degraded!

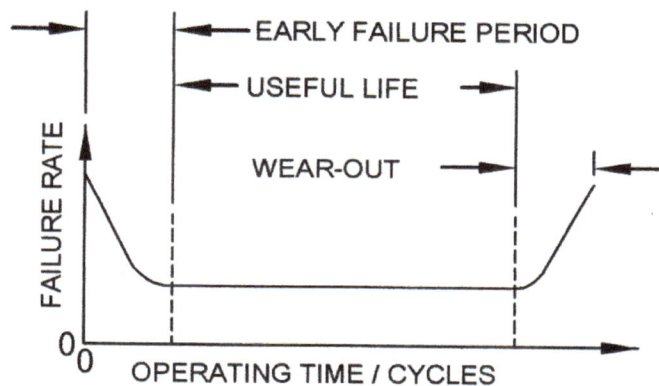

Figure 183 Failure Rate Verses Operating Time

George Michalec's book, "Precision Gearing, Theory and Practice" ,1966, has a very good discussion of the "Nature of Failure" in mechanical systems.

"This idealized bathtub curve is prevalent regardless of the device's nature or complexity. Many electromechanical systems approximate this behavior, including some gear trains. The difference between simple and complex devices is only in the relative height of the bathtub. A complex assembly with many parts has an initially high failure rate because statistically there are many parts and assembly combinations offering opportunities for defects. On the other hand, units with very few parts, such as a gear pair, involve so few parts that initial failure is relatively small."

Precision and Producibility

These elements compete and create the need for the mechanisms engineer and the precision machinist to communicate face to face. I prefer to place my new development jobs into a single shop with a "lead" machinist overseeing the entire job. The shop does not have to be captive or co-located with Engineering but that can also help. This approach is not necessary beyond initial development but it is critically important to a quick development at the lowest possible cost. Here are some of George Michalec's words on the subject:

Integration of Fabrication and Design.

"Even though gear design and fabrication are separate independent operations, there is much value in close integration. The shop must feed back its problems, needs, and capabilities if engineering design is to specify gears in the optimum manner for achieving precision. The common commercial-quality gear presents few problems, but the production of high-precision gears depends heavily upon a host of shop considerations such as availability of machines, test equipment, materials, experience, and know-how.

Limitations in any of these areas, when known to the designer, may permit alternate approaches with better results.

Captive gear shops (those that are part of an engineering design and manufacturing organization) have the advantage of a close working relationship between the two areas. This relationship usually results in efficient handling of challenging precision gear fabrication that requires development and innovations in design and manufacture. Although the independent gear shops are at a disadvantage with their customers, the gap can be made up by their appreciation of this, and by their offering to coordinate shop knowledge with the customer's design engineering".

George Michalec "Precision Gearing Theory and Practice", John Wiley 1966

Developing Precision Capabilities.

"The development of a precision gear fabrication capability is not to be lightly considered. It represents a combination of knowledge and craft acquired through much experience. The true value of precision quality gears becomes more apparent when the uninitiated seek precision gears from unproven sources. Sometimes in a competitive environment a procuring agent believes he can under-price his own internal captive gear shop (or an established vendor gear shop). What is not appreciated is that the established facility has made special efforts to produce precision and is likely to be the least expensive because of available tooling and personnel experienced with the subtleties of the job. Going to a new gear shop solely for a lower price often leads to vendor jumping, with a scattering of limited experience and limited tooling. Under these circumstances no one has an opportunity to become a master of the precision, creating widespread discontent.

If a precision gear is repeatedly made in the same gear shop, there is opportunity for trade-offs of tolerances and deviations, which results in salvaged parts, improved performance, and lower costs. These advantages are lost when piece-parts are procured from several sources."

George Michalec "Precision Gearing Theory and Practice", John Wiley 1966

The man obviously understands what a "tenth" is (see Chapter 4 regarding ball bearings). I agree completely. The only thing which I would change is to replace the word "gear" with the words "mechanism component"

Tolerance -- How Loose is too Loose?

"The closer the tolerance, regardless of the particular dimension, the greater fabrication effort required, which results in increased manufacturing cost. The relationship between tolerance and cost is not linear, for as the tolerance approaches zero the required effort becomes enormous.

Similarly, at the other extreme, fabrication cost decreases with relaxation of tolerance, but a value is reached beyond which little is gained."

George Michalec "Precision Gearing Theory and Practice", John Wiley 1966

If you needed a low-precision metallic cube, tolerance could be set at, say, ±0.05 in. This would allow the cube to be band-sawed and hand-filed. But what a dumb way to create such a part! The obvious right way is to mill the cube, and the mill will easily produce ±0.005 accuracy. Nothing is gained with a looser tolerance, except to encourage sloppy workmanship.

Dual-Function Actuators

A less costly approach to redundancy -- find a way to make one actuator perform two functions. The actuator shown below is capable of deploying a long output shaft which supports a solar array or antenna. Once deployed, the same actuator can provide tracking motion about its axis of rotation.

We normally think of actuators as having an input shaft and an output shaft.
But, they actually have three possible moving elements:
The Grounded Member / The Input / The Output

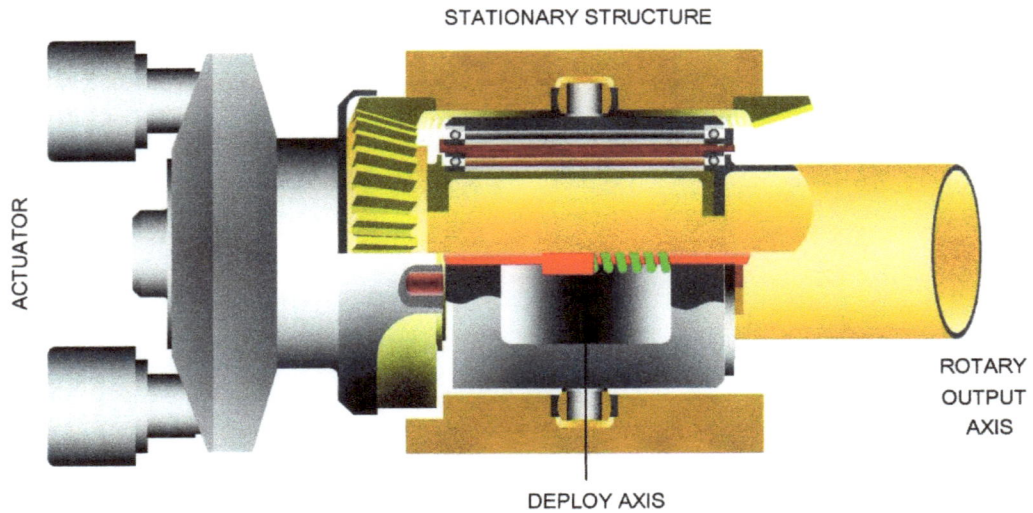

STATIONARY STRUCTURE

ACTUATOR

ROTARY OUTPUT AXIS

DEPLOY AXIS

ACTUATOR BODY ROTATES AND WALKS AROUND RING GEAR
TO DEPLOY BOOM
AT COMPLETION OF DEPLOYMENT, RED LOCKOUT
PIN ENGAGES / LOCKS ACTUATOR BODY AND
FREES ROTARY OUTPUT AXIS

Figure 184 Dual Function Actuators

The Philosophy of Belt and Suspenders Redundancy

One high-quality belt will keep your pants up, but a belt and suspenders provides added confidence. However, achieving true "belt and suspenders" redundancy often requires too much complexity.

Case No. 1: A Redundant Drive

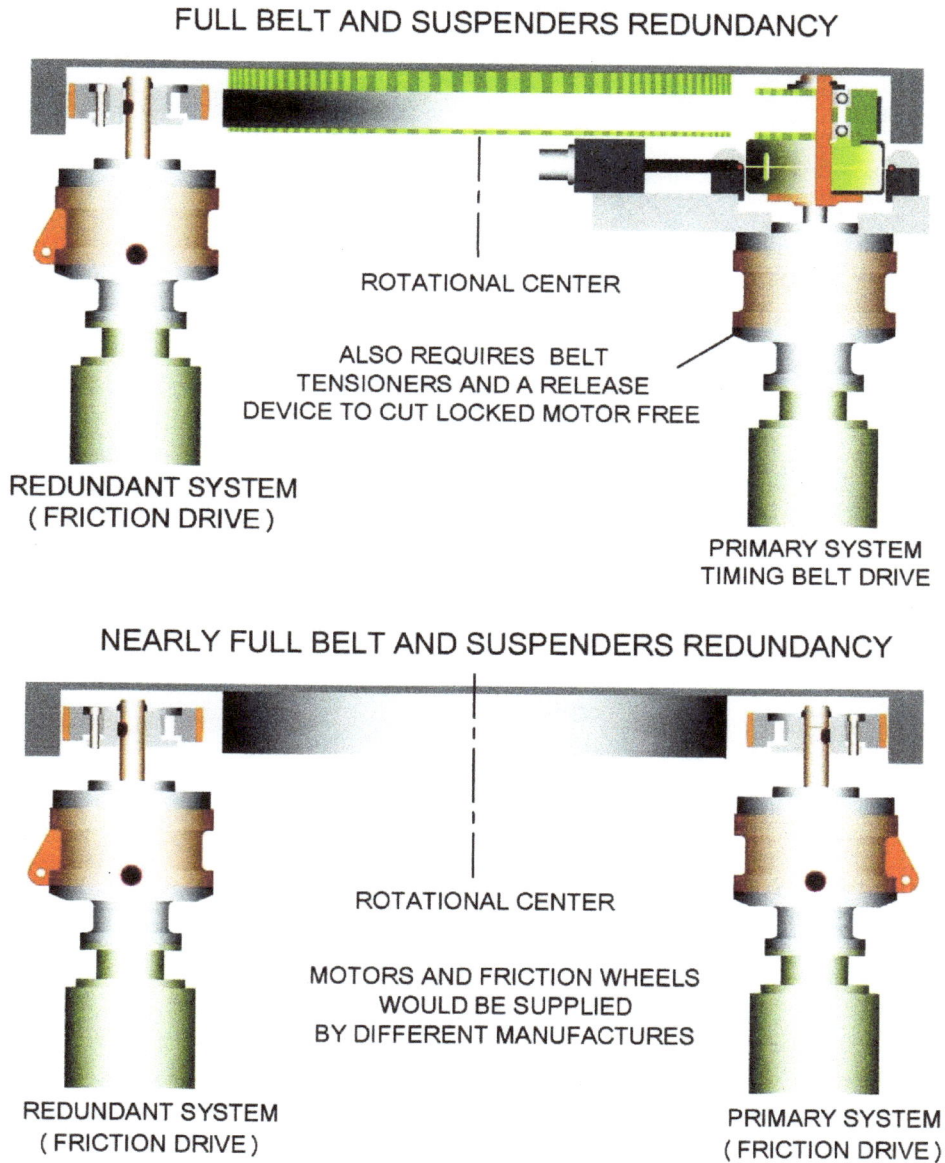

FULL BELT AND SUSPENDERS REDUNDANCY

ROTATIONAL CENTER

ALSO REQUIRES BELT
TENSIONERS AND A RELEASE
DEVICE TO CUT LOCKED MOTOR FREE

REDUNDANT SYSTEM
(FRICTION DRIVE)

PRIMARY SYSTEM
TIMING BELT DRIVE

NEARLY FULL BELT AND SUSPENDERS REDUNDANCY

ROTATIONAL CENTER

MOTORS AND FRICTION WHEELS
WOULD BE SUPPLIED
BY DIFFERENT MANUFACTURES

REDUNDANT SYSTEM
(FRICTION DRIVE)

PRIMARY SYSTEM
(FRICTION DRIVE)

Figure 185 Comparison of Drive Systems

Case No. 2: A Spacecraft Separation System

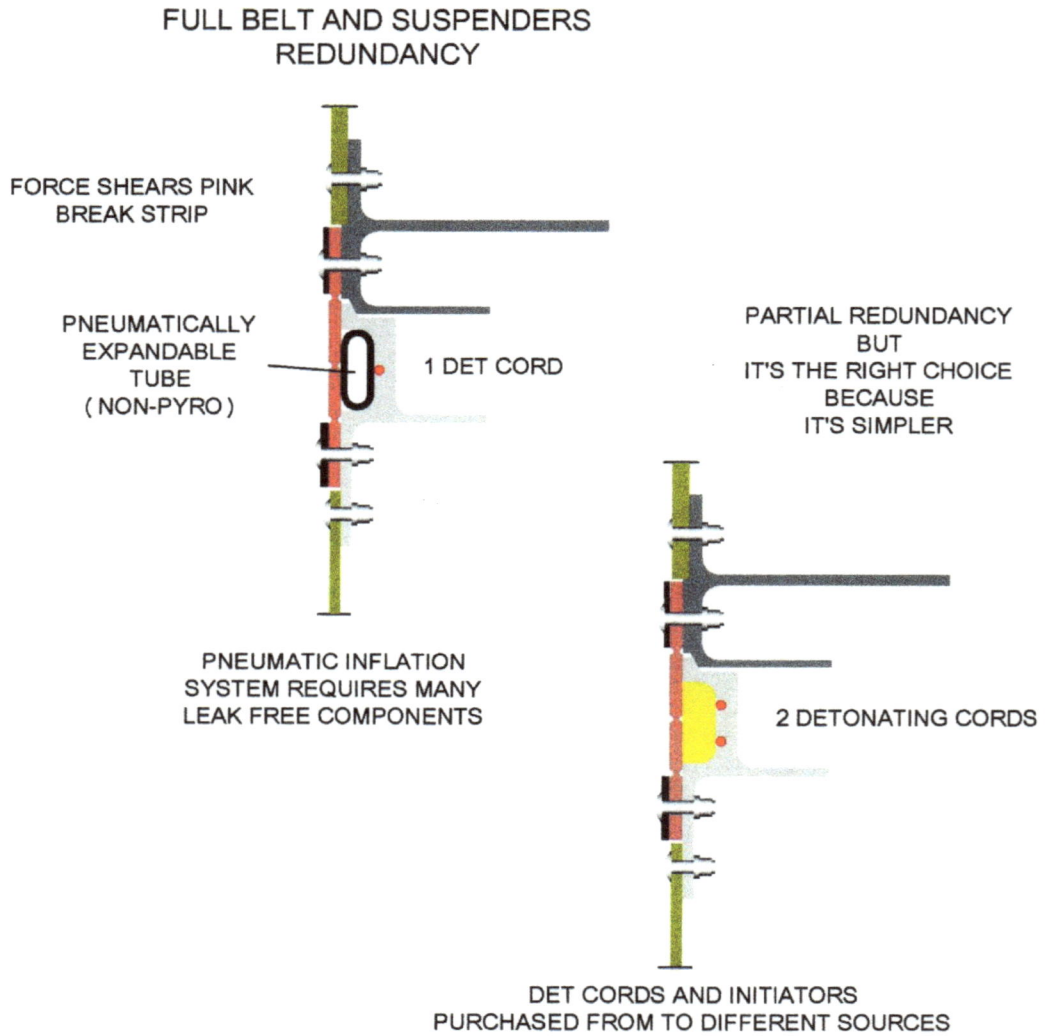

FULL BELT AND SUSPENDERS
REDUNDANCY

FORCE SHEARS PINK
BREAK STRIP

PNEUMATICALLY
EXPANDABLE
TUBE
(NON-PYRO)

1 DET CORD

PARTIAL REDUNDANCY
BUT
IT'S THE RIGHT CHOICE
BECAUSE
IT'S SIMPLER

PNEUMATIC INFLATION
SYSTEM REQUIRES MANY
LEAK FREE COMPONENTS

2 DETONATING CORDS

DET CORDS AND INITIATORS
PURCHASED FROM TO DIFFERENT SOURCES

Figure 186 Comparison of Separation Systems

239

Philosophy of Sailor Proofing

The term "sailor proofing" refers to the art (not science) of rendering a design immune to technician errors. This is one of the most important aspects of a mechanism design. Technician errors usually occur later in the build cycle, when the cost and schedule impacts are enormous.

Sailor Proofing Rules

1. Design systems that are easy to assemble.

2. Sacrifice low cost, and accept a "hard-to-fabricate" design if that will significantly simplify assembly and test.

3. Modularize the design to simplify assembly and repair.

4. Provide an assembly drawing that clearly depicts the assembled system, including critical steps, and warns of high risks.

5. Augment the assembly drawing with step-by-step procedures.

6. Use the development unit to establish procedures, identify high-risk assembly steps, and checkout the test equipment.

7. Carefully design and review ground support equipment (including component fixtures). Don't accept the idea that, "It's not our job". Those folks can break your shinny new toy.

8. Be sure that your top assembly drawing clearly identifies all warnings that must apply to higher assembly levels.

If you work in an environment that prevents you from doing any of the above steps, you can't do your job with maximum efficiency. There will be errors made and fixes required. That means slipped schedules and cost over-runs. The working group will become angry because blame is passed around like political donations in DC. It will become harder and harder for workers to work efficiently. Folks, it's not an engineering problem! It's a management problem. Too many people want to be boss before they are ready.

Concluding Remarks:

Well! This has been quite an adventure. I hope that the information which I provided proves useful to you in the years to come. I know that I would have found similar information very valuable back in 1960 when I was getting started.

I was very lucky to begin working at the dawn of the Space Age. The down side was the lack of a choice of paths to follow. We did not have an opportunity to select "a road less traveled by" as Robert Frost suggested. We had to hack out a trail and do it quickly because the Russians were coming. The first Aerospace Mechanisms Symposium did not occur until 1966. We had, by then, developed Corona, Gambit and were beginning Hexagon. Six years later we had learned how to extend the "on orbit" life of these machines to a point that missions lasting years became a reality.

The people who did these things were not geniuses (or disguised aliens). They were a well shaken-out, hard working, very experienced, group of engineers and managers who had learned how to work well together. Many of them had been working together since the 1940's.

Early in my career (23 years old), I was tasked with transferring Agena D work packages from Sunnyvale California (Lockheed Missiles and Space Division) to Burbank California (The California Division). The Burbank work was done in a barn like open work area with maybe 100 drawing boards stacked side by side. One day while I walked among the "boards", I referred to the Agena D as the "bird". There was an immediate reaction. Many in the group raised from their drawing boards and a few questioned " I wonder what color his bird is". They were referring to their "black bird' the SR-71 but it was a few more years before we all learned about that. Many in that room transferred to Sunnyvale and completed their careers there.

Later when I began to "push work through the system", I suggested that my job was like trying to walk quickly across a large room full of people who were busy talking. I had two solutions: (1) go very slowly and say, "excuse me" over and over or (2) push my way through bumping, shoving and causing hard feelings. I was beginning to have doubts about the company I was working for. Remember what I said in Chapter 1, You are not indispensable and neither is the company you work for!

Life in those years was not without humor. We had one designer who complained bitterly because he was working in an old manufacturing area and there wasn't any tile on the floor. The next morning he found his drafting stool was located on top of four neatly placed pieces of tile. Another time, an engineer shouted orders to a manufacturing tech as he left work, "use a bigger bolt". When the engineer returned he found a 2 inch bolt head attached to his machine with double backed tape. And then there was the engineer who bragged about the mileage he was getting with his new imported car. Each day the mileage seemed to improve. It was actually happening!---------because gas was being added to his tank each day.

If you still want to become a mechanisms engineer after all of my "gloom and doom" talk know that it won't be easy. You will have to really want it bad enough to put up with the good and the bad.

While you are young, you must always be learning new things. Watch out for "one years experience ten times over".

The fact that you have selected this book to read is a good sign because I have now furnished you with the names of dozens of additional books to read. I learned in much the same way---by asking other knowledgeable engineers to recommend "books" which they thought highly of.

Good luck with your career decisions. You will need it because we all are "so soon old and so late smart"!

www.ingramcontent.com/pod-product-compliance
Lightning Source LLC
Chambersburg PA
CBHW060759270326
41926CB00002B/27